WALLACE NUTTING

and the Invention of Old America

WALLACE NUTTING

and the Invention of Old America

Thomas Andrew Denenberg

YALE UNIVERSITY PRESS, NEW HAVEN AND LONDON

in association with
THE WADSWORTH ATHENEUM MUSEUM OF ART

Wallace Nutting and the Invention of Old America is published on the occasion of an exhibition at the Wadsworth Atheneum Museum of Art. The book, exhibition, and public programs are made possible by the generosity of The Henry Luce Foundation, the Connecticut Humanities Council, and Webster.

Designed by Carol S. Cates
Set in Adobe Minion type by Amy Storm
Printed in Italy by Conti Tipocolor

Library of Congress Cataloging-in-Publication Data
Denenberg, Thomas Andrew, 1967–
   Wallace Nutting and the invention of old America / Thomas Andrew Denenberg.
     p.   cm.
Includes bibliographical reference and index.
   ISBN 0-300-09683-6 (cloth: alk. paper)
   1. Nutting, Wallace, 1861–1941. 2. Photographers—United States—Biography.
3. Furniture—Collectors and collecting—United States—History—20th century.
I. Title.
NK2439.N87 D46 2003
770'.92—dc21   2002014448

A catalogue record for this book is available from the British Library.

The paper in this book meets the guidelines for permanence and durability of the Committee on Production Guidelines for Book Longevity of the Council on Library Resources.

10 9 8 7 6 5 4 3 2 1

Frontispiece: Detail of Wallace Nutting, *Elmhurst*, c. 1910, hand-tinted platinum print. The Manville Collection

Whatever is new, is bad.
—Wallace Nutting

Contents

Acknowledgments

Countless individuals and institutions made vital contributions to this book, and I thank them for their ideas, inspirations, and many kindnesses. First and foremost, Richard Candee, Keith Morgan, Pat Hills, Shirley Wajda, Ned Cooke, and Nina Silber dramatically shaped my thinking as I started musing about Wallace Nutting and his world while a graduate student at Boston University, and they continue to do so to this day. My fellow students Cheryl Boots, Shitsuyo Masui, Becky Noel, Mike Sokolow, David Brody, Chris Walsh, David Shawn, John Stomberg, Jeanie Cooper Carson, Melissane Parm, and Sue Gill informed this work and have defined camaraderie for more than a decade.

Many of my initial notions about Wallace Nutting developed while I worked at the Smithsonian American Art Museum on the exhibition *Picturing Old New England*. I thank William Truettner, Roger B. Stein, Bruce Robertson, Dona Brown, and Stephen Nissenbaum for their inspired mentoring. To Bill, in particular, my enduring thanks for sticking with this project and reading countless drafts with his gentle, keen eye. I would also like to express my admiration for Jeana Foley, Jay Gaglione, Judy Maxwell, Merry Forresta, Jeremy Adamson, Virginia Mecklenburg, Pat Lynaugh, and Lerphus T. Brown.

The earliest chapters of this book were drafted at the Henry Francis Du Pont Winterthur Museum with the support of a Lois F. McNeil Dissertation Fellowship. At Winterthur, Gary Kulik, Neville Thompson, Gretchen T. Buggeln, Ritchie Garrison, Brock Jobe, Wendy Cooper, Anne Verplanck, and Pat Elliott critiqued initial ideas and made the museum a home away from home. My fellow residents of Foulsham House, Carolyn White, Eun-young Cho, Liz Siegal, and, later, Mary Beaudry and Wendy Bellion, ignored my unorthodox cooking and provided excellent company.

The Office of Fellowships and Grants at the Smithsonian Institution sponsored the project with a fellowship at the National Museum of American History. At the museum, I would like to single out the late Rodris Roth for her constant enthusiasm and support. I also thank Helena Wright and Pete Daniel for their wise counsel and friendship. Fellow fellows Sarah Johnson, Tim Davis, Roger Davidson, and Natalie Ring provided critical feedback and good-natured support. Also at NMAH, intern Brigham Bowen played a crucial role in this study. Throughout a long, hot Washington summer, Brigham cheerfully chased obscure references and learned far more than he ever wanted to about Wallace Nutting.

This book would not exist were it not for Peter Sutton and Kate Sellers. Peter, former director of the Wadsworth Atheneum, offered me a job and promptly granted me a leave to write the first draft. Kate, now director, has an eye for irony and ensured that I had time to finish the manuscript. When the going got tough, my boss, Betsy Kornhauser, pushed and my colleague Linda Roth shoved. They and the rest of the Atheneum staff ignored my grouchy moods, and I thank everyone at the museum for their encouragement throughout the project.

Sections of this book were presented at an American Studies Association annual meeting, the Historic Deerfield–Wellesley College Symposium, the Delaware Seminar at the University of Delaware, the National Conference on the Colonial Revival at the University of Virginia, and the Yale University Material Culture Study Group. I thank Ken Hafertepe, Jim O'Gorman, Jim Curtis, Richard Guy Wilson, and Ned Cooke for inviting me to participate in these forums and Stephanie Taylor, Elizabeth Hutchinson, and Frank Goodyear III for their comments on these papers. The Wallace Nutting Collectors Club kindly listened to my musings on two occasions. I thank Bill Hamann for including me on the programs at the 1999 and 2000 annual meetings, Joe Duggan for sharing bibliographic material, and Mike Ivankovich for his unflagging enthusiasm.

An outstanding cast of librarians, curators, and archivists contributed to this project from start to finish. My deepest debts of gratitude are owed to Trina Bowman, assistant curator of American Decorative Arts at the Wadsworth Atheneum, Lorna Condon of the Society for the Preservation of New England Antiquities, John Teahan and Bill Staples at the Auerbach Art Library of the Wadsworth Atheneum, and Eugene Gaddis and Ann Brandwein of the Archives of the Wadsworth Atheneum, Steve Gowler, Shannon Wilson, and Loren Ingerson at Berea College, Jennifer Eifrig and Donna Baron of the Webb-Deane-Stevens House, Carl Salmons-Perez at Saugus National Historic Site, Diane Engle and Debra Ervin at the Framingham Public Library, Suzanne Flynt of the Pocumtuck Valley Memorial Association, Brian Sullivan at the Harvard University Archives, and Edouard Desrochers at the Phillips Exeter Academy Archives. My enduring thanks to the private collectors who shared their materials with me, especially Dot Manville, John Baron, and Linda Palmer.

The staff at Yale University Press is remarkble for their patience, humor, and professionalism. For this, I am grateful to Patricia Fidler, Laura Jones Dooley, John Long, Mary Mayer, Michelle Komie, and their colleagues for their kind professionalism. Photographers Ralph Phil and Steve Pitkin came though time and time again.

Numerous people took me in over the course of this project. Many others listened to my complaints. Esther Williams cheerfully lent me her home for two summers. Kay Walsh let me come and go as I pleased (and often provided pizza). Mark Malloy lent moral support as he has since the eighth grade.

Several grown-ups kindly spurred me on with the writing at important moments. They include Abbott Lowell Cummings, John Kirk, Richard Guy Wilson, Leo LeMay, David Dangremond, Roger Gonzales, Put Brown, Dennis Marnon, and Renny Little, who always told me the secret to finishing a project is to make sure you have one rabbit in one hole. Writing a book, even a one-rabbit book, has a surprising effect on an author's memory. I am certain that I have left many important people off this list and hope they will forgive the oversight.

Above all, this book is for Tinka, Allan, Peter, Libby, Elliot, Max, and Amber, who has a much better sense of direction than I.

Chapter 1 *Consumed by the Past*

WALLACE NUTTING AND THE INVENTION OF OLD AMERICA

*W*allace Nutting, a Congregational minister of modest reputation, changed careers in 1904 and became a household name. By the time the 1920s began to roar, the erstwhile clergyman's fluid signature could be found coast to coast throughout countless middle-class American homes, penciled on hand-tinted photographs, branded into reproduction colonial furniture, and printed on the title page of innumerable books and magazines. Historically minded consumers could track their days on Wallace Nutting calendars, send season's greetings on Wallace Nutting Christmas cards, even visit five restored museum houses operating under the Wallace Nutting banner in three New England states. Nutting himself could be found preaching to college students in Kentucky, women's groups in Maryland, and audiences throughout the nation on the idealized values of a time and a place he called Old America (fig. 1.1).

Nutting's Old America, a deft combination of myth and materialism, served as a master narrative for the peripatetic minister's interconnected business and scholarly endeavors. An evocative mélange of invented traditions, Old America gave the entrepreneurial cleric a tap into the developing culture of consumption in the early twentieth century.[1] Old America, part halcyon sermon and part corporate facade, provided the forum for Wallace Nutting the minister to become "Wallace Nutting" the trademark.[2] In hindsight, it is clear that this transition was a harbinger of more recent states of mind and marketing such as Russel Wright's "American Modern" or Martha Stewart's tasteful brand of "Living."[3]

Yet Nutting gave life to his idealized consumer mindscape decades before these later icons of popular culture. He traded on his name and his carefully constructed public image as a flinty Yankee minister-turned-antiquarian to

Opposite: Writing Arm Windsor Chair (fig. 1.3)

1.1
William C. Loring, *Portrait of Wallace Nutting*, 1925, oil on canvas. Wadsworth Atheneum Museum of Art, Gift of Wallace Nutting, 1926.29

build an endlessly self-referential business empire that catered to the culturally conservative needs of middle-class America.[4] He offered this growing and
ever-important population physical mnemonics of a soothing, idealized
American history—a golden-age past that played well in an era of staggering
social change. Not only did such individual purchases as a hand-tinted photograph, a reproduction Windsor chair, an illustrated book, or a chest of
drawers just like Grandmother's take on added value as the conditions of life
in the machine age provoked discomfort and discord, but the package of
interconnected images, texts, and consumer experiences provided a complete
antimodern ideology for the beleaguered middle class (figs. 1.2, 1.3, 1.4).[5]

1.2
Wallace Nutting, *Wentworth-
Gardner House, Portsmouth,
N.H.*, c. 1916, platinum print.
Courtesy of the Society for the
Preservation of New England
Antiquities

1.3
Wallace Nutting, Incorporated,
*#451 Writing Arm Windsor
Chair*, c. 1922, painted pine, ash,
and maple. Wadsworth
Atheneum Museum of Art,
The Elijah K. and Barbara A.
Hubbard Decorative Arts
Fund, 2000.6

1.4
Wallace Nutting, Incorporated,
*#1000, Goddard Type,
Chest-on-Chest.* From *Wallace
Nutting Final Edition
Furniture Catalog* (1937), 50

Old America and New

In a frightening new world of threatening cities, populated by fearsome immigrants and challenging "new" women, Nutting's tangible history lessons for the home were a bracing and popular tonic. Although Nutting himself was a scold and his social prescriptions were often bitter rhetorical pills, decades of service to the Congregational Church in metropolitan cities from Seattle, Washington, to Providence, Rhode Island, sensitized the minister to the pulse of middle-class American culture in the early twentieth century.[6] As daily life evolved into a series of unfulfilling, faceless encounters with institutions rather than individuals, nostalgia became endemic.[7] Mourning the loss of social economy and caught in what historians have described as the "weightless" flux of modernity, the emerging professional class of doctors, lawyers, and corporate managers craved the status accorded by material wealth and the stability provided by history and tradition.[8]

An earlier generation facing similar circumstances might have sought comfort in the church. Indeed, the various Protestant denominations took a decidedly liberal turn in the last decades of the nineteenth century to accommodate the new conditions of modern life.[9] "The Puritans are still Puritans in name," observed writer Henry Mann in 1885, "but their Christianity is of a type adapted to the sensitive and enlightened conscience of a humane and civilized country."[10] The increasingly heterogeneous nation, however, vexed age-old patterns of religious commonality and sent large numbers—including Nutting—looking for new idols.

As middle-class America became an increasingly secular culture at the turn of the century, many sought salvation in consumerism rather than the church.[11] Mail-order merchandisers replaced tract societies; the department store became a house of worship.[12] Liberated by the fluidity of modern social organization and influenced by a myriad of factors including gender and ethnicity—to say nothing of personal aesthetic preference—the middle class sought to purchase goods and experiences that supported a sense of collective identity.

Objects for the home, then as now, were totems—talismans of group behavior and shared experience. Revival styles and suggestive bric-a-brac flourished to fulfill middle-class fantasies of preindustrial community. Indian artifacts, Turkish corners, and Japan rooms all found favor in the decades after the Civil War as worldly eclecticism became the norm—a polyglot style that later provided fodder for countless attacks on the cluttered and sentimental "Victorian" home (fig. 1.5).[13] Out of this heterogeneity emerged a dominant mode based on idealized notions of the American colonial past. Initially represented by the occasional real or invented ancestral object in the parlor, the

1.5
Parlor of the John Curtis family,
Dorchester, Massachusetts,
c. 1895. Courtesy of the Society
for the Preservation of New
England Antiquities

spinning-wheel next to the hearth, the Windsor chair tucked in the cozy corner, physical declarations of filial piety increased in number and expanded geographically to become the nation's preferred style of decoration. By 1900, such incipient historicism had joined forces with nostalgic rituals and nationalist displays to blossom into a full-scale colonial revival.

Inventions of Self, or, From Rockbottom to Industry

Nutting, responding to the nervous tenor of his times, suffered a physical and emotional breakdown in 1904 and in the process of recovering his health transformed himself into an antimodern colporteur of the first rank.[14] Through his photography, writings, and other historical enterprises, he became a beacon of seemingly transcendent American values in an era when new patterns of life challenged daily established beliefs and institutions. He positioned himself as an archetype, a familiar figure within a continuum of native-born, Harvard-educated cultural leaders in New England.[15] Weaving a rich homespun of half-truths in support of his office as a spokesman for the colonial revival and owner of Wallace Nutting, Incorporated, Nutting offered himself to the nation as the perfect Yankee—intelligent, a touch dyspeptic, and always correct.

Getting at the real Wallace Nutting is a task made onerous by the man himself. Between 1936 and 1941, Nutting—a master of self-invention—wrote his autobiography, destroyed most of his business records, and went to his reward.[16] In these three strokes, the minister fixed his myth in print, destroyed all contradictory evidence, and removed the principal witness. Scholars who have since reckoned with Wallace Nutting have largely walked away from the contest, leaving little written that has not been noted before and even less that cannot be traced to the minister's pen.[17] To study the Nutting phenomenon, however, is to plumb the complexities of the man and the contradictions of his times. Lurking just below the text in *Wallace Nutting's Biography* and the host of autobiographical references in Wallace Nutting, Incorporated, advertising copy from the 1920s is a personal history that sheds light on the minister's motivations as well as his penchant for, and remarkable success at, self-invention.[18]

Equal parts memoir, advertisement, and Christian testimony, *Wallace Nutting's Biography* is a case study in chronological impossibilities and willful exaggerations. Titled as if written by another, the book was penned by Nutting and published by Old America, Incorporated, in 1936. Organizing his life into a series of "Adventures," including "Adventures in Picture Making" and "Adventures in Antiques," the minister espoused a dry, almost irritable, positivism while regaling his readers with anecdotes about such varied topics as the restoration of historic buildings, the connoisseurship of antiques, and the joys of marriage. A none-too-subtle subtext in the autobiography hints at ways for the reader to live a Christian life in the godless modern era. Foremost, however, Nutting used the volume to codify and make permanent the self-aggrandizing stories he had been spinning for nearly thirty years.

One of the first questions asked and answered in the *Biography* is that of the minister's ancestry. In an era when many traveled in steerage, Nutting claimed a first-class background. "All were English . . . but Nutting is English Scandinavian (Knott, Knute, Nutting, clan of Knute) from Holland country in East England."[19] Such lineage, art historian Annette Stott has explained, was then the preferred stock. Period historians traced the origins of American institutions to the seventeenth-century Dutch Republic, a time and place of plenty that offered an attractive model for the United States as a relatively young world power. Dutch genesis held such currency that in 1903 Edward Bok, the influential editor of the *Ladies' Home Journal*, declared Holland to be the taproot of American culture.[20] The arrival of Nutting's Anglo-Dutch ancestor in Plymouth Colony in 1639 thus not only established the family name in North America but also provided his progeny with a forebear of the right sort.[21]

Nutting shared his generation's belief in the blue-chip nature of blue blood. As Pilgrim ancestry had evolved into an elite club over the course of the nineteenth century he missed few opportunities to capitalize on this and other impressive branches of his family tree.[22] "Grandmother Nutting was a Whitney," he declared, invoking the name of the storied Yankee inventor as well as the wealthy New Yorker to satisfy readers of history *and* the society pages.[23] This name-dropping was more than mere conceit; as cultural historian Roger B. Stein has demonstrated, genealogy was a useful commodity for writers and artists in the period, and Nutting aired his "old colony" ancestry whenever possible.[24]

In spite of this impressive lineage, Wallace Nutting was born into modest circumstances on 17 November 1861.[25] As a youth Nutting endured hard times when the privations of the Civil War reached the home front. His father, Albion Nutting, joined the Union army when Wallace was just months old and never returned, dying of fever late in the conflict. "It is an irreparable loss not to have a father," Nutting wrote in his memoirs. "A youth can only be half a man without the combination of loving stimulus and restraint which only fatherly watching can give."[26]

Raised by his mother in a small central Massachusetts village known locally as Rockbottom, Nutting spent his childhood in a landscape of loss, dependent on kith and kin.[27] Although he was certainly not alone in this situation, for many had died in the war, Rockbottom was a suggestive hometown for a nostalgic. Historian David Jaffee has described central Massachusetts towns as communities saturated by a wave of politically motivated historical consciousness on the eve of the war. Centennial celebrations and town histories were rituals and texts that "gave the New England elite the opportunity to claim legitimacy as the regions' natural leaders in an unbroken line of succession from the early settlers."[28]

Influenced by the retrospective mood of his childhood surroundings, Nutting clung to the ideal of Rockbottom for the rest of his life even though the name fell out of popular use and the hamlet dropped off the map.[29] This refusal to acknowledge the passing of his childhood home was no doubt the result of a wistful nature. Such petulance, however, was also symptomatic of his generation's interest in the romance of small-town life and Nutting's ability to weave a grand narrative.[30] To a generation raised on formulaic sentimental fiction and success manuals, the image of Rockbottom signified the romantic ideal of small-town New England.[31] As a businessman, Nutting was never one to let such opportunity pass without comment and exploitation. Writing in his autobiography years later, Nutting chronicled his path from

Rockbottom (Massachusetts) to Industry (Maine) in terms reminiscent of both Horatio Alger and John Bunyan.[32] It was not enough for a fatherless country boy to make good by attending Harvard; Nutting sought to raise the ante by casting his life as a modern-day *Pilgrim's Progress.*[33]

Nutting's progress carried him in Maine from Industry to Manchester and eventually to Augusta, with periods in Massachusetts and Minnesota along the way. "My schooling began at four," he declared in his memoirs, as "the modern stupidity of keeping children back had not then arisen." Continuing in this Lincolnesque vein, he noted that "we trudged a mile in snow to school, and the sessions were never suspended for storms, but my older sister and cousin gave me an occasional 'spell' on the sled." Hints periodically appear in this Currier-and-Ives-like bildungsroman that foreshadow the high-strung adult to come. For instance, "frail health" interrupted high school at age fifteen. He "contracted chronic headaches and was sent along to Minneapolis for a winter" as a result of "reading too much and without direction."[34]

Nutting whiled away his years away from school by farming, working in a publishing house, and clerking at such stores as Boston's Bigelow, Kennard and Company, a high-end jewelry emporium.[35] In 1876, the fifteen-year-old joined the throngs who visited the centennial celebrations at Philadelphia.[36] At the centennial Nutting witnessed unique displays of both progressive and retrospective national culture, including the great Corliss steam engine, exhibitions of architecture and photography, and groupings of colonial relics in fanciful "Olde Tyme" interiors (fig. 1.6).[37] These practical experiences were useful. "There would be less academic nostrums advocated," he wrote, "if the professors had enjoyed several years in the world school."[38] Although the adult Nutting made much hay out of his modest beginnings, he in fact spent relatively little time in this self-described school of hard knocks. Prompted by his minister, Nutting returned to his studies and headed off to preparatory school at age nineteen.[39]

An Old American Education

Nutting entered Phillips Academy in Exeter, New Hampshire, in the fall of 1880 and remained at the prep school until 1883.[40] The academy, not yet a bastion of social privilege, boasted a faculty of five, maintained lax standards of student conduct, and clung to a somewhat antiquated program of classical education.[41] For three years Nutting studied Latin, Greek, and mathematics, with three terms of English interspersed in his second and third years.[42] He "enjoyed (sometimes) the teaching of 'Bull' Wentworth," a legendary teacher who served at Exeter from 1858 until 1892.[43] Opinionated and stubborn (the

1.6
New England Kitchen,
Centennial Exposition,
Philadelphia, 1876, in *Frank
Leslie's Illustrated*, 10 June 1876.
Courtesy of Rodris Roth

sobriquet was thought to be short for "Bull Dog"), Wentworth provided Nutting and such classmates as later politician and conservationist Gifford Pinchot with a model of fusty and uncompromising behavior.[44]

Exeter affirmed Nutting's commitment to the church. The academy yearbook for 1881 records that he and three others read essays at the anniversary exercises for the Christian Society, a forerunner of the Young Men's Christian Association.[45] Nutting's leadership role in the Christian Society was preordained, he recalls, for his mother "devoted me to the clerical profession before I was born and it was seldom a question what I would do in life."[46] As a youth Nutting had joined Boston's Park Street Church, an evangelical congregation known for fiery preaching.[47] Exeter, however, set the young man on a path to the Congregational Church. With this serious mission, he traveled to Cambridge and enrolled at Harvard College in the fall of 1883.[48]

At Harvard, Nutting "joined the group of religious men in college, some of whom were looking forward to the ministry."[49] In spite of his early focus and in sharp contrast to his prep school experience at Exeter, studying at Harvard in the mid-1880s exposed Nutting to a broad spectrum of ideas. Nutting's matriculation at Harvard coincided with the tenure of reform-minded president Charles W. Elliott and an era often referred to as Harvard's "golden age."[50] Elliott, who served as professor from 1854 to 1863 and president from 1869 to 1909, shifted the college's curriculum from the classical program of the antebellum generation to an elective-based model that favored the liberal arts and preprofessional training. "None of the former exclusive staples, Greek, Latin, mathematics, logic, and metaphysics, are required," Elliott noted in 1885, "and no particular combinations or selections of courses are recommended by the faculty."[51] The elective system enlarged the undergraduate body, and students increasingly lived outside Harvard Yard and beyond the college's control.[52] Wealthy students lived on the "gold coast" in Harvard Square; others, including Nutting, boarded where they could in Cambridge. The permissive atmosphere pervaded Harvard life: compulsory attendance at chapel ended during Nutting's last year on campus, no doubt to the chagrin of a young man "looking forward to the ministry."

Whereas Elliott transformed the curriculum and the conditions of student life at Harvard, such teachers as Charles Eliot Norton, the first professor of art history in America, dramatically altered the intellectual program of the school on the banks of the Charles River.[53] "Norton," writes art historian Edward S. Cooke, Jr. "always moved from an understanding of the past to a critique of the present."[54] Although the elective system still allowed for gut courses ("all the geology necessary to a gentleman"), Norton and his colleagues challenged students with newly translated great texts, offered them lectures on medieval art and architecture, and established canons of high culture relevant to the new professional classes.[55]

Although these were heady times at Harvard, Nutting held mixed feelings about his alma mater. In his autobiography he complained about entering college "handicapped by frail health" and noted that he "made few acquaintances and never recovered from a sense of being an alien." His Alger-like rise from the backwoods of Maine made good advertising copy when he later sold photographs and furniture, but it resulted in an uncomfortable undergraduate experience. "Harvard is altogether too large, or was, as then conducted, to encourage fellowship among classmates," he remembered.[56] Also hampering Nutting's attempts at camaraderie was his living situation: he served as a "bull dog" for the elderly widow of Maine politician Elihu Washburne, acting as a factotum and boarding in her home.[57] The arrangement gave the future minister entrée to wealthier social classes than those found in Rockbottom or

Industry. Yet it also reinforced his sense of being something of a charity case in Cambridge.[58]

Nutting's outsider status at Harvard was further emphasized during the summer months, for in the warm weather the bespectacled undergraduate held a job, no doubt an alien proposition to students who lived on the "gold coast." Nutting worked in hotels at a number of popular watering holes during his college years. Summer vacation in 1883, for instance, found him on Campobello Island, Maine. The next year it was Nantucket, followed by Martha's Vineyard, then out West to Cheyenne Mountain in Colorado.[59] This exposure to the culture of summer proved to be as important as any Harvard lecture, for it gave Nutting the opportunity to meet individuals such as Lyman Abbott, perhaps the most influential Congregational minister of his day.[60] More important, "summering" sowed the seeds of Old America, for Nutting's photography business grew out of postgraduate return trips to these resorts in the late 1890s. And yet the most significant result of Nutting's summer in the Rockies was personal: it was there in 1886 that he met his future wife, a vacationing New Englander named Mariet Caswell.[61]

Nutting left Harvard after three years to fulfill his mother's dream by enrolling at Hartford Theological Seminary in 1886. In choosing Hartford, Nutting opted for a conservative graduate training. Founded in 1833 as a "counterseminary" to the increasingly liberal (read evangelical) divinity school at Yale, Hartford hewed to an orthodox, Old Calvinist theology that held that salvation was predetermined.[62] Hartford was a poor fit, however, and 1887 found him in New York City attending Union Theological Seminary.[63] Union, established jointly by Presbyterians and Congregationalists in 1836 as an "institution independent of all official church control," suited Nutting for the remainder of his schooling.[64] Shifting institutions also set Nutting on a five-year course of travel, for Union Theological Seminary was but one result of a broad alliance between the two denominations. Another outcome, writes historian Sidney Ahlstrom, was the development of "little New Englands" throughout the country as the church advanced into the American West.[65] Such communities needed ministers. Ministers required wives.

Adventures in Matrimony

Writing of his 1888 marriage to Mariet Griswold Caswell, Nutting displayed many of the ambivalences held by society (and portrayed in his photographs) when it came to changing gender roles in the modern age (fig. 1.7).[66] "In the vicissitudes of life my wife has been queen of the kitchen as well as the drawing room," he declared, indicating a commitment to traditional notions of domestic organization tempered by an awareness of the ever-increasing presence of women in the public sphere.[67] Just as Wallace Nutting later adapted to the conditions of modern life by leaving the ministry and promulgating a consumer-based antimodern ideology for middle-class America, so, too, did Mariet Nutting turn from nineteenth-century minister's wife to twentieth-century helpmate—a change in role but not image.

Mariet Caswell presented an ideal candidate for the position of minister's wife in the waning years of the 1880s. A young widow, she was descended from a distinguished New England family, having been born "in the old Griswold homestead" in Buckland, Massachusetts, in 1853. Although her famous second husband was ever solicitous, making their marriage the subject of his sermons and dedicating a chapter to "Adventures in Matrimony" in his autobiography, a newspaper article from 1941 noted of Mariet Nutting that "while her husband was alive she kept herself in the background."[68]

Such public identification as Wallace Nutting's helpmate notwithstanding, Mariet's contribution to the invention of Old America far outstripped her credited work of "loving and being loved, serving and being served." It was she, for example, who struck upon the subject and formula for her husband's success when she suggested that he try his hand at interior photography. She made "those 'Colonial' pictures attractive by providing fair young women decked out in the finery or the sweetly homely garb of the ancient day," he wrote (fig. 1.8).[69] Mariet Nutting designed and produced the hooked rugs that appear in the minister's photographs and furniture catalogs, creating an ethos of sympathetic marketing between product lines (fig. 1.9).[70] The Nuttings' patronage of Berea College, where students worked their way through school in the shop and at the loom, was largely her initiative.[71] Above all, however, Mariet Nutting's public persona became a marketing tool for Old America. As a seemingly old-fashioned minister's wife, she provided a voice of quiet authority in a time of social change.

The Minister's Nerves

Married, respected, and reasonably well off, the Nuttings were fully committed to the bourgeois values of the new middle class. The young minister and his slightly older wife dressed well, vacationed in the right places, and quickly converted to new patterns of life brought about by technology.[72] As bicycling became popular in the 1890s, Nutting pedaled into the countryside with his companions. When photography developed into a middle-class hobby, he became a dedicated amateur, carrying his cumbersome camera on coaching trips along the back roads of northern New England's summer resorts. The

1.7
Mariet Nutting in the 1930s. From
Nutting, *Wallace Nutting's Biography*, 17

1.8
Wallace Nutting, *Private and Confidential*, c. 1910, hand-tinted platinum print, tipped into *Old New England Pictures* (1913). Auerbach Library, Wadsworth Atheneum Museum of Art

1.9
"An All Curly Bed Room, Rug by Mrs. Nutting." From *Wallace Nutting Final Edition Furniture Catalog* (1937), 99

1.10
Wallace Nutting, *Stevens Duryea Car at York Cathedral* (Mariet Nutting in rear seat), c. 1915, hand-tinted platinum print. The Manville Collection

Nuttings were early and enthusiastic converts to automobile culture, buying a car and hiring a chauffeur as soon as they were able (fig. 1.10).[73] Few fads missed their attention, and the increasingly nervous minister invested a good deal of energy in remaining au courant.

This constant search for rewarding leisure masked Nutting's increasing agitation. As the minister of a middlebrow denomination, Nutting often served as the principal therapeutic voice for the managerial classes of his community. The demands of pastoral care took a severe toll, and relaxation eluded the minister (and much of the middle class). No amount of preaching, pedaling, touring, or Kodaking could stave off the challenges that pervaded modern life (fig. 1.11). High-strung and sickly, Nutting stepped down from the pulpit of the Plymouth Congregation Church in Providence, Rhode Island, in 1904 and looked to his hobbies—principally photography—for relief.[74]

Consumed by the Past

Though he had retired from the ministry, Wallace Nutting continued to cloak himself in the mantle of an old-time parson and preach about the virtues of the past and the evils of the present. His initial forays into amateur photography struck a resonant chord, and by 1918 he was delivering his new liturgy in a variety of media—photography, books, reproduction furniture—even in the evocative domestic environments of his chain of museum houses. Scratch the surface of these historicizing endeavors, however, and the irony of Nutting's worldview appears with modern brilliance. The minister from Rockbottom relied heavily on new patterns of consumerism, a phenomenon dubbed "the culture of consumption" by historians Jackson Lears and Richard Fox, to preach the theology of Old America. Although he professed disdain for all things modern and proffered historical objects and values as palliatives for contemporary social maladies, Nutting built his businesses on modern technology and mass consumption. It is no surprise, therefore, that Wallace Nutting, Incorporated, developed from the nascent efforts of a sickly shutterbug into an organization closely resembling a modern, vertically integrated corporation.[75]

At its high-water mark in the 1920s, Wallace Nutting, Incorporated, was a close ancestor of the biography-based business empires developed by corpora-

1.11
Eastman Kodak Company,
"Take a Kodak with You,"
c. 1910, chromolithograph.
Private collection

tions in the era of late capitalism.[76] Well before marketing experts extolled the virtues of product tie-ins, Nutting offered the public a series of closely themed, historically referential commodities and experiences. Just as Martha Stewart's television shows promote her magazine, which in turn advertises her retail lines, Nutting's writings and photographs often referred to other historical and commercial interests.[77] By the early 1920s he offered romantic vignettes for the wall, inspirational (and illustrated) tales of stalwart early Americans for the shelf, and authentic furniture for the homes of latter-day Pilgrims. As with Russel Wright's forward-looking American Modern line of

1.13
Wallace Nutting, Incorporated,
*#733 Goddard School Desk and
Bookcase.* From *Wallace Nutting
Final Edition Furniture Catalog*
(1937), 40

1.14
Wallace Nutting, *Elmhurst*,
c. 1910, hand-tinted platinum
print. The Manville Collection

1.15
House and Garden (November
1939), cover. Courtesy of The
Winterthur Library, Printed
Book and Periodical Collection

housewares, there was a bit of Old America to fit every budget. Nutting's customers could buy into his ideology and aesthetic at a mere fifty cents for a small hand-tinted platinotype; matching silhouettes of George and Martha Washington would set them back a couple of dollars; or, in a show of commitment, consumers could buy a monumental reproduction mahogany desk-and-bookcase in the style of the famous Townsend-Goddard shop of eighteenth-century Newport, Rhode Island, for a little under a thousand dollars (figs. 1.12, 1.13). Between these extremes stood a myriad of images, objects, texts, and experiences that contributed to the totality of Old America (fig. 1.14).

As a consumer-friendly myth, Old America outlived its creator. Nutting died on 18 July 1941, thus missing the final suburbanization of the United States (fig. 1.15).[78] His entrepreneurial vision of the colonial past, however, enabled this process by providing images, objects, and texts that ensured a place for history and sentiment in the modern cultural landscape. Nutting's books remain in print today; his photographs still grace the walls of countless homes. Persistent and persuasive, Wallace Nutting's Old America is a graphic example of how middle-class America consumes, and is consumed by, the past.

Chapter 2   *Spinsters, Widows, and a Minister*

Amateur Photography in a
Professional World

Wallace Nutting's mass-produced vision of Old America held a dominant place in American visual culture for almost half a century. Signed, matted, and framed, his sentimental photographic views appealed to a broad middle-class audience seeking a traditional, often historically suggestive aesthetic for the home (fig. 2.1). These softly hued platinum prints offered consumers a middling genre of art, more respectable than the chromolithograph yet far less expensive than an oil painting or watercolor. Surprisingly, the history and cultural work of these domestic art photographs remains largely unstudied.[1]

By dint of sheer numbers, the minister's photographs command attention. Nutting claimed in 1936 to have produced ten million individual views.[2] A year later, in his last furniture catalog, he raised the ante to eleven million.[3] The views were distributed, he wrote, "in all states and countries [including] Japan, China, England, France, Sweden, Italy, and India."[4] Ever prone to exaggeration, the elderly minister clearly improved the figures, but not by much, as any habitué of antique shops and country auctions can tell you today. Although an exact tally is made impossible by the destruction of Nutting's business records shortly after his death, these sentimental scenes of idyllic streams, rugged coastlines, and fair colonial maidens enjoyed great currency in the years before World War II.[5]

Nutting demonstrated a keen and precocious awareness of photography's commercial potential. He began to copyright his images just four years after taking up the camera in 1897, eventually protecting more than seventeen hundred individual images between that year and 1937.[6] His largest catalog, the so-called Expansible edition of 1915, offered more than eight hundred views in a number of standard sizes with varying prices to fit a variety of budgets. Nutting boasted that he exposed fifty thousand individual glass-plate negatives in

Opposite: Detail of fig. 2.11

2.1
Wallace Nutting, *An Old Fashioned Village*, c. 1905, hand-tinted platinum print. The Manville Collection

the course of his career, composing "all but two" himself.[7] Although this claim may well be another example of his hyperbole, his "Office Book," a master log of negatives, runs to some 358 pages and contains more than ten thousand entries.[8] Some of these negatives were abject failures, selling but a handful of prints. Other scenes sold in multiples of a thousand.[9] A single view of a Welsh cottage, romantically titled *Larkspur*, "has been sought for by the hundred thousand," wrote Nutting in 1927 (fig. 2.2).[10]

Numbers aside, "Nuttings" were so popular that they were subject to counterfeit and reproduction. Unscrupulous operators purchased Nutting platinotypes and reissued them in cheaper formats, and large graphic houses such as Tabor Prang Art Company and a host of legitimate commercial artists offered hand-colored photographs (figs. 2.3, 2.4).[11] Nutting rued that his work "proved a serious and disastrous temptation to pirates" and warned the under-handed that "all infringements will be prosecuted to the extent of the law."[12] Of his competitors, one-time Nutting employee David Davidson of Providence,

2.2
Wallace Nutting, *Larkspur*.
From *Wallace Nutting
Expansible Catalog* (1915), 451

Rhode Island, Charles Sawyer of Concord, New Hampshire, and Fred Thompson of Portland, Maine, were well known in their day.[13] Although many others produced hand-tinted photographs in the early twentieth century, none of Nutting's rivals struck the balance between commerce and aesthetics needed to achieve the breakaway success of the minister from Rockbottom.

2.3
"Grandpa's and Grandma's
Bed," c. 1925 (sold by J. J.
Newberry Company 5-10-25
Cent Stores). Private collection

2.4
Tabor Prang Art Company,
hand-tinted photograph,
copyright 1906. Private
collection

The Camera Cure

Overwhelmed by the conditions of the modern age, beset with neurasthenia, Nutting took up photography as a means of escape. He sought fulfillment in amateur artistic endeavors and, like many other middle-class Americans, readily accepted Eastman Kodak's offer: "You Push the Button, We Do the Rest."[14] For most of the camera-toting population, leisure-time Kodaking was the end of the story. Department store clerks brought inexpensive Brownies and Bull's Eyes along on picnics in the park while middle managers carried more elaborate view cameras into the mountains on summer vacation. The Victorian family album was thicker for their efforts; few were concerned with turning a profit or developing an artistic reputation.

For the more adventuresome amateur, however, the possibilities were almost endless; commercial interests made photography a particularly well-organized hobby.[15] Camera clubs sprang up in major cities in the 1880s, often supported by manufacturers of photographic supplies, and specialty journals vied for the attentions (and dollars) of the dabbler.[16] Amateurs could send their work into these magazines for critique by leading figures in the arts, such as Charles H. Caffin and Sadakichi Hartmann, or include their best efforts in local and national exhibitions and hope to win a prize.[17] Some tried to sell their work—so many, in fact, that the National Convention of Professional Photographers called on its delegates to petition their respective state legislatures to criminalize the practice in 1913.[18] For the rank-and-file amateur, however, photography provided a sense of artistic achievement, created community among like-minded individuals, and became a rallying point for the variety of outdoor activities prescribed for well-being in the period.

As middle-class America adopted the ethos of the rugged outdoor life, photography wed the curative recreations of touring, camping, bicycling, and nature study—all forms of taking the view while taking in the fresh air of the countryside. Nutting, tired in mind and body, desperately needed the air. As a Congregational minister, he was often the principal therapeutic voice in his community. This singular position made him particularly susceptible to neurasthenia, the scourge of the Victorian "Brain-Worker."[19] First identified in 1869 by New York neurologist George M. Beard, neurasthenia plagued the developing middle class in post–Civil War America.[20] The disease, as Beard defined it in *American Nervousness, Its Causes and Consequences*, was a clinical grab bag of symptoms. Neurasthenia could manifest itself as "insomnia, flushing, drowsiness . . . bad dreams . . . pressure and heaviness in the head . . . [and] nervous dyspepsia." Worse yet, it could induce "desire for stimulants or narcotics . . . fear of closed places, fear of society, fear of being alone, fear of fears

. . . [and a] lack of decision in trifling matters."[21] Vague by modern standards, Beard's diagnosis was accorded great currency in the half-century before the rise of Freudian psychoanalysis.[22] Followers included physicians of national reputation, such as S. Weir Mitchell, as well as arbiters of New England literary culture, including William James, Charles Eliot Norton, Henry Adams, and Thomas Bailey Aldrich.[23] One of the best-known documents of the disease today is a work of fiction, Charlotte Perkins Gilman's story of 1892 "The Yellow Wallpaper," rather than a medical treatise.[24] Gilman's chilling tale chronicles one woman's descent into madness brought about by the affliction and the isolating rest cure frequently prescribed in the period.

Photography as Therapy

"When a pastor in Providence," Nutting remembered in his autobiography, "I took long bicycle rides on Monday."[25] Increased interest in physically challenging leisure activities had led to the development of the safety bicycle in the early 1890s.[26] An improvement over earlier velocipede or high-wheeler bicycles, it allowed neophytes (such as middle-aged ministers) and women of genteel repu-

2.5
Eastman Kodak Company, "Cartridge Kodaks, Perfectly Adapted to Use Awheel," in *Century Magazine* (June 1897)

tation to take to two wheels. Advertisements for the new bicycles specifically targeted women and individuals suffering from the nerves.[27] An advertisement in the *Ladies' Home Journal* in 1892 could not be more explicit. "I never enjoyed summer before," exclaims the waving woman pictured in the ad, "always felt ambitionless—My Columbia [bicycle] is my healthful constitutional—I'm simply happy."[28] Seeking this healthy happiness, Nutting initially found only frustration.

Preoccupied by the demands of pastoral care, Nutting admitted that he "went too fast and far and became exhausted instead of rested." When his wife asked him what he had seen on these ostensibly relaxing jaunts into the countryside, Nutting confessed that he had noticed nothing of the landscape, thus depriving himself of the benefits of two-wheeling. "It appeared that if a camera was used in these journeys," he wrote, "they would be shorter and more useful."[29]

Like many camera-toting bicyclists, Nutting discovered that pedaling and Kodaking were sympathetic palliatives (fig. 2.5).[30] The two avocations built up the constitution and fed spiritual needs. An article in *The Wheel: A Journal of Cycling and Recreation* of 1887 summed up the promise of the camera cure. "The benefits derived from the practice of amateur photography cannot be overestimated. . . . It entices one into the open air and sunshine and leads into pleasant rambles. . . . It stimulates one to exercise by bringing new scenes constantly to the notice and cultivates the taste by bringing one into communion with the beauties of nature, and it suggests ideas to the imagination that are both beautiful and wonderful. In fact, it brings out that which is best and noblest in man."[31]

Photography as a Sport

Serious photographers found little use for bicycle-riding amateurs and their crude hand cameras. Indeed, as more photographers sought to make a living as artists, they quickly distanced themselves from such bourgeois dilettantism. Alfred Stieglitz, then leading the charge for photography as an art form, waxed sarcastic in the *American Annual of Photography of 1897*.[32] "Photography as a fad is well-nigh on its last legs, thanks principally to the bicycle craze. Those seriously interested in its advancement do not look upon this state of affairs as a misfortune, but as a disguised blessing, inasmuch as photography has been classed as a sport by nearly all of those who deserted its ranks and fled to the present idol, the bicycle."[33]

Stieglitz, pompous and territorial in his classification of amateur photography as a "sport," penned this editorial during the early days of his storied battles for artistic respect—a critical war that included founding the journal *Camera Work*, opening the exhibition space known as 291, and serving as paterfamilias of the Photo Secessionists.[34] The development of the Photo

Secessionists, a cadre of mostly New York–based photographers who sought status as modern artists, has obscured the cultural work of contemporary amateur photography, including the efforts of a dabbling minister who, ironically, published an article entitled "Photography as a Sport" in 1900.[35]

"Photography," wrote Nutting, "appeals to more people than any other sport." "All the subtle stealing up on the game, all the careful study of the hour and the place are as necessary for the camerist as for the gunner or fisher." Sprinkled among technical tips and compositional recommendations in the article were clever homilies and an overt moral program. Nutting recommended bringing along "a companion to double your joys and divide your sorrows (and incidentally carry part of the luggage)." He warned his readers that "a tipsy photograph is worse than a tipsy man, for the picture can never reform." Nutting's article is more than mere ministerial jocularity, however. Writing for a national audience, he neatly defined the camera cure and provided a rationale for thousands, including himself, to take to the hills to "catch the permanent beauty" and "ephemeral joys" of photography.[36]

Spinsters and Ministers

Nutting's initial photographic efforts were in direct dialogue with the work of other amateur photographers in turn-of-the-century New England. A series of images taken on the farm of Charles Vilas in Alstead, New Hampshire, is typical of his early work (fig. 2.6). Following conventions of nineteenth-century agricultural genre scenes, Nutting's view of an aging farmer in his barn established his bona fides as an amateur limner of timeless folkways. The Yankee old-timer, dressed in a simple smock, tends his animals in time-honored manner. Nutting was by no means alone in composing such nostalgic images. Countless other photographers trained their lenses on similar scenes with like results—many of them women.

The sport of photography was specifically recommended to the fairer sex, and so Nutting's early photographic peers were often female. "Amateur photography is of special interest and importance to women," wrote W. S. Harwood in 1896. "Many a ruddy cheek there is whose hue has been won on long camera tramps, many an elastic step which would have been slow and halting, many a spirit dull and languid, but for the leading of the lens."[37] Photography, moreover, allowed women *without* means to cross the line from amateur to professional.

The career of Chansonetta Stanley Emmons personifies the new female shutterbug. Born in rural Maine to a family of Yankee inventors (her twin brothers developed a dry-plate photographic technique and the Stanley Steamer automobile), Emmons moved to Boston and taught art in the public schools in the mid-1880s.[38] While in Boston, she studied under J. G. Enneking

2.6
Wallace Nutting, *Vilas Farm—Alstead*,
c. 1905. From *New Hampshire Beautiful*
(1923), 112

and J. G. Brown, two painters noted for their rural views of an idealized "old" New England.[39]

In 1898, now a forty-year-old widow, Emmons took her eye and her camera to northern New England. Returning to summer in Maine, she began to chronicle rural life, portraying the state's rustic ways and aging inhabitants in a highly nostalgic light. Emmons's *Shelling Corn* dates to 1901 (fig. 2.7). In this view, a graybeard sits in a summer kitchen, shelling corn. A young girl at his side builds a cabin out of dried cobs. Evoking a similar timeless atmosphere as Nutting's *Vilas Farm, Shelling Corn* is typical of countless ruralizing photographic efforts that depicted the voyage of life at the turn of the century. From leading modernists, such as Stieglitz or Clarence White, to young widows seeking to fill their days in a productive and meaningful way, photographers held such nonspecific old-time imagery in high regard at the turn of the century.

Other photographers sought a more focused look at the past. The work of Mary and Frances Allen of Deerfield, Massachusetts, adds historical specificity to the amateur image. Although the sisters initially took up photography as a hobby in much the same way as Emmons, they quickly moved beyond amateur exhibitions to market their talents to a broader audience. Through publishing and catalog sales, the Allen sisters soon spanned the gap between amateur and professional.[40]

The Allens' conjoined careers show how historically minded amateurs evolved into artists by serving the public interest in photographic representations of quaint customs and rural ways. Born in 1854 and 1858, respectively,

2.7
Chansonetta Stanley Emmons, *Shelling Corn*, 1901. Photo courtesy of the Stanley Museum, Kingfield, Maine

2.8
Frances and Mary Allen,
Deerfield Street, Looking North,
c. 1900, platinum print.
Pocumtuck Valley Memorial
Association, Memorial
Hall Museum, Deerfield,
Massachusetts

Frances and Mary Allen attended the State Normal School in Westfield and launched careers as teachers. When they began to lose their hearing in middle age, the sisters retired to the family homestead in Deerfield. "Put out to pasture," to use Nutting's phrase, the Allens took up photography.

As descendants of early settlers, the Allen sisters enjoyed a certain authority in Deerfield, where the past was rapidly becoming an important commodity. Passed over by the railroad at midcentury, the historic center of Deerfield had withered as commercial activity shifted south to the railroad crossing at South Deerfield and north to the industrial center of Greenfield. What remained of the village, a street of venerable eighteenth-century homes, took on economic importance in its own right, however, as "local promoters put their dilapidated buildings and grass-grown streets to work, creating 'old' Deerfield" (fig. 2.8).[41] Deerfield the backwater became Deerfield the watering hole as tourists began to flock to the picturesque community.

The Allen sisters, arbiters of old Deerfield, began to sell their views to tourists in the 1890s, inspired perhaps by Emma Lewis Coleman, a pioneering photographer and life partner of the preservationist C. Alice Baker, who summered in

Emma L. Coleman, *Spinning Woman, Deerfield, Massachusetts*, c. 1885. Courtesy of the Society for the Preservation of New England Antiquities

town (fig. 2.9). The sisters printed a series of catalogs and eventually sold their images to national publications.[42] In 1902 the *Ladies' Home Journal* elected the Allens to a pantheon of "the foremost women photographers of America."[43]

A two-page spread in the *Ladies' Home Journal* in 1906 featuring the Allen sisters and Nutting illustrates the close circles of influence in amateur photography. Not only did the Allens and Nutting share an interest in composing historical vignettes by this date (Nutting later called these scenes "colonials"), but they also held the common belief that this genre of photography should be rendered in crisp detail. In this way, the Allens and Nutting moved away from the mainstream mode of amateur representation—that of the soft-focus, Pictorial mode—and sought a heightened sense of realism for their increasingly "authentic" historical imagery.

Nutting later articulated his reasoning in his book *Photographic Art Secrets*: "A very wide vogue has come in for seeking the softness of a mezzotint by using an imperfect lens. Nevertheless, in the last analysis, very few persons really prefer a picture produced in this manner. The writer has tried the soft focus in many instances. In not one of them has he ever found an appreciable response from the public." By 1927, when the book was published, this seemed a fair assessment. Nutting continued, however, and in typical fashion, betrayed a pattern of thought and practice evident throughout his career as an

2.10
Wallace Nutting and Clifton
Johnson in *Woman's Home
Companion*, 29, no. 11
(November 1902): 28–29

entrepreneur. "A better way [to achieve a pictorial image] is here suggested. Let the focus be as sharp as the conditions will allow, but let the softness of the focus, if desired, be obtained by the interposition between the paper and the plate, in printing, of a thin, transparent surface, like a sheet of white celluloid. The effect can be scarcely be distinguished from a picture made with a soft focus. This method, however, has the advantage, that from the same plate prints may be made in either sharp or soft focus." In short, Nutting wanted to play for both teams. He could offer a pictorial image to those interested in art, but he also kept a sharp negative to sell to a magazine.[44]

And sell he did. Commercial images were important to Nutting in the early days of his business, and his work appeared cheek by jowl with the efforts of such well-known photographers as Stieglitz, the Allen sisters, and Clifton Johnson. In November 1902, Nutting and Johnson were featured in *Woman's Home Companion* in a montage entitled *Thanksgiving at the Old Homestead* (fig. 2.10).[45] One month later, Nutting's *Old Fireplace on Christmas Morning* appeared as the centerfold in the December issue of *Country Life in America*, which featured Stieglitz's *Christmas Tree* as a frontispiece.[46]

2.11
Wallace Nutting, *Nuttinghame Blossoms*, c. 1908, hand-tinted platinum print. The Manville Collection

Nuttinghame

Nutting, like Emmons and the Allens, desired the status and income of a professional photographer. Carrying on at the pulpit but increasingly incapacitated by his nerves, he struck a deal with a local print shop in Providence, Rhode Island, and began to sell platinotypes of birches and blossoms he had taken in northern New England.[47] By 1904 he had raised enough capital to retire from the ministry and to move to New York City—then, as now, the place to live for a serious artistic photographer. He lasted one year.

After his disastrous sojourn in the city, which included a period marked by further illness, Nutting again fled to the country. In typical fashion, he shaded the episode with a mixture of candor and folksy obfuscation in his autobiography. "When physicians turned me out to grass at forty-four for nervous weakness, the charm of a farm was so strong in me that I induced a

2.12
Barn-studio at Nuttinghame,
c. 1915. Courtesy of the
Southbury Historical Society

good-humored but doubtful wife to go farm hunting."[48] Weakened in mind
and body by the pace of life in New York, he moved with his wife to Southbury,
a rural town in southwestern Connecticut, in the summer of 1906.[49]

In Southbury, the Nuttings purchased and restored a fallow farm and
became acolytes of the country life movement.[50] They drained the land,
improved the house—modestly christening it Nuttinghame—and for a time
attempted to lead the lives of genteel farmers (fig. 2.11). As early as 1885 such
back-to-the-land activities had attracted the attention of cultural critics.
"Many of the rich manufacturers are farmer's sons, Dick Whittingtons from
the country towns, and they have a fellow-feeling for the neighbors and the
homes of their boyhood. Indeed, they frequently invest a share of their wealth
in the purchase of ancestral acres, and convert the gambrel-roofed cottage
into an elegant summer retreat."[51] Kate Sanborn gently lampooned the phenomenon in 1892 in her book *Adopting an Abandoned Farm.* "Weary of boarding at seashore and mountain, tired of traveling in search of comfort, [and]
hating hotel life," Sanborn, like thousands of Americans, made the move
"from Gotham to Gooseville."[52]

The Nuttings, however, were no wealthy manufacturers when they moved
to Southbury. The need to make a living curtailed the agricultural fantasy
almost immediately. Photography, not farming, provided the daily bread at
Nuttinghame. The new barn, intended for animals when built, was converted
into a studio and became the center of a remarkable commercial enterprise
(fig. 2.12). "When my picture venture grew," Nutting later explained, "we
moved out from the house, cleansed the cement basement floor, where the

2.13
Wallace Nutting's colorists,
c. 1912. Local History
Collection, Framingham
Public Library

farm animals had been kept, and finished the barn above into two stories, the first for work rooms, the second for dormitories for the girls from a distance who colored the pictures. With a chaperon and a cook we had under one roof a dormitory, a studio, offices, and, in the basement, storage."[53]

Nuttinghame was a unique hybrid—part utopian community, part company town. At times it resembled the living experiments associated with the Arts and Crafts movement such as the Roycroft shops in East Aurora, New York, Rose Valley outside Philadelphia, and New Clarvioux in Montague, Massachusetts.[54] But the presence of Nutting's paid young, female colorists also made Nuttinghame something of an idealized factory village. The paternalistic structure of life at Nuttinghame, which included a dormitory with chaperone, lectures, sermons, and an emphasis on the outdoor life, recalled the movement of New England girls from the farm to mill towns to better their lot in the early industrial revolution. Commercial forces would soon change the rosy picture—just as it did in the nineteenth century.

Although Nutting claimed to have employed up to a hundred colorists at a time, there is scant evidence to support this assertion. Surviving photographs depict groups of ten to twenty colorists (fig. 2.13). Ruth Flood Brown, interviewed at age ninety-five, worked for Nutting for a number of years beginning in 1914. Brown estimated that there were perhaps twenty other colorists, though she also described other departments within the organization that could have added to the tally of employees.[55]

Coloring Life

Nutting's young female colorists initially worked in an upstairs hallway at Nuttinghame. They boarded nearby in the rural community and treated the endeavor much like attending school.[56] The experiences of Sarah Shortt were typical of Nutting's early colorists. Shortt was born on 13 June 1890 in Southbury, Connecticut.[57] After graduating from high school in June 1908, "Nutting sent his secretary up to my house and asked me to come talk to him about working," she recalled. Shortt described Nutting's restoration of the house and conversion of a long hallway into a gallerylike studio on the second floor. Windows along one wall let in sufficient light, and there was room for about six girls to work at a time. All had a "sense of art" but were trained by a head colorist that Nutting had brought up from New York City. Of the six girls, Shortt remembered that one came from Torrington, far up Connecticut's Brass Valley, three came from New York, and the rest were locals. They boarded in local Southbury homes, although Nutting also provided a small cottage "a little distance from the house" that he used as a dormitory, complete with a "mother" in charge.

A select group of Nutting's colorists and other workers from Nuttinghame worked as models in his photographs. Recalling one view, *An Ivied Porch, Nantucket*, Nutting colorist Sarah Shortt remembered, "The model was a very graceful girl. I think it was Nutting's maid."[58] Asked if she had appeared in any photographs herself, she answered, "No. I wasn't that popular—I didn't have the figure." Gertrude Brown, later of Westboro, Massachusetts, recalled, "Esther Swenson sat right behind me, also Daisy Ryder who was Mr. Nutting's model at that time. She was a blonde and wore her hair piled high in her pictures. She was in many of the colonial and some garden scenes. The little girl seen with her in some of the colonials lived in the house right behind the Nuttings."[59]

Nuttingholm

Nutting moved his operation from the Southbury farm to Framingham, Massachusetts, in 1912.[60] Attracted to the city's central location, the Nuttings moved into an Italianate house, calling it Nuttingholm, perhaps in an effort to ameliorate the unpopular Victorian style with a romantic Anglophilic name (fig. 2.14). This house was larger than Nuttinghame and, like the earlier country house, was at first Nutting's de facto commercial headquarters. For a time colorists worked in Nuttingholm, then moved into a studio building made of reused timber and other historic building materials on the grounds. Both

THE WALLACE NUTTING HOME. FRAMINGHAM. MASS.   22

2.14
Nuttingholm, c. 1917, postcard
view. Private collection

solutions proved to be inadequate, and by World War I, Nutting was operating
two major factory spaces.

Five years after the move to Framingham, Nutting opened another large
studio in Saugus, Massachusetts, adjacent to a historic house that he would
restore to become a link in his chain of colonial picture houses. Writing to
Jennie DeMerit, a young woman who had helped Mariet Nutting make a dress
some two years earlier, Nutting hoped to induce DeMerit to join the enterprise: "We are moving to Saugus, nine miles from Boston, three miles from
Lynn," he declared. "There are some pleasant residences around Cliftondale,"
he continued. "I want someone to sign my pictures and do similar work. It is
rather agreeable and I am willing to pay what it is worth." Although Nutting
admitted that it was "impossible for me to say accurately," he estimated that
the salary would be around sixty dollars a month.[61]

Production techniques perfected in Southbury carried over in Framingham and Saugus. Colorists were trained to follow models approved by Nutting himself (fig. 2.15). Stationed by windows, the prints were delivered en
masse from another part of the facility, where they were printed out, several
to a page, depending on their size (fig. 2.16). The toothy platinum paper, sized
with amyl acetate, also called banana oil, provided a ready surface for the

THE UNBROKEN FLOW

SKY PRUSSIAN BLUE:CHINESE WHITE
SUNSET ALIZARIN SCARLET:INDIAN YELLOW
DISTANCE MAUVE:GRAY GREEN
TREES GRAY GREEN:HOOKERS NO. 1 GREEN:INDIAN YELLOW:SAP GREEN
TREE TRUNKS SEPIA
FOREGROUND YELLOW OCHRE:BURNT SIENNA:HOOKERS NO. 1 GREEN
REFLECTIONS THE SAME AS ABOVE

2.15
Wallace Nutting, coloring
model for *The Unbroken
Flow*, c. 1920. The Manville
Collection

2.16
Wallace Nutting's colorists
at their workstations, c. 1915.
From MacKeil, *Wallace
Nutting*, 13

2.17
Wallace Nutting, *The History
of the Revolution—Webb House*,
untinted and uncut platinum
print, after 1916. Local History
Collection, Framingham
Public Library

Windsor and Newton pigments applied with sable brushes.[62] The prints were tinted color by color, according to Ruth Flood Brown. Workers would mix a blue for the sky, for instance, and color many skies before moving on to green trees or a yellow dress (fig. 2.17). In this way, colorists were participating in an assembly-line occupation of piecework rather than any individual artistic form of expression.[63]

One advantage of coloring platinum prints was that the process allowed Nutting to remove any offending evidence of the twentieth century. A colorist recalled that Nutting wrote out instructions on the back of a model photograph for his employees to "remove post and wire."[64] This was a far less physical process than the alternative he suggested in 1927, when he recommended that photographers "always carry a hatchet" to remove any offending sapling.

Nutting thus sought to clean up the view by retouching the prints and removing the telephone or telegraph poles and wires.[65]

Retouched by brush or pruned with a hatchet, Nutting's photographs stand as a paradigm of middle-class cultural production. Evolving out of the amateur photography movement, his hand-tinted platinum prints achieved wildfire market success and became the vehicle for the minister from Rock-bottom to branch out and develop his Old American business empire. By 1915—when he issued his largest catalog—Nutting's middle-class art held sway in American visual culture.

Chapter 3   *Middle-Class Art, or, The Expansible Old America*

"Not so long ago," Wallace Nutting wrote in 1921, "it was impossible to purchase a natural, tasteful picture without going to great expense." Fine art was simply beyond the reach of most Americans. "There were millions," he continued, "who knew beauty when they saw it but could not indulge in the works of old masters, or new masters for that matter." As for more affordable media, "the watercolors of twenty years ago were numerous and shall we say startling."[1] Domestic art, for all but the wealthy, consisted of one form of simulacrum or another. Mass-produced statuary groups provided a sentimental conversation piece for the parlor; chromolithographs and inexpensive stenciled landscapes adorned the walls of countless middle-class homes (figs. 3.1, 3.2).[2]

The diffusion of a modern artistic sensibility, however, altered notions of popular art. Although "chromos" were promoted as educational and uplifting, critics grumbled about their derivative nature and sentimental subject matter.[3] As early as 1870 the *Nation* weighed in on the issue: "The chromo-lithographic imitation of oil painting is a type of everything in bad art that is most disgusting to the artist and to the cultivated."[4] By 1900, for the work to be art it required the singular touch of the master. Etchings passed muster and print clubs flourished, but the simple demographics of an expanding nation posed challenges to new notions of high art.[5] Photography provided an attractive answer to the riddle of a middling aesthetic.

As an art form unto itself, photography's reputation had waxed and waned since its invention in 1839. Initially, photographers were considered commercial tradesman, "bread and butter practitioners" in Nutting's words.[6] Those who pushed the media beyond portraiture for the first fifty years or so were odd men out. The development of Pictorial photography, a style that celebrated artistic intervention in the photographic process, breathed life into the field in the 1890s. Concurrent advances in technology, including the diffusion

Opposite: Detail of fig. 3.40

3.1
L. Prang and Company,
Spring, after Alfred Thompson
Bricher, c. 1869, chromolitho-
graph. Private collection

3.2
John Rogers, *"Why Don't You
Speak for Yourself, John?"* 1885,
painted plaster. Smithsonian
American Art Museum, Gift of
Mrs. Genevieve Wisel
in memory of Dan Wisel

of dry-plate technology, led to an active amateur scene and made photography a popular negotiation between the arts understood to be high and low in
the period. By the turn of the century, amateurs, artists, and commercial houses
provided a range of photographic images for the home.

Domestic art photography, Nutting's own bread and butter from 1904
until his death in 1941, coopted the popular notion that for an object to be art
it had to be a unique and singular expression.[7] Relying on a cult of personality
("none genuine without my signature," read his advertisements), colored by
hand, and offering recognizably artistic scenes, Nutting's hand-tinted platinum
prints combined Victorian desires for mass-produced decoration with modern

demands for the real thing.[8] Nutting was clear about his role as a middle-class tastemaker. "I am under no illusions as to my pictures. I am not an artist, and it is most disagreeable to me to be called one. I am a clergyman with a love of the beautiful." Though pious and self-deprecating, Nutting's language reveals his growing contempt for popular media. "My pictures," he continued, "have at least made the chromo less popular and they are honest and carefully marked by artisanship, if not art."[9] Nutting thus sought to stake out a place between what historian Miles Orvell has called the "culture of imitation"—the nineteenth-century world of the "chromo"—and developing sensibilities of high art.[10] By combining photography, a mechanical form of expression, with watercolor, a medium long associated with the heroic sensibilities of plein air painting, Nutting popularized a form of representation more respectable than the chromolithograph yet far less expensive than an oil painting.[11]

Catalog Sales

Nutting owed his success as a purveyor of art for the middle-class home to the development of a sophisticated delivery system. As early as 1904, the recently retired minister issued catalogs of his photography. "Wallace Nutting pictures," he wrote, "had their origin in the love of an amateur for the beauties of our incomparable countryside."[12] His amateur days were soon over. In 1908 he brought out another catalog, and larger editions followed in 1910 and 1912. The offering of 1912 ran to ninety-seven pages and contained more than eight hundred views interspersed with Nutting's commentary. The effort and expense of producing such a lavish catalog ruffled his Yankee sensibilities. "This book is out of date even now that it is new," he grumbled. Catching himself in the same paragraph, Nutting waxed poetic, "but in the sense that the beautiful is eternal the book will always be fresh."[13]

In 1915, Nutting mailed the *Expansible Catalog*. Issued in a clever, flexible format that allowed for almost unlimited growth, the *Expansible* edition represented a new level of maturity for the business (fig. 3.3).[14] Before the move to Framingham in 1912, Nutting relied on a cobbled-together sales program largely based on independent prints shops, traveling salesmen, and local representatives who may or may not have had access to his latest catalog.[15] The new edition rationalized customer relations by giving retailers an up-to-the-minute list of images in a versatile format. In a new streamlined process, the catalog was shipped to an authorized dealer, usually a local department or jewelry store, along with an advertising sign and a representative group of framed platinotypes.[16] After paging through the volume, figuratively wandering the landscape with Nutting, the customer selected view, size, and frame and

A Marlboro Shore   Q and C 3459   Cross Road Shadows   C 3515

A Sheltered Road   Q and O 3147   Early May   Q, S and P 3067   Up the Hill   Q and S 3025

We have been accused of overcoloring the birch trunks.　It is hard to believe that the birch is so white. We do not color the trunks at all, except where the outside bark is missing.　At first the exposed bark is red brown, but turns dark gray to black.

11

3.3
A typical page from the
Expansible Catalog (1915), 11.
Auerbach Library, Wadsworth
Atheneum Museum of Art

12

13

14

15

16

17

3.4
Framing options, *Expansible Catalog* (1915), 979. Auerbach Library, Wadsworth Atheneum Museum of Art

executed the order. The print was then drop-shipped from Framingham directly to the buyer's door (fig. 3.4).

Surviving examples of the 1915 catalog contain approximately eight hundred thumbnail views and often include inserts that advertise related initiatives, such as Nutting's ill-fated chain of house museums.[17] The ability to add to the catalog as well as its flexible pagination reveals that Nutting had expansive plans for the growth of Old America. Thousands of new views could be added without changing either the organizational scheme of the catalog or, more important, the narratives created by the categorization and juxtaposition of images.

Throughout the *Expansible Catalog* Nutting played off established conventions of visual culture to give middle-class consumers a traditional view for the home.[18] Late-nineteenth-century photographers, writes art historian Paul Sternberger, can be grouped broadly into two camps: those who sought

3.5
Wallace Nutting, *The Guardian Angel*, 1910, hand-tinted platinum print. The Manville Collection

approval by employing the "grammar of art" and those who advocated an "anti-photographic" or Pictorial style.[19] The former relied on formal similarities to well-known artistic traditions, such as the landscape theories of the French painter Claude Lorrain or the use of light in seventeenth-century Dutch genre scenes. Although Nutting appeared quite willing to experiment with an antiphotographic, soft-focus aesthetic, as in such images as the allegorical *Guardian Angel*, most of his work sought to exploit well-known visual traditions (fig. 3.5). Less cryptic but equally symbolic, Nutting's photographs traded in convention. To scan the pages of the *Expansible Catalog* was tantamount to taking a short course in Western visual culture.

3.6
Wallace Nutting, *Spring by the Lake*, c. 1916, hand-tinted platinum print. Wadsworth Atheneum Museum of Art, Gift of David W. Dangremond, 2001.5.2

The (White) Birch

The *Expansible Catalog* opens with the land—more specifically, the trees. Images like *A Sheltered Road, Silver Birches*, and *The Bridesmaids of the Wood* invited Nutting's customers into the book and provided a naturalistic portal to Old America (fig. 3.6). Nutting's forest, however, is populated by a specific species, the white or paper birch. The birch is a telling citizen of the forest, not only a forceful formal ally to the photographer, but also rife with symbolic connotations. The most northern and Yankee of trees, the birch was celebrated in art and literature ranging from Willard Metcalf's painting *A Family of Birches* of 1907 to Robert Frost's poem "Birches," written in 1913 and published in the *Atlantic Monthly* in August 1915 (fig. 3.7).[20]

The landscape architect Frank Waugh explained the importance of the

white birch in early-twentieth-century environmental thought. "Birches come quickly into 'new' land," he wrote in 1901 in *Country Life in America*, "where the trees are felled or cultivation lost. They are pioneers, with the dash-and-go, the jaunty air and the instability of frontier character. They come and go quickly . . . they never lost character, or tell a misleading story of the passing of the old and the coming of the new order in the plant world."[21] Consumers who purchased Nutting's photographs imagined themselves as latter-day pioneers, jaunty in their suburban homes and seeking traditional values represented by the country road, stone wall, and placid stream in a modern America overgrown with cities and reforested with immigrants.

Chronologically, the birch pictures represent some of Nutting's earliest work. He began the series in 1900—three seasons after picking up the camera.[22] Summering in northern New England, mostly "in and about Woodstock," Vermont, Nutting "made studies of birches, elms, and pastoral

3.8
Childe Hassam, *Church at Old Lyme, Connecticut,* 1905, oil on canvas. Albright-Knox Art Gallery, Buffalo, New York; Albert H. Tracy Fund, 1909

scenes."[23] So important was this early series to the minister that he included the line "First Birch pictures, 1900," in his résumé—an entry weighted equally with his marriage, honorary degrees, and numerous successes in business.[24] As with his earliest Barbizon-inspired amateur efforts, Nutting followed aesthetic conventions of the day when composing the birch scenes. His pictures thus

3.9
Wallace Nutting, *Old Lyme Congregational Church*, c. 1914, platinum print. Courtesy of the Society for the Preservation of New England Antiquities

appear in ready conversation with the work of contemporary easel painters, especially those in impressionist circles.

Nutting's hand-tinted images reproduced the calming worldview of the impressionists but made it available to a wider audience. A painting such as *A Family of Birches* might cost $5,000 or more when painted in 1909.[25] *A Silent Shore* could be had for as little as $1.50 in 1915, though Nutting preferred to sell a larger print, and framing options added to the price.[26] Bypassing traditional galleries and exhibitions, Nutting delivered a product that performed the same cultural work as Metcalf's painting, but at a price the expanding middle class could afford.

The close geographic circles of art-making in New England, coupled with Nutting's interest in tying his artisanship to popular conventions of high art, produced a homogeneous visual culture. Childe Hassam, perhaps the quintessential interpreter of the New England nostalgic, painted *Church at Old Lyme, Connecticut*, in 1905 (fig. 3.8). Within ten years, Nutting offered images of the interior (fig. 3.9) of this venerable and iconic house of worship. Nutting

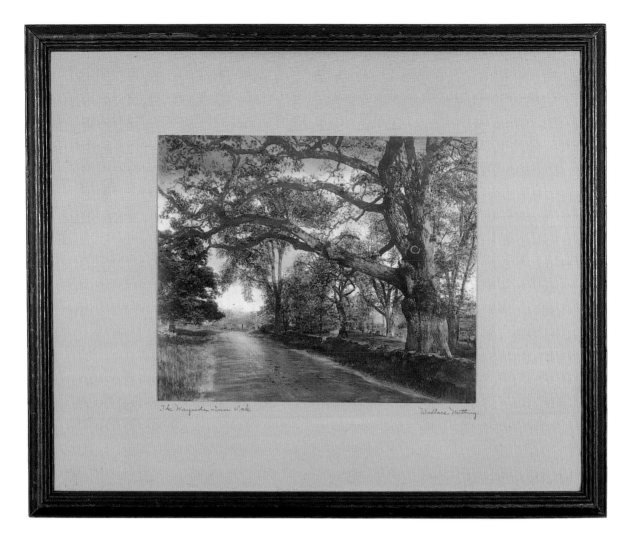

3.10
Wallace Nutting, *The Wayside Inn Approach*, before 1915, hand-tinted platinum print. The Manville Collection

included *The Wayside Inn Approach* as photograph 592 in the *Expansible Catalog* in 1915; Hassam offered his patrons the etching *Wayside Inn Oaks in Spring* in 1926 (figs. 3.10, 3.11). Nutting's stately view of *A Colonial Three Decker* slightly predates Willard Metcalf's *Captain Lord House, Kennebunkport, Maine*, yet both provided cover for the fact that modern New Englanders lived in three-deckers of a very different sort (figs. 3.12, 3.13). Nutting's title, sarcastically referring to a contemporary "spec built" form of worker's housing, preaches about the virtues of the past and the perceived vices of the present (fig. 3.14).[27] As moralizing visual inventions, Nutting's landscapes and architectural scenes pale when compared to his figural studies—especially his images of women.

3.11
Childe Hassam, *Wayside Inn Oaks in Spring*, 1926, etching on paper. Smithsonian American Art Museum, transfer from the National Museum of American History, Division of Graphic Arts

The Old-Fashioned Girl versus the New Woman

"Colonials," idealized images of women in historic dress, fill one-fifth of the 1915 catalog (fig. 3.15). Although a handful of men appear sporadically throughout the catalog, they are invariably assigned supporting roles in moralizing tableaux and are marginalized by dint of age. Male children shade Nutting's women in maternal light while bearded patriarchs "sparking" with their wives testify to the enduring values of marriage (fig. 3.16). Most of Nutting's views depict young women in their late teens or early twenties—women of marrying age. As idealizations of traditional female behavior, they speak volumes about period concerns surrounding the changing roles of women in the early twentieth century. These old-fashioned girls all reckon with the New Woman.[28]

The New Woman gave many people pause. Termed a "revolutionary demographic and political phenomenon" by historian Carroll Smith-Rosenberg, the New Woman was the daughter of the modern industrial age. Single, athletic, and possessing an increasingly public persona, the New Woman demanded attention and received plenty of notice. "Eschewing marriage, she fought for professional visibility, espoused innovative, often radical, economic and social reforms, and wielded real political power."[29]

3.12
Wallace Nutting, *A Colonial Three-Decker*, before 1915, hand-tinted platinum print. Courtesy of the Society for the Preservation of New England Antiquities

Inextricably part of the modern scene, the New Woman was particularly threatening to cultural conservatives like Nutting. Whereas an earlier generation of strident social reformers, temperance workers, and suffragettes could be dismissed as members of the radical fringe, the New Woman became normative and appeared especially dangerous as a result.[30] "Her quintessentially American identity," notes Smith-Rosenberg, "her economic resources, and her social standing permitted her to defy proprieties, pioneer new roles, and still insist upon a rightful place within the genteel world. Repudiating the Cult of True Womanhood in ways her mother—the new bourgeois matron—never could, she threatened men in ways her mother never did" (fig. 3.17).[31]

The Modern Priscilla

Reacting to the challenges of the New Woman, Nutting placed great emphasis on the creation of a visual genealogy for the helpmate. In an age of independent, bicycle-riding, vote-demanding women, Nutting looked back and rehabilitated a nineteenth-century symbol of domestic tranquillity based on hearth and home. He found his archetype, a literary cliché of the capable colonial housewife, in Priscilla Mullins, the central character of Henry Wadsworth Longfellow's epic poem *The Courtship of Miles Standish*, written almost fifty years earlier, in

3.13
Willard Leroy Metcalf,
Captain Lord House, Kenne-bunkport, Maine, c. 1920, oil on canvas. Courtesy
of the Florence Griswold
Museum, Old Lyme,
Connecticut; Gift of Mrs.
Henrietta Metcalf

3.14
*Lawton Street, Lynn,
Massachusetts*, c. 1911.
Courtesy of the Peabody Essex
Museum

3.15
Wallace Nutting, *The Morning Mail*, 1912, hand-tinted platinum print, tipped into *Old New England Pictures* (1913). Auerbach Library, Wadsworth Atheneum Museum of Art

1858.[32] In hundreds of carefully constructed photographic costume dramas, Nutting brought Priscilla and her sisters to life for a generation of Americans concerned with modernity and women's changing roles (fig. 3.18).

Longfellow's "Puritan pastoral," which he based largely on such popular histories as Charles W. Elliott's *New England History* (1857) and Alexander Young's *Chronicles of the Pilgrim Fathers* (1841), had launched Priscilla into popular consciousness as the ideal wife and mother.[33]

> *Praise of the virtuous woman, as she is*
>   *described in the Proverbs,—*
> *How the heart of her husband doth safely*
>   *trust in her always,*
> *How all the days of her life she will do him*
>   *good, and not evil,*

3.16
Wallace Nutting, *Cornered*,
copyright 1902, hand-tinted
platinum print, tipped into
Old New England Pictures
(1913). Wadsworth Atheneum
Museum of Art

3.17
From Charles Dana Gibson,
Pictures of People (New York:
R. H. Russell, 1896)

3.18
Wallace Nutting, *A Virginia Reel*, 1912, hand-tinted platinum print. The Manville Collection

How she seeketh the wool and the flax and
  worketh with gladness,
How she layeth her hand to the spindle and
  holdeth the distaff,
How she is not afraid of the snow for her-
  self, or her household,
Knowing her household as clothed with
  the scarlet cloth of her weaving! [34]

Producing and providing, Longfellow's Priscilla became the middle-class domestic ideal: she had spurned the rough adventurer Miles Standish in favor of the thoughtful John Alden (a prototypical Victorian Brain-Worker in Pil-

3.19
A. Brown and Company,
*The New England Kitchen,
Brooklyn Sanitary Fair*, 1864,
chromolithograph. Wadsworth
Atheneum Museum of Art

grim garb). In conjunction with John Greenleaf Whittier's beloved mother
from the 1865 epic *Snowbound*, Priscilla became the ur-wife and mother for
America's turbulent age of industrialization.[35]

Priscilla and her fellows were celebrated at every turn, leaping off the pages
to appear time again in nineteenth-century visual culture. Her saintly actions
were acted out in *tableaux vivants* at United States Sanitary Commission fairs
throughout the North during the Civil War (fig. 3.19).[36] After the war, she was
enlisted as a historical mother figure at the 1876 centennial celebrations in
Philadelphia—a national birthday party attended by fifteen-year-old Wallace
Nutting (fig. 3.20).[37] William Dean Howells, writing in the *Atlantic Monthly*,
noted that "Massachusetts, [erected an] Old Colony House of logs, which we
found thronged by pleased and curious visitors. There are many actual relics of
the Pilgrim days, all of which the crowd examined with the keenest interest;
there was among other things the writing-desk of John Alden, and at the corner of the deep and wide fire-place sat Priscilla spinning—or some young lady
in a quaint, old-fashioned dress, who served the same purpose. . . . That was
altogether the prettiest thing I saw at the Centennial."[38]

Popular at the fair, images of Priscilla and other spinning women were
soon ubiquitous in American visual culture.[39] Painters of national reputation
committed her likeness to canvas (fig. 3.21). Regional photographers such as

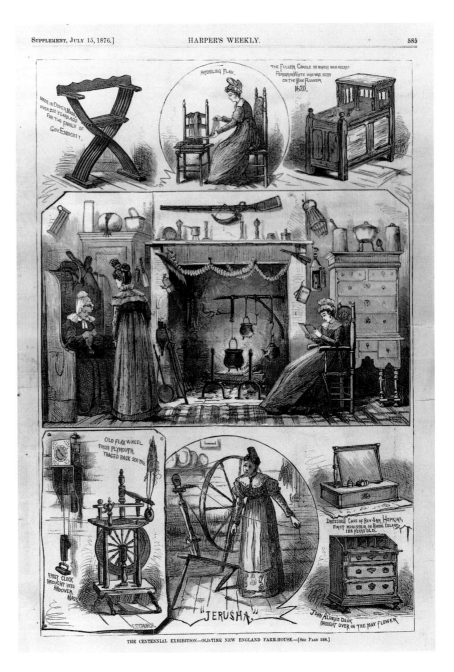

THE CENTENNIAL EXHIBITION—OLD-TIME NEW ENGLAND FARM-HOUSE.—[SEE PAGE 588.]

3.20
Harper's Weekly, 15 July 1876.
Courtesy of The Winterthur
Library, Printed Book and
Periodical Collection

Emma Lewis Coleman staged similar scenes (see fig. 2.9) in the 1880s. John
Rogers, the sculptor who specialized in mass-market statuary groups, reproduced a scene from Longfellow's tale verbatim when he included "Why Don't
You Speak for Yourself, John Alden" in his catalog (see fig. 3.2). The mythic
mother even appeared on stage as the female lead in such dramatic episodes
as "The Mayflower Period," an act in the National Society of New England
Women's 1897 "Dramatic and Scenic Reproduction of American History."[40]

3.21
Thomas Akins, *In Grand-mother's Day*, 1876, oil on canvas. Smith College Art Museum, purchased from the artist, 1879

Women, Productive and Genteel

Nutting's Pilgrim mothers were clearly heiresses to a long tradition of colonial helpmates. Not only did the minister directly connect his oeuvre to midcentury Pilgrim tales through such photographs as *A Chair for John*, *A Pilgrim Daughter*, and *Rose Standish*, but he also pushed beyond mere literary parody to develop a visual vocabulary of traditional female behavior for his own generation. Genteel and productive, Nutting's old-fashioned girls served as a caution to modern housewives, lest they forget the perceived virtues of their grandmother's day.

Nutting's depictions of domestic life focus on women as producers within
a preindustrial household economy. An iconic example of this rubric is *Trimming the Pie Crust* (fig. 3.22). Taken at the Cooper-Frost-Austin House in Cambridge, Massachusetts—one of the earliest properties acquired by the Society
for the Preservation of New England Antiquities—*Trimming the Pie Crust* is
one of a number exposed during one photographic session. Nutting's model,
in apron, cap, and temporally ambivalent old-fashioned dress, takes the viewer
along through several steps of baking an apple pie in an open hearth. In varia-
tions on the same pose, she rolls the crust, trims the pie, and places it in the
beehive oven. Easily recognizable props, including a wool wheel, ladder-back
chair, and small worktable, surround and contain Nutting's model. Other Nutting scenes, taken slightly later in his Chain of Colonial Picture Houses and
other historic houses, depict women sewing, weaving, spinning, cooking, drawing water, minding children, and demurely toiling at other domestic chores

(fig. 3.23). Cast to populate the invented Old America, these women belie the fact that the upper classes enjoyed the assistance of domestic servants and textile production had long since moved out of the middle-class home. In fact, Lewis Hine's reform-minded visions of mill girls came far closer to capturing the realities of manufacturing textiles in the twentieth century than did Nutting's paeans to the golden age of homespun (fig. 3.24).[41]

After productivity, according to Nutting, gentility was the paramount female virtue. Providing traditional modes of behavior for the modern era, Nutting's ladies of the parlor take strolls, read books, write letters, drink tea, await suitors, or engage in such delicate pursuits as regarding their fine china (figs. 3.25, 3.26). An anonymous author, writing in *Old New England Traits*, offered the opinion that "pictures of past manners, if truthfully portrayed, can hardly fail to be both interesting and useful. We heard plenty of stories, in our youth, of a higher style of living in colonial days . . . the gold embroidered garments, the laced ruffles of the gentleman, and the highly ornamented, but rather stiff garniture in which the ladies with their powdered heads saw fit to array themselves, as they now present themselves to us on the living canvas of Copley."[42]

Nutting's living canvas reified gentility by providing images that closely resembled the iconic interiors of the Boston school (figs. 3.27, 3.28). Just as his therapeutic views of historic buildings and trees demonstrated kinship with the work of Metcalf and Hassam, so his interiors followed the portrait conventions of Edmund Tarbell, Frank Benson, Joseph DeCamp, and William Paxton. Elegant and refined, the women portrayed by the Boston School are invariably depicted in a hushed, hermetic parlor, far removed from the hustle and bustle of modern life.[43] As with the young sewers in Tarbell's *New England Interior* or the woman looking at her china in DeCamp's *Blue Cup*, they embroider, mend, read, or regard ancestral objects in much the same way as Nutting's Old American actors (figs. 3.29, 3.30).

Views of the Bedchamber

A sense of purpose pervades Nutting's images of colonial women and sets his work apart from that of his predecessors and contemporaries (fig. 3.31). Earlier photographers had worked in a similar vein, but although a few such as Emma Coleman or Mary and Frances Allen sought to aestheticize disappearing "old-time" practices, none sought to proscribe behavior quite as Nutting did. His visual tributes to pretty, traditional girls in an era of unsettling suffragettes and unspeakable flappers were part of the overall ideology of Old America—a system of values that led Nutting to criticize modern female taste

3.23
Wallace Nutting, *Weaving a Rag Rug*, c. 1915, hand-tinted platinum print. Courtesy of the Society for the Preservation of New England Antiquities

3.24
Lewis Hine, *Fourteen-Year-Old Spinner, Berkshire Cotton Mills, Adams, Massachusetts*, 1916. Courtesy of the Library of Congress, Prints and Photographs Division

3.25
Wallace Nutting, *The Merchant's Daughter*,
copyright 1911, hand-tinted platinum
print, tipped into *Old New England
Pictures* (1913). Auerbach Library,
Wadsworth Atheneum Museum of Art

3.26
Wallace Nutting, *Colonial
China* (Wentworth-Gardner
House, Portsmouth, New
Hampshire), copyright 1915,
platinum print. Courtesy of the
Society for the Preservation of
New England Antiquities

in the most private of arenas—the bedroom. "While some would point out that there is a revival of good taste," wrote the minister of his era, "the ugliness and bareness within and without modernistic walls may more than balance" this rejuvenation. Of his many worries, "the ugliness of the pajama-class outline sadly points to the lack of taste where women should be most sensitive to it—the charm of good lines was clearly a thing of the past."[44]

Nutting's horror at the thought of a woman in pajamas is telegraphed in the buttoned-up aesthetic of his colonials. In relying so heavily on images of the fairer sex, however, he risked a charge of voyeurism. Although his models occasionally displayed the nape of a neck in a time-honored sensual pose, the overall Nutting program left little room for titillation or base thoughts (fig. 3.32). His interest in women, he claimed, was purely a business decision. "No one cares for an interior without a person posed in it," he wrote, "the person must be a woman and in the background. If she is prominent, nobody wants the picture, but she must be in it."[45]

Compared to other artists of his day, Nutting encoded his photographs with a highly oblique sexuality. Two images, Thomas Wilmer Dewing's *Spinet* from about 1902 and Nutting's *Spinet Corner* from before 1912, illustrate the

sublimated nature of the minister's interest in this most human of behaviors
(figs. 3.33, 3.34). Dewing, a denizen of the forward-thinking art colony at Cor-
nish, New Hampshire, and a particular favorite of the libertine critic Sadakichi
Hartmann, presents a bare-shouldered musician playing with natural aban-
don, the chords rising from her instrument to animate the very wallpaper,
hinting at a primal force.[46] Nutting's spinet player, by contrast, is the picture
of reserve. Posed in quiescent tribute to the Dutch interiors of the seventeenth
century, she is a long way from bringing the wallpaper to life (fig. 3.35).[47]

3.30
Wallace Nutting, *For the Honored Guest*, c. 1910, hand-tinted platinum print. Courtesy of the Society for the Preservation of New England Antiquities

The Moral Landscape

As with his figural scenes, Nutting often prescribed a moral to accompany his landscapes, adding to the didactic nature of the *Expansible Catalog*. Most individual lessons are transparent; Nutting offered the viewer an interpretation in the titles he assigned to each print. Of particular interest in this regard are his "Blossom" pictures—views that depict upland apple trees in full bloom (fig. 3.36). These scenes were frequently marketed as a wedding gift—Nutting reminded his customers that "an apple blossom used at a wedding fades before the ceremony is fairly completed." However, "a picture of blossoms to be on the wall of the happy couple will continue to remind them even to their golden or diamond jubilee of the glad and sacred occasion that joined their lives."[48] Nutting sought to enlist the land itself to aid in a crusade to strengthen the bonds of the traditional nuclear family. In doing so, Nutting mixed morals, aesthetics, and economics in his views of the New England landscape.

Dozens of blossom pictures in the 1915 catalog carry such matrimonial titles as *Decked as a Bride*, *Honeymoon Windings*, and *Honeymoon Cottage*. One can excuse a Congregational minister a certain interest in the subject of matrimony, but why was Nutting so profoundly focused on the question? One answer lies in the period perception that the institution of marriage was itself under threat at the turn of the century. Not only did recent immigrants bring new religious traditions to the United States, but the general secularization of

3.32
Wallace Nutting, *Ol' Bill
Speare's*, copyright 1913,
platinum print. Courtesy of the
Society for the Preservation of
New England Antiquities

3.33
Thomas Wilmer Dewing,
The Spinet, c. 1902, oil on canvas,
Smithsonian American Art
Museum, Gift of John Gellatly

3.34
Wallace Nutting, *The Spinet
Corner*, 1912, hand-tinted
platinum print, tipped into *Old
New England Pictures* (1913).
Auerbach Library, Wadsworth
Atheneum Museum of Art

3.35
Jan Vermeer, *The Concert*,
1658–1660, oil on canvas.
Isabella Stewart Gardner
Museum, Boston

everyday life was perceived to be loosening the marriage bond. Divorce statistics buttressed these fears. In the 1880s, about the time Nutting was called to his first congregation, divorce rates stood at about one in twenty-one marriages. By 1890, one in twelve marriages ended in divorce. By 1924, the figure was one in seven. Furthermore, those seeking marriage in the Protestant church were fewer in number with each passing decade. "Religiously sanctioned weddings," writes historian Lynn Dumenil, "accounted for 85 percent of the marriages in 1890, but only 63 percent in 1923. As marriage itself became less sacred, there was a rise in marriage dissolutions."[49] If the very trees in Nutting's photographs could be enlisted to combat contemporary social ills, it comes as no surprise to discover political meaning in the minister's architectural views.

3.36
Wallace Nutting, *Decked as a Bride*, 1910, hand-tinted platinum print. The Manville Collection

Pilgrim Prehistory

The first man-made structures encountered in the *Expansible Catalog*, other than the odd barn or shed in a distant landscape, are a handful of English cottages and a small grouping of Romanesque bridges, mostly from Italy and England. Abbeys, cathedrals, and idyllic river views follow in great number. The product of Nutting's extensive travels, these foreign scenes are extensions of the nineteenth-century mania for photographic scenes of English and Continental antiquities (figs. 3.37, 3.38). "By 1900," writes Miles Orvell, "vicarious experience had become a major commodity . . . and the habit of [photographic] surrogates had grown strong and indelible in American life."

3.37
Wallace Nutting, *The Conscious Stones*, c. 1915. From the *Expansible Catalog* (1915)

3.38
Wallace Nutting, *The Pergola Amalfi*, copyright 1904, hand-tinted platinum print. The Manville Collection

3.39
Wallace Nutting, *The Mills
at the Turn*, before 1915,
hand-tinted platinum print.
The Manville Collection

Indeed, within "twenty years of the invention of photography in 1839 it became commonplace to speak of the practical advantages and pleasures of 'touring' without having to leave home."[50] Nutting's tourist scenes, however, provided more than mere simulation of travel in the English countryside. Often referencing Shakespeare and the romantic poets, they established a learned ancestry for their purchasers. Particularly important were views of the Low Countries.

Old America, as illustrated in the *Expansible Catalog,* is especially rife with Dutch imagery.[51] One catalog illustrates twenty-one separate views of windmills, canals, city scenes, and hearty peasant women. Scenes such as *The Mills at the Turn* and *The Canal Road* initially seem out of step with Nutting's nativist program, but to look more closely at turn-of-the-century American visual culture is to come face-to-face with what Annette Stott has termed "Holland Mania" (fig. 3.39).[52] Citizens of all stripes, relates Stott, were drawn to an ancestry that allied the ideals of the historic seventeenth-century Dutch

3.40
Wallace Nutting, *A Warm Spring Day*, before 1906, hand-tinted platinum print. The Manville Collection

Republic (democracy, commerce, tolerance, and plenty) with the ideology of the Progressive era. In particular, the American middle class came to identify with the Netherlands as an alternative, more benign heritage than that offered by the ever-shifting reputation of the Puritan fathers. "Many younger writers of the early twentieth century," notes historian David Hall, came "to perceive American culture as suffering from the blight of a repressive parochialism stemming from the founding of New England" by the Puritans.[53] Dutch heritage offered the middle class a convenient way out of this unsavory reputation.

On one level, Nutting's images of the Netherlands provided reassuring and unchallenging art for the home. "Holland," he wrote, "to those persons who love the quaint, abounds in themes, such as canals, old cottages, cheese markets, city halls, and genre subjects."[54] For those customers who read the popular historian John Lothrop Motley, however, parallels to the modern world were evident and imbued the pictures on the wall of the middle-class home with significance. The Dutch, to those "in the know," were peace loving and merely enjoying the fruits of their honest trade when the Spanish (read

3.41
Wallace Nutting, *Topsham
Banks*, c. 1905, platinum print.
From *Maine Beautiful* (1924), 121

Catholics) besieged them in the seventeenth century. How many middle-class Americans, fearing latter-day immigrants, sympathized with the plight of their adopted ancestors? "Many" is the answer provided by such groups as the Immigration Restriction League, an organization of predominantly wealthy Bostonians founded in 1894 to lobby for policies and regulations that would "close the gates" to "undesirables" from foreign lands.[55]

Pastoralism

Nutting's conservatism, so evident in his European views and colonials, carried over into a series of pastorals. "The relation of a farm to the study of the beautiful," he wrote, "was well known to artists, who, like Constable, have enthralled generations by their depiction of country life."[56] His *Warm Spring Day* continued in this lengthy tradition of bucolic imagery (fig. 3.40). Although Barbizon influences run high in his pastorals, Nutting-the-gentleman-farmer certainly did not have to travel to France to seek the timeless landscape of agrarian life. It was in his own backyard. Nutting's writings belie the sort of farm he ran in Southbury. "The cattle were selected for beauty of black and white banding; the horses bought for handsome heads. The sheep and lambs because we loved them. If an animal would not pose for a picture, it was not for us."[57]

Highly traditional but no less calming, such imagery enjoyed popularity well into the twentieth century, as evidenced by Nutting's claim that *A Warm Spring Day* was "by far the most popular sheep picture ever made. It has been pirated and one pirate has even signed his name to it."[58] The therapeutic qualities imbued in such imagery are again made explicit by the minister, who placed his motivations in a most modern context. "Who," he asked, "possessing a cow and a cornfield, needs to know what Wall Street is doing?"[59]

The Frontier of Old America

Having defined his patrons as refugees from the modern world of Wall Street, in his "marines"—views of the rugged shoreline and surging sea—Nutting extended the fantasy of Old America to a coastal frontier. There is a marine to match every mood, from the calming waters of a glassy harbor to the rugged clash where land meets sea. "The endless phases of the sea," Nutting wrote in 1898, "merit our delighted devotion."[60] Indeed, along with birch pictures, views of streams, and pastoral scenes, coastal compositions appear to have been among Nutting's earliest photographic interests (fig. 3.41). The sea can be a calm, soothing presence, as in the sheltered waters of *Southwest Harbor*

3.42
Wallace Nutting, *Impassible
Barriers*, c. 1905, platinum
print. From *Maine Beautiful*
(1924), 17

and *The Rhode Island Coast*, but usually it is a source of primal conflict. Images like *Impassible Barriers* (fig. 3.42) evoke a rugged, moody realism. Indeed, *Impassible Barriers* looks very much like a photographic interpretation of the later work of Winslow Homer, typified by *High Cliffs, Coast of Maine* of 1894 (fig. 3.43).

The importance of such rugged imagery is suggested in the writings of Ralph Henry Gabriel, an early scholar of America and the sea. Writing in the 1926 series *The Pageant of America*, Gabriel noted, "In reality America had two frontiers, one working steadily across the continent and the other pushing out finally to the farthest ends of the oceans. The men and women of each knew the same hand-to-hand struggle with nature."[61] The rugged coast pictured by both Homer and Nutting is thus also a frontier zone. For Homer it provided the backdrop for upper-class fantasies about the strenuous life. For Nutting this was the shoreline of his beloved Old America, the primal landscape of yeoman farmers and their hearty wives. In Nutting's cosmology they gave birth to a golden century of genteel manners, forms, and customs later lost to the machine, the city, and the heterogeneous helter-skelter of modern American life.

Like the potshards of a past civilization, Nutting's photographs outlived the minister to litter the postwar middle-class landscape. Re-classified as

3.43
Winslow Homer, *High Cliffs, Coast of Maine*, 1894, oil on canvas. Smithsonian American Art Museum, Gift of William T. Evans

kitsch, the tinted photographs became symbols without meaning. Although Nutting recycled numerous images in the 1920s and 1930s in his popular travelogues, a series of volumes that ran from *Vermont Beautiful* to *Ireland Beautiful*, the hegemony of high modern aesthetics consigned his apple blossom wedding presents to the attic after World War II. The *Expansible Catalog*, however, provides a guided tour of Nutting's hopes for Old America. From upland orchards, reflecting ponds, and winding roads to the parlors of genteel coastal towns and out onto the rugged Atlantic, the "minister with a love of beauty" provided a photograph to fit every aesthetic in the opening decades of the twentieth century. A middle-class art, Nutting's photography prescribed traditional modes of decoration and behavior for the generation that built suburban America.

Chapter 4	*Picture Houses, Period Rooms, and Print*

WALLACE NUTTING AND THE PLACE OF HISTORY

A keen student of business practice, Wallace Nutting moved to diversify his company on the eve of World War I when he organized "The Wallace Nutting Chain of Colonial Picture Houses."[1] His interest in gathering these consumer-friendly museums stemmed, first and foremost, from his needs as a photographer and entrepreneur. Stymied by the time, effort, and expense involved in seeking out "authentic" interiors to photograph, Nutting decided to acquire a select number of historic buildings to streamline the process.[2] These properties, he wrote in a brochure of 1915 introducing the endeavor to his customers, would serve as "a proper setting for quaint pictures with attractive background and furnishings." He therefore gave "his hobby the rein" with a "daring and unique plan" to purchase five houses, "each notable for some outstanding merit."[3] Illustrated in photographs and opened to tourists, the chain of picture houses became the physical location of Old America.

From the outset, Nutting designed the Chain of Colonial Picture Houses to provide a narrative journey. Each stop on this tour of Old America (in photographs or in person) taught the latter-day pilgrim a lesson about the past. From the rugged (and entrepreneurial) seventeenth-century environment of Broadhearth in Saugus, Massachusetts, to the patriotic air of Hospitality Hall in Wethersfield, Connecticut, and the genteel elegance of the Wentworth-Gardner House in Portsmouth, New Hampshire, Nutting's picture houses provided a history course for the consumer age.[4] Nutting commodified the past and defined a market-based attitude toward museums and historic preservation that not only stood in sharp contrast to the activities of his contemporaries in the nascent preservation movement but presaged today's much-lamented era of commercialized "Mickey Mouse history."[5]

Opposite: Detail of fig. 4.14

Preservation for Profit

Unlike such Progressive era preservation organizations as the Society for the
Preservation of New England Antiquities (invariably shortened to SPNEA),
Nutting founded his Chain of Colonial Picture Houses as an integral part of a
profit-making business.[6] SPNEA, like many smaller organizations, relied on
patriotism and the theory of associationism for funding and cultural relevance.[7] Historic houses should be saved, it was thought, to provide object
lessons for the increasingly heterogeneous American public. Preservation was
a patriotic duty, good citizenship the benefit. This "aesthetic moralism," according to historian Patricia West, served the needs of multiple constituencies.[8]
Activist women searching for a voice in the public sphere, culturally conservative community leaders, and dilettantes all found a home in the nascent
house museum movement. Organizations that took on multiple sites, including SPNEA, soon discovered a need to professionalize their operations and
standardize practices.

    In developing a sustainable preservation economy, SPNEA fostered "today's
broadly accepted standards of professionalism," writes historian William Murtaugh.[9] Reacting to the earlier, more creative, restoration philosophies of such
architects as Joseph Everett Chandler, William Sumner Appleton set the ball
rolling away from imaginative projects like Chandler's 1908 renewal of the Paul

4.2
The Paul Revere House, Boston, Massachusetts (after restoration), c. 1915. Private collection

Revere House in Boston or his 1910 renovation of the House of the Seven Gables in Salem, Massachusetts (figs. 4.1, 4.2).[10] Appleton, the founder and long-serving "corresponding secretary" of SPNEA, worked toward a day when documentation of historic fabric, reversible treatment, and transparency of process would hold sway.[11] In doing so, he facilitated the adoption of professional codes and ethics that led to modern, nonprofit, historic preservation.[12]

Nutting, on the other hand, placed his faith in the market. Despite the minister's frequent public protestations that he entered the museum business for purely altruistic reasons, the five picture houses owed their existence to his ledger book.[13] Two years after calling the project "a labor of love" in 1915, Nutting admitted to Appleton "the advantage of obtaining pictures in the houses which justified perhaps an investment of $20,000 will be availed of in a few months so that the source of advantage will be nullified." After providing the desired interior views, the houses would be required to float on their own bottoms, though he did concede that it "is some advantage to have the houses shown as it is an advertisement of my pictures."[14] Using the houses to advertise his prints and furniture offered Nutting yet another opportunity to cross-market his lines of historically inspired domestic accessories.

The efforts of Wallace Nutting, William Sumner Appleton, and the legion of other men and women intent on preserving the past in the early twentieth century were spurred by a mix of often-contradictory motivations. Historic sites were dedicated to promoting good citizenship as well as healthy sales. Good, bad, or indifferent, all early preservation efforts shared a nexus in the developing middle-class culture of heritage tourism.

The Past Is (Not) a Foreign Country: Touring Old New England

Leisure travel had a long and distinguished history before Appleton, Nutting, and their colleagues took up the preservation cause. In the eighteenth century, well-bred tourists and antiquarians sought "the view" and investigated ruins throughout the landscape of Britain and the Continent.[15] In the early nineteenth century, as art historian Kenneth Myers and others have demonstrated, tourism developed into a common pastime and dramatically affected how middle- and upper-class Americans understood their world.[16] By the 1840s pilgrimages to destinations such as New Hampshire's Mount Washington or the cabin of the unfortunate Willey family were common.[17] Leisure touring picked up pace after the Civil War, and by the turn of the twentieth century, "tourism," writes geographer John Jakle, "became a great universal."[18]

"By 1900," agrees historian Dona Brown, "the tourist industry had penetrated almost every corner of New England, from the coast of Maine to the hill towns of Connecticut."[19] The new industry, according to Brown and Stephen Nissenbaum, ironically depended on the economic engines of modern America.[20] The factories that propelled New England to fiscal and cultural preeminence after the Civil War left a profound imprint upon the cultural geography of the region. Rural towns, depopulated to staff the factories, propel westward expansion, and fill the burgeoning urban centers, were left as fallow reminders of earlier, presumably simpler, days. Sociologist Dean MacCannell has written perceptively of the crossroads of tourism, preservation, and modernity. "A touristic attitude of respectful admiration is called forth by the finer attractions, the monuments, and a no less important attitude of disgust attaches itself to the uncontrolled garbage heaps, muggings, abandoned and tumbledown buildings, polluted rivers and the like. Together, the two provide a moral stability to the modern touristic consciousness that extends beyond immediate social relationships to the structure and organization of the total society."[21]

MacCannell's theorizing is compelling, but Brown cautions that "nostalgic touring was not necessarily backed by a coherent ideology." Tourism crossed class lines and served many needs. "It was more often a mixed bag of unexamined impulses and emotions that motivated nostalgic tourists. Travelers who felt stifled in their parlors and libraries might hope to experience some of the dangers and difficulties once faced by hardy pioneers. Those who were uncomfortable with the industrial order's mechanization and regimentation were drawn to places where independent farmers and artisans performed traditional tasks with simplicity and dignity. Those beset by alien faces and languages in their home cities might search for a place where 'Anglo-Saxon' purity still prevailed."[22] Nutting, himself a tourist of the first rank and a businessman adept at providing images that entreated the middle class out into the landscape, moved to capitalize on this need for therapeutic relaxation. He promoted the Chain of Colonial Picture Houses as a narrative journey for those "beset by alien faces and languages." The trip, he took pains to assure the public, would be comfortable and time efficient. "The houses can, so far as distance is concerned, easily be seen in one day. From Saugus to Haverhill, is about twenty miles; thence to Newburyport fourteen miles; thence to Portsmouth twenty miles, or fifty-four in all, or sixty-four reckoned from Boston."[23]

Relying once again on the moral authority invested in his position as a former clergyman, Nutting assured his customers of the content and value of his enterprise. "More can be learned in one day's careful examination of these houses and their furnishings than a considerable course in architecture and the rummaging of shops for years could give."[24] Nutting was careful to distance his endeavor from earlier, lurid tourist spots such as the Willey cabin or more modern roadside attractions, and he catered to "anyone who desires to be informed and not at the mercy of the unscrupulous." With the chain of picture houses, claimed Nutting, "the benefit of a very costly experience is offered to the public." Waxing altruistic, the minister neglected to mention the twenty-five-cent admission fee.

Forging the Chain

Nutting tested the waters in the mainstream preservation community when he began to assemble his chain of houses. Indeed, William Sumner Appleton of SPNEA played a key advisory role in the acquisition of the properties and their subsequent restoration.[25] Appleton, passionate about his cause, left no stone unturned (or arm untwisted) in his efforts to preserve the landscape of his ancestors as "a constant incentive to patriotic citizenship" in the modern era.[26] As early as 1914, Appleton was enticing Nutting: "I have lately come across a house which I consider the best of the year 1700, or previously, that I have ever seen."[27]

Though he viewed Nutting as a potential ally, Appleton early on expressed concern about the minister's ability to hew to a modern preservation ethos. Writing to Nutting, Appleton noted, "I would be perfectly willing to suggest that house to you as a possible purchase." Having proposed the acquisition, the preservationist proceeded to dun the minister. "But if I did mention it to you I should want you to agree in advance that you would carry out the plan you suggested in the beginning—of turning the house over to the Society immediately on acquiring it, and doing nothing to it except what our experience has taught us is the proper thing to do to such a house." Appleton was explicit about his concerns. "I don't want to take any chance of its being over-repaired or wrongly repaired, or restored to something very attractive indeed."[28]

Anticipating Nutting's lack of long-term commitment, Appleton decried restoration work "done with the intention of selling." "The house in such a case would, of course, be treated as a real estate venture. One of our members does exactly that with houses, and I think he does it remarkably well, but at the same time there is very great risk of injury through the succeeding buyer."[29] Nutting clearly bristled at Appleton's implications and with some justification. If the minister was associating with the "right sort" and reading the proper literature, including such professional publications as the White Pine Series of Architectural Monographs, why was Appleton being so dogmatic?[30] His rejoinder was defensive and foreshadowed the eventual rift between the two antiquarians. "Relating to your statement that this is a commercial enterprise with me, I will say that is true but only partly true. I and my friends are both persuaded that I shall be some thousands of dollars to the bad owing to my love of these things. I shall be glad if I get back eventually what I am investing . . . if I were working for a commercial investment alone the only one of these houses that I could have bought is the Bartlet house. I do not want to pose as a public benefactor any further than I am, but it is only justice to recognize this aspect of the matter."[31]

The crux of the dispute lay in conflicting ideologies. To the end of his life, Nutting believed that historic *character* should be the preeminent concern of the antiquarian. Appleton placed his faith in a more scientific approach, that of evolving professional preservation. As late as 1936 Nutting expressed such heretical sentiments as "The acquisition of old paneling and its installation in rooms which perhaps never had any, is legitimate. If the dwelling is substantial there is nothing but praise in the effort to give it a good old dress."[32] Nutting

4.3
Halliday Historic Photograph
Company, *The Ironworks House*
(before restoration), c. 1900.
Courtesy of the Society for the
Preservation of New England
Antiquities

himself bought and sold such interior woodwork—no doubt to Appleton's
discomfort—in his efforts to create the golden glow of a mythic colonial environment for his customers and clients.[33] In brokering such architectural frag-
ments, Nutting confirmed Appleton's suspicions. Emotion, rather than ana-
lytic method, motivated the minister. When the Chain of Colonial Picture
Houses became a poorly timed reality during World War I, the schism
between the two men grew deeper.

Appleton, often called to play the role of referee in the early New England
preservation community, increasingly found Nutting hard to handle. He was
well used to mollifying egos among his troika of "consulting architects,"
Joseph Everett Chandler, Norman Isham, and Henry Charles Dean, but Nutting's commercialism and controversial behavior soured the relationship in
the end.[34] By 1919, Appleton was confiding to his friends that Nutting was "an
impossible man to deal with."[35] Appleton formed his opinion in short order
after he and Dean assisted Nutting with the renewal of a seventeenth-century
house in Saugus, Massachusetts.

The Business of America Is Business

Nutting's initial purchase and most dramatic restoration was the Appleton-
Taylor-Mansfield House in Saugus, Massachusetts (fig. 4.3). The structure's
metamorphosis reveals much about Nutting's likes and dislikes and unravels

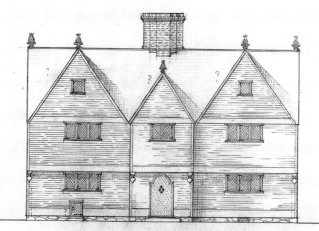

Iron Works Ho.
Saugus, Mass.

some of the complexities of the early preservation movement. Fueled as much by the minister's need to create a dramatic centerpiece for his commercial operations as by a desire for historical accuracy, Broadhearth, as Nutting romantically rechristened the building, stands with other first-period icons such as Boston's Paul Revere House and Salem's House of the Seven Gables as a group of structures restored to meet decidedly modern needs during the Progressive era.[36]

The Old Iron Works House, as the structure itself was known locally, was by no means a Wallace Nutting discovery. Indeed, as early as 1879 Edward Whitfield, an illustrator with an antiquarian bent, included the building in his *Homes of Our Forefathers, Being a Collection of the Oldest and Most Interesting Buildings in Massachusetts*, an important architectural concordance for early preservationists.[37] The Saugus property came to Nutting's attention through his correspondence with Appleton.[38] Nutting and Appleton, still on speaking terms, had been discussing the possibility of a joint venture, and by 1915 several properties north of Boston were under consideration.[39] On 4 February, Nutting told Appleton that he "might be interested in the Boardman house, buying it under an agreement to fix it up and allow it to be visited by the Society members."[40] Although the proposed collaboration came to naught (and the relationship to grief), both Appleton and Nutting focused their attention more closely on Saugus. In that same year SPNEA took the dramatic step of purchasing a historic structure for the first time (the so-called Scotch Board-

4.5
William Sumner Appleton,
*The Ironworks House Being
Surveyed*, 1915. Courtesy of the
Society for the Preservation of
New England Antiquities

4.6
William Sumner Appleton,
*The Ironworks House During
Restoration*, 1915. Courtesy of
the Society for the Preservation
of New England Antiquities

man House), while Nutting acquired the well-known Old Iron Works House on Central Street.[41]

Appleton's SPNEA was an awkward five-year-old in 1915, an institution striving to present a coherent ideology and program. Steward of four historic houses (all north of Boston), the society existed by the sheer will of Appleton, and finances were always precarious. In this environment, Nutting's money-making business looked promising to the preservationist, but Appleton shied from commercial solutions and preferred low-yield (and low-impact) uses for SPNEA structures. Early SPNEA properties were used as tea rooms and rented out to caretakers for their own protection, but the organization was anything but entrepreneurial with its holdings. Nutting, by contrast, saw his new Saugus property as another opportunity to market his vision of Old America.

The minister purchased the building on 2 March 1915.[42] Nutting immediately executed a series of prerestoration photographs and commissioned the Boston architect Henry Charles Dean to oversee the project. Dean produced a set of measured drawings of the structure and another group of drawings to suggest various renovation trajectories (fig. 4.4).[43] Dean's conception of the house with a projecting porch found favor, and in the summer of 1915 Nutting and his architect commenced the transformation of the old tenement into Broadhearth. Appleton, kibitzing, documented the restoration with his camera (figs. 4.5, 4.6) as the project moved into autumn.[44]

Broadhearth, postrestoration, became the center of Nutting's historical and commercial activities, serving as the "authentic" facade for a second photography studio, a furniture factory, and a forge (figs. 4.7, 4.8). On 4 October 1917 the *Saugus Herald* reported that Nutting had purchased the Scott woolen mill "and seven houses" abutting his property (fig. 4.9).[45] The newspaper further noted that Nutting planned "to employ 200 hands at first" making furniture.

4.7
Halliday Historic Photograph
Company, *The Ironworks
House*, 1923. Courtesy of the
Society for the Preservation of
New England Antiquities

4.8
Sign from Broadhearth, c. 1915.
Courtesy of the Department
of the Interior, National Park
Service, Saugus Ironworks
National Historic Site

The site's convenience and importance as a hearth of American industry were key selling points. "This house being so near the centers of travel is capable of giving most conveniently an idea as correct as can now be had of American life in its *first generation*—as it was instituted by the original settlers. Further, as America has come to have the first place in production and working of iron products, this house has a pre-eminent interest, not only as an original and noble type, but as the earliest relic of our greatest industry."[46]

Nutting moved to capitalize on this "earliest relic" when, probably in late 1917, he set up a blacksmith shop at Broadhearth (fig. 4.10). Writing two years later, he explained that the "object of entering into the ironwork (business) was that it was impossible to find anywhere in American a good assortment of Colonial designs, correct in detail and with the early feeling."[47] Having "experienced difficulty in restoring old houses and finding the types required," Nutting secured the services of Edward Guy, a "descendent of a line of forgemen of five generations."[48] The romance of preindustrial craftsmanship again motivated the minister. Writing of the original Saugus ironworks, he longed for a time when the "age of chivalry had passed away and the modern-time machinery had not come in. Simplicity and strength mark the productions of our forefathers at the forge."[49] Nutting's use of an ambivalent tense is telling, for he explicitly wanted to blur the boundaries between new and old at Saugus. He issued a catalog of *Early American Ironwork* in 1919 and sought to capitalize on the historically referential nature of the small house movement

4.10
Alfred Shurrocks, *Old Iron Forge House*,
c. 1925. Courtesy of the Society for the
Preservation of New England Antiquities

4.11
Wallace Nutting, *Early American Ironwork*
(1919), cover. Auerbach Library, Wadsworth
Atheneum Museum of Art

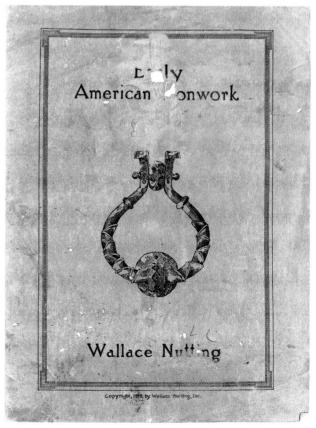

by providing hardware for new construction projects as well as to those involved in restoration work (fig. 4.11).

Failing to make an economic go of it, Nutting pulled up stakes in Saugus in 1920.[50] After trying to interest SPNEA and other museums in the property, he sold Broadhearth to an antiques dealer from Boston and moved his operations, including the forge, to Ashland, Massachusetts. Rather than move his entire staff to the new locale, Nutting pointedly left his English blacksmith behind. The break with Guy elicited no small amount of attention in antiquarian circles and led to the final schism with Appleton as well.[51] Offended that Nutting published his work without credit in *Furniture of the Pilgrim Century*, Guy issued an open letter on 1 April 1922 that accused Nutting of representing the reproductions as period iron. Nutting clearly reused photographs from his 1919 commercial catalog in the scholarly *Pilgrim Century* just as he would reuse his art photographs in the *States Beautiful* series in the mid-1920s. Appleton, his patience long since exhausted, suggested that SPNEA would like to postpone publication of a Nutting article in the journal *Old Time New England* until the minister had cleared up the matter. "The brief delay in printing your article will give you ample time to answer that letter of Mr. Guy's which I was sorry to receive," wrote Appleton.[52] Nutting was intractable. "Please to return at once my article and photos," he demanded. "You stand, in this and other matters, in a poor position to suggest that it is necessary to reply to attacks of an employee discharged for cause."[53] Although Nutting and Appleton eventually reconciled, their correspondence was never again so frequent or so cordial.

The Past Patriotic

Second only to Broadhearth in the minister's heart and pocketbook stood Hospitality Hall (fig. 4.12). Known locally as the Joseph Webb House, Nutting purchased the Wethersfield, Connecticut, mansion on 9 February 1916.[54] Like Broadhearth, the house enjoyed a considerable reputation before it caught Nutting's attention. Indeed, historian Douglas Kendall has pointed out that the "aura of a shrine or proto-tourist attraction began to surround the site" in the days of the early Republic as John Warner Barber, a chronicler of antiquarian attractions in the Nutmeg State, included the building in his *Connecticut Historical Collections* as early as the 1830s.[55] Fearing that the building might be torn down, a group of local citizens purchased the mansion in April 1915 with the evident intention of turning it into a memorial library.[56]

In Boston, William Sumner Appleton closely followed the fate of the house as it changed hands. Writing to Nutting in a conspiratorial tone, the preservationist tried to goad the minister into acquiring the house. "I shall ask

4.12

Hospitality Hall. Webb-Deane-Stevens Museum, Wethersfield, Connecticut. Courtesy of the Society for the Preservation of New England Antiquities

you please not to let anyone know that I am putting [this] letter in your hands." Concerned that the Connecticut preservation community was moving too slowly, Appleton complained, "All I know of the situation is that the place is for sale and it should be preserved, for it is eminently worth it." As for the price, he suggested, "If you should flash three $1000. bills before him it might possibly do the trick."[57]

Nutting passed on the first opportunity to purchase the house. The local consortium overpaid in his estimation, and he wanted nothing to do with a bidding war. He complained to Appleton about the situation, knowing full well how to press the antiquarian into action. "My only fear is that they may do things which they ought not. The house ought not to be fitted up with shelves for a library."[58] Writing back immediately, Appleton expressed his fears and pledged to apply pressure to the citizen's group. "About the Webb house in Wethersfield, I feel as you do, that its dangers are about to begin, and shall certainly write a diplomatic letter to the town librarian urging them to go slow in changing it."[59] Bowing perhaps to outside pressure, the citizens group reversed their decision and sold the house to Nutting amid much local publicity (fig. 4.13).

An excellent financial accounting survives for the Wethersfield restora-

HISTORIC WEBB HOUSE RESTORED BY WALLACE NUTTING

Famous Place Where Washington Planned and Slept.

ARTIST TAKES IT BACK TO OLD DAYS.

Wethersfield's Celebrated Building Soon To Be Opened to Public.

There is an old house in Wethersfield—it stands on the main street, not 200 feet from the town post office, and is familiar to everybody in the town and to many Hartford people as well—in which George Washington was entertained, and in which an alliance between the governments of this country and France was formed; also in which Washington and his generals planned the Yorktown campaign, which ended the Revolutionary War. The house is called Hospitality Hall and is the historic Webb House.

A Massachusetts man bought the place three months ago, and he expects to open it to the public July 4, or a few days later. He has spent many thousands of dollars in improving it so that the interior, at least, looks almost as it did during the Colonial period.

The man who bought it is Wallace Nutting, an artist and photographer. He was formerly a minister and preached in Congregational churches both in the East and West. Since his retirement from that field he has been very successful in producing Colonial pictures by photography and color work.

Built in 1752.

Hospitality Hall was built in 1752. The building is of the gambrel-roofed type Colonial in appearance, but

WALLACE NUTTING

Artist who has Restored Historic Webb House in Wethersfield

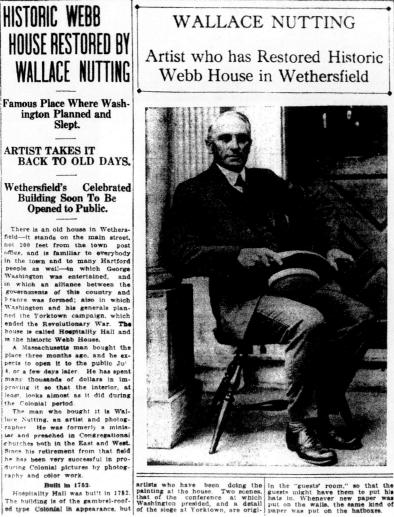

artists who have been doing the painting at the house. Two scenes, that of the conference at which Washington presided, and a detail of the siege at Yorktown, are origi-

In the "guests' room," so that the guests might have them to put his hats in. Whenever new paper was put on the walls, the same kind of paper was put on the hatboxes.

4.13
"Historic Webb House Restored," *Hartford Daily Courant*, 3 July 1916

---

tion. Between 6 April 1916 and 3 July 1919, Nutting invested $3,572.09 in building expenses and utilities at the house.[60] He made monthly payments totaling $413.28 and $1,446.66, respectively, to mason E. A. Smith and G. W. Dodge, the project carpenter. Unlike the Saugus property, a longtime tenement by 1915, the minister wrote Appleton that the previous owner "Welles was penurious to say no more and so left the house unchanged & would not 'repair' that is modernize it."[61] A happy result of this neglect is that Nutting believed the house to be substantially intact, and the contractor's fees reflect discreet projects—the chimney, a shed, select interior fabric—rather than the wholesale renewal undertaken in Saugus.

Nutting made a quick study of the property before commencing. "The ell," he wrote, "was presumed by Isham (who takes up the house in detail in his book on Conn. houses) to be considerably older than the house." After rebuilding the chimney mass, Nutting turned his attention to the interior woodwork. "The Sitting Room mantel was changed when the fireplace in it was reduced & a poorer later mantel put in (about 1870) but I have a beauty of the period of the house (1745–50) with fine scroll top (came out of old house in Providence) which I am putting in."[62] Nutting, according to Kendall, "considered the original woodwork in the Webb parlor of little interest, and in its place substituted paneling acquired when the Marsh House, another Wethersfield landmark, was torn down."[63]

Though Nutting had no qualms about moving historic fabric around the community or the region, his standards of workmanship were exacting. "The carpenter placed the poor roll moulding on the back parlor fireplace in my absence and contrary to my instructions and I have gotten through employing him. As it is the room is not much shown and I am leaving it the way it is until I can get some proper moulding to apply in the proper place."[64]

The dominant feature of the restoration of the structure was clearly the introduction of a series of historical murals in the Northeast Parlor and the so-called Council Room (fig. 4.14). The work of three Hartford painters, Walter

Korder, Louis Donlon, and Edwin Yungk, the parlor murals depict the famous council of war between George Washington and the comte de Rochambeau that reportedly took place in the house in May 1781.[65] Other scenes depict the two men at the Siege of Yorktown as well as Nutting's other picture houses. By including the other links of the chain on the walls of Hospitality Hall, Nutting literally painted his businesses into American history (figs. 4.15, 4.16).

On 24 June 1916 the first admission fees were recorded in Nutting's account book—seventy-five cents for three visitors.[66] Visitation remained strong throughout the first year that Hospitality Hall was open to the public. June brought 150 people to the house, July added 176, August peaked at 308, and the remaining months of the year saw the numbers slide from 280 to 53 by the holidays.[67] Predictably the number of visitors climbed throughout the spring to reach a high point again of 251 in July 1917. In the first two years of its existence, some 2,000 people visited the museum.[68] Not every link in the chain enjoyed the exposure or visitation of Broadhearth or Hospitality Hall. All were important to Nutting's narrative concept, however, and contributed to the consumer platform of Old America.

4.16
Wall mural in the Joseph Webb
House depicting the Hazen
Garrison, c. 1916. Photograph
courtesy of the Webb-Deane-
Stevens Museum

An Entrepreneurial Frontier

Picking up on the Saugus story of intrepid capitalists-in-the-wilderness, the
Hazen Garrison in Haverhill represented a darker tale for Nutting and his
patrons (fig. 4.17). "Historically the place is of peculiar interest," wrote the
minister. "As the Saugus 'Iron Works' House marks the beginning of the iron
industry so the Hazzen [sic] House is said to be the first edifice used as a shoe
factory. The owner had his office in a little room at the front of the upper hall,

4.17
Arthur C. Haskell, *The Hazen Garrison House*, c. 1935. Courtesy of the Society for the Preservation of New England Antiquities

and through the house his workmen carried on a business which from small beginnings was the parent of our immense leather manufactories."[69] Nutting's conception of the structure as a hybrid fortified house and factory clearly informed the restoration.

The idea of a fortified factory must have held symbolic appeal to many at the time.[70] Standing in Haverhill, a shoemaking city not far from the large urban mill towns of Lowell and Lawrence, Nutting's little garrison house seemed to be an ancestral answer for factory owners coping with an increasingly unruly immigrant workforce (read Indians) and the possibility of strikes (read sneak attack). That the "parent" of the regional shoe industry required masonry walls might well have seemed an inspired idea to some in the period.

Nutting's rhetoric and restoration sought to heighten the sense of frontier danger. He outlined his plan for this structure and its sisters in a letter to Appleton. It called for him to "restore them to their original shape in finish and to furnish them absolutely in period." He continued, "There will not be

4.18
Wallace Nutting, *Slanting Sun Rays*, c. 1915, hand-tinted platinum print. Wadsworth Atheneum Museum of Art, Gift of David W. Dangremond, 2000.5.1

anything in the Garrison house or the Iron Works House which could not have been purchased or in existence within twenty years after they were built" (fig. 4.18). As with the Saugus property, Nutting wrote, "it will be proper to state that Mr. Dean is assisting in this matter and that the plans at the Garrison house are entirely his own" (figs. 4.19, 4.20).[71]

Nutting expended considerable capital on the Haverhill house, but the museum failed to thrive.[72] Although John Greenleaf Whittier's birthplace, already a literary shrine, was nearby, Nutting's house was somewhat off the beaten path when it came to attracting the necessary tourist audience, and there is little evidence that he ever successfully integrated the site into his overall program. Nutting's other houses all contributed to the larger business in some way. They served as an entry to the chain (Hospitality Hall), a headquarters (Saugus), or, in the case of the Cutler-Bartlet House in Newburyport, a showroom for Nutting products.

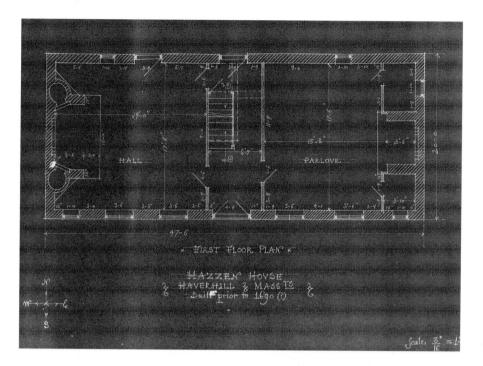

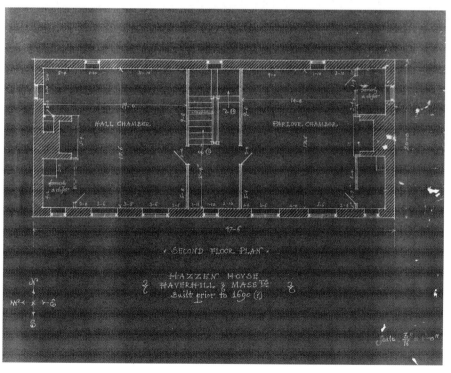

4.19
Floor plan of the Hazen Garrison House, first floor, c. 1915. Courtesy of The Winterthur Museum

4.20
Floor plan of the Hazen Garrison House, second floor, c. 1915. Courtesy of The Winterthur Museum

4.21
Wallace Nutting, *Cutler-Bartlet House*, c. 1915, platinum print. Courtesy of the Society for the Preservation of New England Antiquities

Gentility for Sale

A casual comment to Appleton about the Cutler-Bartlet House in Newbury-port summed up Nutting's interest in his assembly of houses. "I don't like the house so well for art purposes," he wrote in February 1915. "It is hardly sufficiently quaint."[73] That "quaintness" topped Nutting's list of attributes, ahead of accuracy or originality, speaks volumes about his restoration priorities. He further tipped his hand two years later, remarking, "I felt that our pictures did not look well in the house[s] and I have taken down every one except those in the upper stories at Newburyport."[74] More picture gallery than house museum, Cutler-Bartlet reveals the interconnected nature of Nutting's projects.

The kinship of the houses to the photography business is evident in the way Nutting advertised the museums. He employed a uniform program of signage, placing white wooden signs of historic pattern in front of each restored building (figs. 4.8, 4.21, 4.23). Nutting also made widespread use of

4.22
Wallace Nutting, *Cutler-Bartlet House* (second-floor chamber showing Wallace Nutting prints), c. 1915, platinum print. Courtesy of the Society for the Preservation of New England Antiquities

print media, including a series of brochures designed to be interleaved into the 1915 *Expansible Catalog*. In this way the photography catalog took on greater significance: not only could a patron purchase a view from Nutting, but he or she could visit the very site where the picture had been taken.

In Newburyport, a venerable town noted for its Federal architecture, Nutting took this concept one step further when he installed his platinotypes throughout the Cutler-Bartlet House (fig. 4.22).[75] "All the pictures of the various houses may be seen," he wrote, keen to advertise the other houses in the chain. "Old lanterns light the gallery and the halls, so that they may be seen to advantage on dark days." (Not coincidentally, by the time the gallery was created in the Cutler-Bartlet House, Nutting was selling tin lanterns from the Saugus property). "Pictures are to some extent colored in the house," explained the minister, "though the main studio is not here."[76]

The Past in Place

The northernmost link in the Chain of Colonial Picture Houses was the Wentworth-Gardner House in Portsmouth, New Hampshire (fig. 4.23). Overlooking the Piscataqua River and the Portsmouth Naval Shipyard on the opposite shore, the house stood at the edge of the Puddle Dock neighborhood, the city's immigrant district. Nutting was keenly aware of the setting's unsavory reputation and admitted as such to Appleton. "The drives are through a poor

4.23
The Wentworth-Gardner House,
c. 1917, postcard view. Courtesy
of the Society for the Preservation of New England Antiquities

quarter, [but] it is not a slum and not a disreputable quarter and there is a
chance that the approach could be very much improved," he argued.[77]

Dean again prepared a set of plans and appears to have shepherded the
restoration of the house in the fall of 1915 although the architect and the minister found the house to be in far superior condition to their other efforts (figs.
4.24, 4.25).[78] For the most part the renewal of the house was a question of
details. Nutting informed Appleton, "I don't know that I wrote you, but we
found that the banisters and posts were not original." He was delighted to continue "but we have found them in the house where they were and have paid
$350.00 for them and gotten them back." In addition, Nutting "bought back
some carvings which went on the panels in the parlor." Rather smugly, he
declared that the "house, therefore, now is to be put back just as it was, with
the exception of a few broken tilings which I shall replace."[79]

Appleton wrote to Nutting the following autumn and congratulated him
on a job well done. "Yesterday afternoon I was in Portsmouth as the guest of

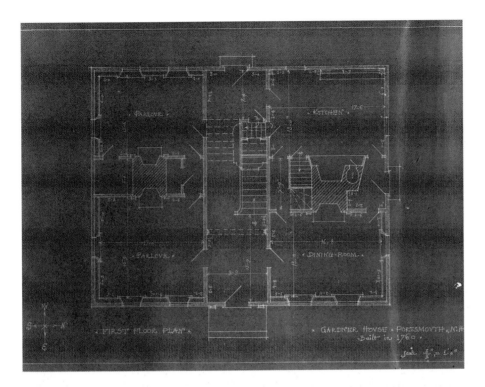

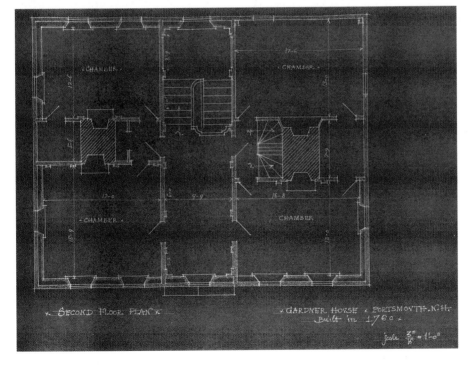

4.24
Floor plan of the Wentworth
House, first floor, c. 1916.
Courtesy of The Winterthur
Museum

4.25
Floor plan of the Wentworth
House, second floor, c. 1916.
Courtesy of The Winterthur
Museum

4.26
Wallace Nutting, *Wentworth-Gardner House* (second-floor chamber showing Wallace Nutting prints), c. 1916, platinum print. Courtesy of the Society for the Preservation of New England Antiquities

Mrs. Barrett Wendell and after going over the Bos'n Allen house I went over yours." The preservationist approved heartily. "I want to say right off that I think you have done a wonderful work there . . . you certainly have proved yourself a first class friend of New England antiquities."[80]

Appleton, a master of the left-handed compliment, clearly wished to broach the issue of encroaching commercialism with the minister (fig. 4.26). "Mrs. Wendell was afraid that your pictures were somewhat of a discordant note as introducing modern work with the old. Of course this is so to a certain extent, but on the other hand, I feel that your pictures have a better right in any of your houses for the simple reason that the pictures made the houses, as I understand it, and the more pictures you sell the more houses you will be able to buy. The house owes the pictures a great debt of gratitude and the only way it can repay that is by giving them wall space. So that although the pictures may be archaeologically out of place, to one who knows their story they seem eminently in place."[81] Unfortunately for Nutting, not even discordant notes could save the house. The chain was not making money. "The war has put me back very badly," he confided to Appleton, "and it was a necessity that I should not only sell the furniture but an act of prudence that I should sell one or more of the houses.[82] The days of the picture houses were numbered.

The Portsmouth house, eventually shuttered by Nutting, became a point of much discussion within the preservation community. In his correspondence with Appleton, Nutting mooted several schemes to save the buildings. First and foremost, he attempted to interest SPNEA in the enterprise, but the price was far too steep for the perpetually strapped institution. Nutting then suggested moving the Portsmouth house. "You mention the scheme of moving it, that is entirely feasible floating it on two scows, put together as one."[83] Getting little reaction from Appleton, Nutting pushed the panic button. He offered to sell the building's interior paneling to a museum for use as a period room.[84] Crying crocodile tears, he reported, "I think no one could regret more than myself the taking down of the house to re-erect in a Museum, as I understand the purpose to be, yet 'needs must where the devil drives.'"[85]

Responding to Appleton's shocked rejoinder, Nutting let the cat out of the bag. "As for the Portsmouth house," he confirmed, "it is the Metropolitan Museum that is acting there."[86] The New York museum loomed large in New England, for in the run-up to the installation of the American Wing in 1924, Metropolitan agents were scouring the region in search of woodwork for use in period rooms. The installation, a culmination of more than a decade's worth of exploratory exhibitions and supported by the cream of New York society, opened to great fanfare. Hidden in the ruckus, however, were the voices of the New England preservation community who repeatedly cried foul at the museum's efforts to cart off regional patrimony.[87] Appleton, Chandler, and their local compatriots repeatedly frustrated the museum's efforts to strip paneling from period houses.[88] Nutting, having realized his goal of staging photographs in his houses and faced with declining visitation, was looking to sell off the Chain of Colonial Picture Houses and knew exactly how to get a rise out of William Sumner Appleton. Mere mention of the Metropolitan galvanized the preservation community and guaranteed that the picture houses would remain in New England. The days of Nutting's ownership, however, were over.

Breaking the Chain

The Chain of Colonial Pictures Houses all but ruined Wallace Nutting. Early on in the enterprise he complained to Appleton about his lot in life. "It is true that my business is pretty good, but I have not invested funds to live upon like most persons who cultivate the passion for antiques."[89] In spending lavishly on the restoration of the Saugus and Wethersfield properties, Nutting incurred considerable debt. Geopolitical events then delivered the coup de grâce. America's intervention in World War I effectively removed Nutting's customer base as voluntary rationing of gasoline went into effect during the winter of 1917–1918—a move that swiftly curtailed tourism that summer.[90] With the motoring set at war or stuck at home, Nutting folded his enterprise, sold the houses piecemeal, and turned his attentions elsewhere.[91]

The demise of the chain was hardly the end of Nutting's interest in museums,

however. In fact, the breakup set in motion a sequence of events that led to his subsequent involvement with a much larger institution: the Wadsworth Atheneum in Hartford, Connecticut (fig. 4.27). For five years after breaking up the chain of houses Nutting flirted with the private exhibition of his furniture in various locations in Framingham, advertising the collection and then closing the doors as his needs and interests were met. Finally, in 1924 Nutting negotiated a deal with financier J. P. Morgan, Jr., that saw the collection first placed on loan and then given to the Wadsworth Atheneum in 1926. In one swift move, Morgan and Nutting created an "American Wing" for Connecticut—copying the much-publicized 1924 addition to the Metropolitan. In doing so, Nutting's reputation as an authority on early American life became an institutionalized reality.

The Rise of the Period Room

Despite his widespread name-recognition from his picture business and furniture marketing, Nutting's reputation as a connoisseur and historian of early American furniture is based largely on his association with the Wadsworth Atheneum. Founded in 1844 by Daniel Wadsworth, an early collector of American paintings, the Atheneum was one of the nation's most venerable museums by the 1920s.[92] A true athenaeum in the classical sense, the institution was simultaneously an art museum, a library, and a natural history collection. As a Victorian "cabinet of curiosities," the Atheneum collected historical relics, including furniture of local significance. Wadsworth himself encouraged such practice when he commissioned a set of reproduction eighteenth-century chairs in the late 1830s, donating several to his namesake institution.

In October 1921, however, the Hartford museum signaled a shift in direction when it organized an exhibition of American furniture from the collection of George Dudley Seymour.[93] Seymour, an Atheneum trustee, lent the museum "a considerable number of the most interesting pieces from his unusual and comprehensive collection of New England furniture," according to the *Hartford Courant*.[94] The collection was displayed in the lecture room of the Morgan Memorial, a 1915 addition to the original Atheneum donated by J. P. Morgan, a Hartford native.[95] The newspaper reported enthusiastically that the exhibition contained "characteristic examples of the furniture which the well-to-do of early times had and used in their homes."[96]

Americana programs followed the installation. In 1923, for example, the museum hosted a loan exhibition of pewter. "Some sixty collections have furnished the 450 to 500 pewter objects," noted the *Hartford Daily Times*.[97] Also that year George Francis Dow, curator of the Society for the Preservation of New England Antiquities, presented a lecture with the whimsical title "Side-Lights on Colonial Houses."[98] The Seymour installation and Dow lecture are significant moments in the history of the Atheneum for they reflect the growing importance of Hartford as a center of antiquarian activities and presaged a much larger commitment to the decorative arts just around the corner.

The watershed occurred in December 1924. Nutting, having sold a half interest in his collection to J. P. Morgan, Jr., transferred the furniture to the Atheneum for display.[99] "The first consignment of the collection, consisting of four court cupboards, three of which are unique in design and execution, arrived last night from Framingham by motor truck," announced the *Hartford Courant*.[100] The newspapers made much of the fact that moving the furniture, iron, and treen took several weeks because of its size and fragility. The collection opened to much pomp and circumstance on 16 February 1925—a scrapbook kept by the Atheneum archived more than thirty articles from local dailies and weeklies. "Walking among these things of old times," wrote the *Courant*, "we are able to translate ourselves to a surprising degree into the lives of our forebears."[101] Nutting, listed as the "joint owner" of the furniture, no doubt beamed with pride. His goal of allowing modern customers to walk into the past was realized not in a picture house but in the museum period room.

4.28
The Wallace Nutting Collection of Early American Furniture, Morgan Building, c. 1928. Archives of the Wadsworth Atheneum Museum of Art

4.29
The Wallace Nutting Collection of Early American Furniture, Morgan Building, c. 1928. Archives of the Wadsworth Atheneum Museum of Art

4.30
The Wallace Nutting Collection of Early American Furniture, Avery Building, c. 1935. Archives of the Wadsworth Atheneum Museum of Art

Morgan subsequently purchased the second half of the collection, and on 16 January 1926 the trustees of the Atheneum formally accepted the Wallace Nutting Collection of Early American Furniture at the annual meeting. The collection was reinstalled in the basement of the Morgan Memorial in a series of semipermanent period rooms according to the latest tenets of museum practice (figs. 4.28, 4.29). Within years, however, the Atheneum initiated an ambitious expansion program and constructed the Avery Memorial. Completed in 1934, the Avery stood as one of the pioneer International Style interiors in America. The brainchild of Atheneum director A. Everett "Chick" Austin, the Avery was designed to provide the most up-to-date museum environment in the country. In a strikingly precocious move, Austin and Wesleyan University professor Henry-Russell Hitchcock programmed the second floor of the building with selections from the Nutting Collection, thus moving from the idea of the period room to embrace the modern, masterworks format of decorative arts installations (fig. 4.30).[102]

Although Nutting's foray into the museum business was short-lived, it is a key chapter in the story of Old America and a significant moment in the history of historic preservation in its illustration of a market-driven approach to the salvage, restoration, and presentation of American architecture. As a commercial enterprise, the Chain of Colonial Pictures Houses stood in graphic contrast to the Progressive era initiatives of such regional organizations as SPNEA and the many smaller community-based associations and societies founded to preserve and interpret local historic buildings. That Nutting eventually found the house museum to be a disappointing bedfellow is perhaps to be expected, given the undercapitalized and poorly organized nature of the field. His involvement with the chain of houses led to greener fields, however, both at the Wadsworth Atheneum and in publishing.

Armchair Tourism

In the years between the demise of the Chain of Colonial Picture Houses and the installation of his collection at the Wadsworth Atheneum, Wallace Nutting finally hit on a product that required relatively little capital outlay—the book. Rather than tie up his resources in the purchase and restoration of historic buildings, Nutting took a lesson from his failure and established a publishing company. Although he eventually came to use the publishing house for a number of furniture books, such as *The Clock Book* and the revised 1924 edition of *Furniture of the Pilgrim Century*, the principal mission of Old America Publishing was to market and distribute his travelogues. Beginning in 1922 with *Vermont Beautiful* and running though the publication of *Virginia Beautiful* in 1930, Nutting dipped back into his trove of photographs from the turn of the century and formed a series of books designed to be a "perfect gift book, travel book, auld lang syne book, picture book [and] library book" (fig. 4.31).[103]

The ten books in the series continued Nutting's narrative journey though the fields of Old America and exported the idea of the Chain of Colonial Picture Houses to a national audience. Rather than appealing to the few who could afford "brass and gas" touring cars, *Massachusetts Beautiful* and its companion titles provided an illustrated ramble though the historic corners of each state to a broad readership (fig. 4.32). Haphazard in organization, the volumes bob and weave though Nutting's Old America. A description of a venerable tree is followed by the critique of an old house; all the while the author maintains a running commentary on all that is wrong with the present and right with the past. As a group, the books are snapshots of the postwar tourist culture.

"It is difficult to live on scenery," wrote Nutting in 1923, "though certain American states come near doing that."[104] This bon mot, like all the minister's

4.31
Wallace Nutting, *States Beautiful Books*, first editions, 1920s. The Manville Collection

declarations, is delivered with dyspeptic accuracy. By 1923 whole regions of New England did indeed support large populations with a tourist economy. Nutting, however, was equally guilty. With his travel series, he established another venue from which to distill profit from his earlier professional, artistic, and commercial activities. Uniform in size, design, and narrative content, the books proved to be quick to write for a camera-toting minister with a ready body of text left over from twenty years of preaching.

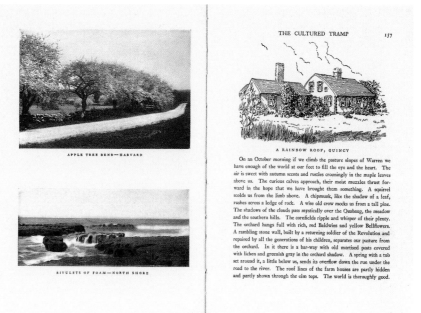

APPLE TREE BEND—HARVARD

A RAINBOW ROOF, QUINCY

On an October morning if we climb the pasture slopes of Warren we have enough of the world at our feet to fill the eye and the heart. The air is sweet with autumn scents and rustles crooningly in the maple leaves above us. The curious calves approach, their moist muzzles thrust forward in the hope that we have brought them something. A squirrel scolds us from the limb above. A chipmunk, like the shadow of a leaf, rushes across a ledge of rock. A wise old crow mocks us from a tall pine. The shadows of the clouds pass mystically over the Quabaug, the meadow and the southern hills. The cornfields ripple and whisper of their plenty. The orchard hangs full with rich, red Baldwins and yellow Bellflowers. A rambling stone wall, built by a returning soldier of the Revolution and repaired by all the generations of his children, separates our pasture from the orchard. In it there is a bar-way with old mortised posts covered with lichen and greenish gray in the orchard shadow. A spring with a tub set around it, a little below us, sends its overflow down the run under the road to the river. The roof lines of the farm houses are partly hidden and partly shown through the elm tops. The world is thoroughly good.

RIVULETS OF FOAM—NORTH SHORE

4.32
Wallace Nutting, *Massachusetts Beautiful* (1923), 156–157

Baedekers for the armchair traveler, the states beautiful series was by no means a novel invention. At any moment from the turn of the century until World War II authors could be found scouring New England intent on producing similar books. Charles Goodrich Whiting, Clifton Johnson, and Helen Henderson were but a few of Nutting's competitors.[105] As with his earlier photography business, Nutting adopted an existing format and soon owned the market. At the height of the Depression, when symbols of distinctive American places and traditions found great popularity, Nutting released second editions with an updated graphic standard (fig. 4.33).[106]

Nutting's books provided a cost-effective way to create a sense of place for his middle-class audience.[107] Juxtaposing images, text, the occasional line drawing, and bit of verse, the ten volumes reinforced the mythic landscape of Old America for an increasingly suburban nation. "A field road like the one shown in the picture will lead the way to all sorts of joys," wrote Nutting in *Connecticut Beautiful*, "if only we allow the imagination to build and inhabit its structures."[108] The structures built by those who followed Nutting through his Chain of Colonial Picture Houses, books on furniture, period rooms at the Wadsworth Atheneum, and across the states beautiful shape America to this day. By creating a past implied at every turn by a heterogeneous and layered consumer experience, Nutting made history a part of everyday life in the modern era.

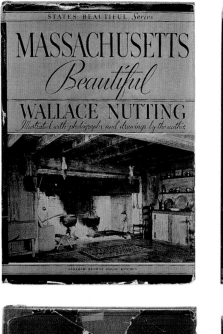

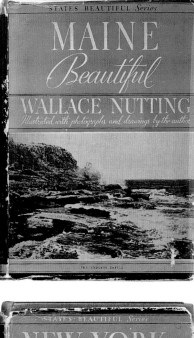

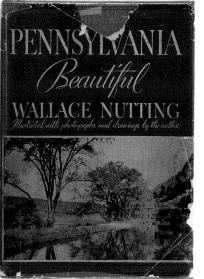

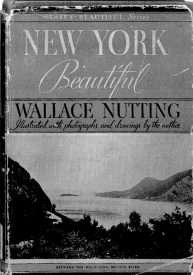

4.33
Wallace Nutting, *States Beautiful Books*, second editions, 1930s. Auerbach Library, Wadsworth Atheneum Museum of Art

Chapter 5

Pilgrim Furniture of the Modern Century

*T*hose who know the pictures," Wallace Nutting observed, "want the chairs."[1] With the opening of a furniture studio in 1917, Nutting attempted to secure yet another profit line for his growing empire by selling authentic reproductions of the chairs, chests, cupboards, tables, and miscellaneous forms he had gathered to serve as props for his photographs and furnishings for the Chain of Colonial Picture Houses (fig. 5.1). Eventually the proprietor of three separate factories, author of six volumes on furniture, and contributor to myriad antiquarian magazines, Nutting organized the fledgling Americana market to fit his commercial needs.[2] By writing books for the collector while providing catalogs for the consumer, Nutting effectively linked culture and commerce to add value to his holdings and become one of the foremost twentieth-century authorities on American decorative arts.

Wallace Nutting Furniture, active from 1917 to 1945, is a textbook study in modern business practice. By diversifying his booming photography business into a series of related fields, Nutting followed a path blazed by the storied tycoons of the Gilded Age. Andrew Carnegie, for example, owned not only his steel mills but the means of supply and distribution as well. John D. Rockefeller's Standard Oil flowed from the ground to the point of consumption without ever leaving the hands of his holding company.[3] In perhaps the most complete example available, Henry Ford sought to control (and secure a profit from) every stage in the life of his automobiles—from extraction of raw material to manufacture, sale, and warranty repair. This new model of corporate organization provided unprecedented wealth in the decades that bracket the turn of the twentieth century—an era in which Nutting eschewed the pulpit and embraced the culture of consumption.

The paradigm *almost* worked for Nutting. Like the well-known captains of industry, Nutting encouraged consumerism through a cult of personality,

Opposite: Crests for #340, #380, and #394 Chairs (fig. 5.22)

5.1
Wallace Nutting, Incorporated,
#911 Sunflower Cupboard,
c. 1925. From *Wallace Nutting
Final Edition Furniture Catalog*
(1937), 35

advertised widely, controlled diverse product lines within his market, and satisfied public demand by turning out products at an acceptable quality and price point for his customer base. Unfortunately for Nutting, sound business theory does not always result in successful practice, and the furniture business failed to thrive when measured by profit alone. Although his illustrated lectures were well received and his books, including *A Windsor Handbook* (1917), *Furniture of the Pilgrim Century* (1921), *The Clock Book* (1924), and the three-volume magnum opus *Furniture Treasury* (1928–1933), remained standard texts for decades, Wallace Nutting Furniture barely earned its keep.[4] Indeed, the furniture business operated as a break-even enterprise for much of its twenty-eight-year history, often dipping into the red.[5]

In spite of its marginal economic contribution, Nutting's furniture company paid an important dividend: it dramatically bolstered his reputation as a connoisseur of the decorative arts. The company provided an intellectual home and economic hub for the minister and gave him a masculine forum to recover a reputation tarnished by his earlier emotional breakdown and subsequent failure in the house museum business.[6] The furniture company became "the center of Old American life," a central point on Nutting's compass and one that he literally tried to plot in his advertisements (fig. 5.2).

5.2
"The Center of Old American Life," c. 1927, Wallace Nutting advertising graphic. Local History Collection, Framingham Public Library

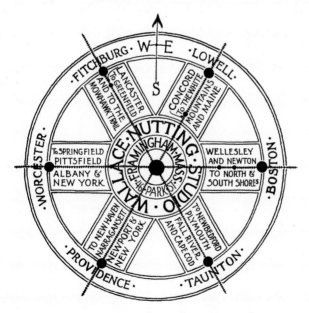

Wallace Nutting
Period Furniture

LOCATION OF SHOP
46 PARK ST., FRAMINGHAM, MASSACHUSETTS

THE CENTER OF OLD AMERICAN LIFE

B Y THE above it appears that my shop is at the crossroads of the ancient Commonwealth of Massachusetts. Though the land reaches the railway station, a walk of two blocks is required. Cross the track to the north side and take the first left.

5.3
Wallace Nutting, Incorporated, *#992 Savery School, High Chest of Drawers*. From *Wallace Nutting Final Edition Furniture Catalog* (1937), 47

Nutting's failure to turn a profit in this arena is a puzzle, given the runaway success of his earlier photography business and the demand for historically inspired domestic goods during the building boom that followed World War I.[7] With the rise of the colonial revival suburb, a national movement composed of a myriad of historical styles ranging from the rugged "Pilgrim Century" to the genteel Federal era, Wallace Nutting's furniture line should have been a roaring success. Few manufacturers enjoyed the name recognition of the well-published minister-turned-photographer. None successfully established links between sympathetic product lines.[8] The problem lay not with the market or the marketing, however, but with the minister.[9]

Nutting's finely crafted persona as a flinty Yankee cleric hampered effective business practice. Inflexible standards of quality and poor strategic thinking all but guaranteed a stunted economic life for his furniture company.[10] Espousing an idealized Arts and Crafts–inspired philosophy that made him unwilling to cut corners, Nutting produced an expensive product and severely limited his customer base as a result.[11] Even at the height of middle-class prosperity in the late 1920s, only the well-off could afford his more substantial case furniture. Indeed, Nutting's two top-of-the-line offerings in 1930, a mahogany desk and bookcase with a price of $1,800 and a "Philadelphia" high chest of drawers for $1,230, represented a considerable outlay in a period when a lawyer or physician could expect to take home between $5,000 and $6,000 a year (fig. 5.3).[12]

Surviving examples show, however, that such monumental casework was the exception rather than the rule in Nutting's production schedule.[13] His bread-and-butter offerings consisted of smaller, more affordable articles such as reproduction Windsor chairs, turned stands, joined stools, and diminutive tea tables designed to fit the domestic space and budget of the middle class.[14]

Certain offerings, such as the minister's interpretation of a seventeenth-century carved box, were modest and affordable, yet rich in symbolism, for they gave twentieth-century customers an opportunity to physically mark their place in history (figs. 5.4, 5.5, 5.6). As Nutting expanded his line, a Hadley chest and other carved forms offered the latter-day Puritan "space for initials" and a place in the continuum of Old America.[15]

Redeeming the Windsor

"All persons of taste and discernment will be glad that at last someone has had the courage to undertake the redemption of the Windsor chair," wrote Wallace Nutting in 1918.[16] That "someone," of course, was himself. Ostensibly drawn to the Windsor's elegant lines, democratic "American" heritage, and ease of construction, Nutting's interest in the form reveals a pattern wherein the entrepreneurial minister popularized an area of study, commodified the subject, and then profited from his status as an authority in the field.[17] Nutting assembled a collection of chairs, deployed them throughout his businesses, published an authoritative guide to the form in 1917, and issued a catalog from which customers could order reproductions in 1918.

Nutting's eye for the Windsor form is readily evident in his popular photographic "colonials." *At the Fender*, copyrighted in August 1904, is one of Nutting's earliest attempts at a historical vignette (fig. 5.7).[18] Crude in comparison

5.4
"BC" Box, Springfield, Massachusetts, c. 1700, oak and yellow pine. Wadsworth Atheneum Museum of Art, Wallace Nutting Collection, Gift of J. Pierpont Morgan, Jr., 1926.352

5.5
Wallace Nutting, Incorporated, *#901 Oak Box*, with "space for initials," c. 1927. From *Wallace Nutting Furniture, Rugs, and Iron*, rev. ed. (1927), n.p.

with later scenes, *At the Fender* depicts a woman seated in profile in front of a hearth, engrossed in her sewing. A Federal-era banjo clock marks time while the fire burns brightly beneath the neoclassical mantle. French scenic wallpaper signifies that the room is a high-style parlor from the second or third decade of the nineteenth century. Of the many icons present, however, one stands out—the chair to the left of the model. Bathed in sunlight, a common bow-back side chair draws the viewer's eye from the woman at her knitting to the minister's future product.

Nutting's depiction of a Windsor chair in *At the Fender* presaged an endless number and variety of the form in his colonials. Scanning the pages of the *Expansible Catalog* offers a typology of the style (fig. 5.8). A chair is never just a chair, however, but an opportunity to preach about the past and turn a

5.6
Carving Template, 1930,
pencil and paper. Wadsworth
Atheneum Museum of Art,
American Decorative Arts
Purchase Fund, 1999.47

profit in the present. The use of such icons, according to art historian William Truettner, was an important contribution to the creation of a colonial visual culture in the modern era. "Reproduced with surprising frequency in turn-of-the-century images," such objects were important props in the creation of an idealized past.[19] A chair, therefore, had multiple uses in Nutting's cosmology as photographic prop, history lesson, investment, and template for reproduction.

In the course of furnishing his Chain of Colonial Picture Houses, Nutting purchased some 140 Windsor chairs.[20] "We have expended about $10,000 to reclaim them from the degradation into which they have fallen," he claimed.[21] Nutting installed most of the chairs in a gallery at the Cutler-Bartlet House in Newburyport, although others were distributed throughout the chain. At Broadhearth in Saugus, for instance, Nutting appropriately kept what he considered the "earliest forms" in the kitchen lean-to of the seventeenth-century structure.[22]

In Newburyport, Nutting blended the divisions of his business when he fitted out "a little picture gallery" at the Cutler-Bartlet House to advertise his photographic interests and "practically filled" the room with Windsor chairs (fig. 5.9).[23] "Students," he offered, "are at liberty to sketch [the chairs] . . . to their heart's content, provided they do the owner the courtesy to procure his photographs rather than make their own." Nutting's sole motivation, according to the catalog, was to encourage "the diffusion of a proper familiarity with good lines."[24] Of course, such altruistic promotion of "good lines" also promoted an appreciation of his newly introduced product line. Cutler-Bartlet was more showroom than museum. Tourists, who presented themselves at the front door, paying twenty-five cents for admission, became fully informed consumers by the time they exited the house. Not only did they experience Wallace Nutting's vision of Old America in a tangible environment, but they could buy into this history by ordering the platinotypes on the wall and furniture just like the pieces on display.

5.7
Wallace Nutting, *At the Fender*, 1904, hand-tinted platinum print, tipped into *Old New England Pictures* (1913). Auerbach Library, Wadsworth Atheneum Museum of Art

5.8
Wallace Nutting, *A Delicate Stitch*, c. 1910, hand-tinted platinum print, tipped into *Old New England Pictures* (1913). Auerbach Library, Wadsworth Atheneum Museum of Art

5.9
Wallace Nutting, *Cutler-Bartlet House* (hallway showing Windsor chairs), c. 1918. From Wallace Nutting, *Correct American Windsors* (1918), 1

Humbug Furniture

As with his earlier hand-tinted photographs, Nutting clearly felt that the public required education to appreciate his products.[25] With the exception of a limited number of historically correct copies of original objects, forms understood to be "colonial" in the early years of the twentieth century were a hybrid lot. They included earlier, highly imaginative interpretations, such as chairs manufactured from obsolete spinning-wheel components as well as the overblown classical forms and Renaissance details of "Centennial Furniture," ably decoded by curators Christopher Monkhouse and Rodris Roth (fig. 5.10).[26] "Colonial" furniture also included loose adaptations of historic forms and styles manufactured by such large furniture companies as Danersk (fig. 5.11).[27] These pieces particularly provoked the minister's ire. "One of our greatest public libraries," he exclaimed, "is also furnished by a notable firm of architects with chairs of mongrel pattern and bad construction."[28]

Writing of this hybrid furniture, Nutting oscillated between avuncular storytelling and biting, almost profane criticism. "It is like the bug put together from six bugs and brought to the professor with the bland inquiry by the student, 'Please tell us what this bug is?' The professor fixes on it for a moment a sardonic look, and says, 'Yes, gentlemen, it's a humbug.'" Having made his point with ministerial humor, however, Nutting proceeded to castigate

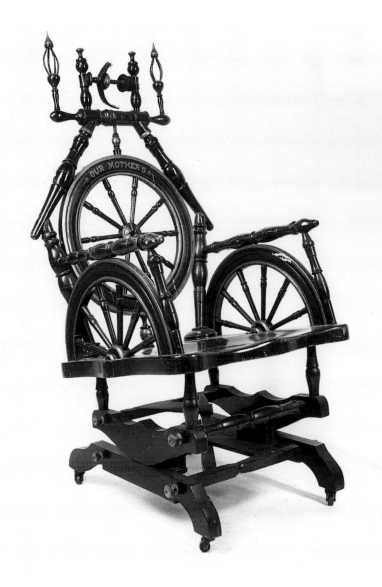

5.10
Spinning Wheel Chair, c. 1885,
painted maple and pine.
Courtesy of the Strong
Museum, Rochester, New York

peddlers of such furniture in the same breath. "The designer . . . selects a
Queen Anne foot, an Elizabethan leg, a King James bracket, a George I frame,
a George II crest, a Victorian seat, and puts it all together and says 'There you
are!' There you are indeed. He calls it Jacobean. It is Jack."[29]

By providing access to accurate examples of early American furniture,
Nutting offered his products as morally superior specimens for the home of
good taste. In linking his chairs to his interior "colonial" views, Nutting also
hoped to rule out "humbugs," incipient eclecticism, and the unfortunate mix-
ing of periods. "To my thought," he once confided to William Sumner Appleton, "antique furniture in a modern house is like a jewel of gold in a swine's
snout."[30] Beyond mere decoration, Nutting thus sold a product complete with

5.11
Erskine-Danforth Corporation,
Danersk Furniture. From
Antiques (January 1932): 37

suggested patterns of behavior. His photographs served as a de facto owner's manual for the furniture, demonstrating not only proper interior design for the modern colonial home but a sense of decorum as well.

Making History

Wallace Nutting's furniture company employed makeshift production facilities, an ethnically heterogeneous workforce, and conspicuously modern shop practices for the duration of its existence.[31] The company carried on for twenty-eight years, employing perhaps as many as twenty (often foreign-born) multiskilled woodworkers in a series of adapted industrial spaces in Saugus, Ashland, and Framingham, Massachusetts. Although the company never achieved the level of organization (or profits) of a Gardner, Massachusetts, or Grand Rapids, Michigan, manufacturer, Nutting's furniture studio consistently exploited the latest in commercial woodworking equipment.[32]

Nutting first located the business in a mid-nineteenth-century brick mill

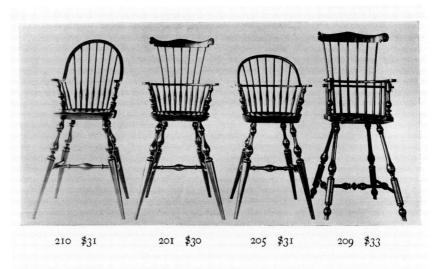

210 $31   201 $30   205 $31   209 $33

5.12
Windsor chairs in *Wallace
Nutting Final Edition Furniture
Catalog* (1937), 90

next to Broadhearth (see fig 4.10). The mill, owned for years by the woolen manufacturer F. Scott and Son, was situated on the Saugus River and gave Nutting room to house an expanded photography business as well as the new woodworking shop.[33] The new endeavors, in conjunction with the restored museum-house and a working forge operated by blacksmith Edward Guy, created a formidable compound. At Saugus, Nutting devoted areas to outright display (Broadhearth), performance (Guy's shop), and pure production (the Scott mill). As in Newburyport, the combination offered the public multiple opportunities to consume relics of the past (wrought-iron hinges, hand-tinted "Pilgrim Century" interiors, Windsor and Carver-type chairs) complete with a set of rituals and behaviors for their interpretation and use.

Off-stage in the brick mill, the furniture-making initiative appears to have been well under way by November 1917. Toward the end of that month William Sumner Appleton wrote to Nutting, complimenting him for his "very attractive [furniture] line" at the Brooks Read Gallery in Boston.[34] The furniture line, as exhibited in Boston and inspected by Appleton, officially appeared a year later in Nutting's first catalog, *Correct Windsor Furniture*. A chatty booklet, *Correct Windsor Furniture* offers considerable detail about shop practice in the original Saugus factory. Turning, for example, the fundamental operation in Windsor production, was accomplished by hand because "machines cannot cut the extremely deep stems or delicate lines," according to Nutting. Likewise, "seats are finished by hand," with three to four seats being "a day's work for a good man."[35]

The initial product line was cleverly conceived. Although Nutting offered a variety of Windsor chairs, representing period understanding of local and regional variation in American seating furniture, the principal difference from one model to the next came in the pattern of turning (fig. 5.12). Nutting could therefore offer the sixty-eight varieties in *Correct Windsor Furniture* without dramatic investment in tooling. Indeed, the chairs, stools, and cradles that made up his initial offering could have been produced with only a lathe, band saw, planer, and steam box for bending bows, although the inventory probably also included a table saw and joiner for dimensioning stock.[36]

A clue as to the level of capital equipment available in the Saugus factory comes from an accident report in the local newspaper. "A light delivery truck, the property of Wallace Nutting, Central Street, was badly damaged Saturday morning when a big five-ton truck backed down the yard of the studio into the delivery truck."[37] That Nutting's activities at Saugus required a modest commercial vehicle clearly demonstrates that he oversaw a business of respectable size. In a twist of high historical irony, however, Nutting's little truck was clearly no match for larger commercial forces.

Ashland, the Great American Idea

With the decline and eventual breakup of his Chain of Colonial Picture Houses, Nutting sold the Saugus compound and its contents. He was far from through with the furniture business, however, and sometime around 1920 Nutting moved the operation closer to his central Massachusetts home and installed the business in an old cannery in Ashland, an industrial community just north of Framingham (fig. 5.13). From this adapted space, Nutting issued an expanded furniture catalog in 1921 called *The Great American Idea*. Despite the failure of the Chain of Colonial Picture Houses, a financial reverse that

5.13
Wallace Nutting's Ashland Factory, c. 1920, postcard view. The Manville Collection

5.14
The Parmenter Cupboard, c. 1695, oak,
maple, and pine. Wadsworth Atheneum
Museum of Art, Wallace Nutting
Collection, Gift of J. Pierpont Morgan, Jr.,
1926.291

5.15
The Parmenter Cupboard, as found by Wallace Nutting, c. 1920. Archives of the Wadsworth Atheneum Museum of Art

also prompted Nutting to liquidate a portion of his collection through John Wanamaker's department stores, Nutting moved to expand his reproduction business by diversifying forms and taking on increasingly more complex pieces.[38] In Ashland, Nutting began to rebuild his collection around a predominantly seventeenth-century furniture theme, a body of objects that he used to illustrate *Furniture of the Pilgrim Century* and that served as prototypes for the expanded reproduction line. One of the most famous objects acquired and reproduced at Ashland was the so-called Parmenter Cupboard.[39]

The Parmenter Cupboard, or, A Machine in the Studio

The Parmenter Cupboard is an excellent case study in the synergy between Nutting's efforts as a scholar, connoisseur, and manufacturer of early American furniture (fig. 5.14). "Discovered" in Sudbury, Massachusetts, in the early 1920s, the cupboard had been cut down in the early nineteenth century to serve as a sideboard (fig. 5.15).[40] It was "pieced," or restored, by Nutting's cabinetmakers,

5.16
Carving template for the *#910
Cupboard*, c. 1928, pencil on
cardboard. Courtesy of The
Winterthur Museum

5.17
Wallace Nutting, Incorporated,
#910 Cupboard. From *Wallace
Nutting Final Edition Furniture
Catalog* (1937), 34

and a series of carving patterns were taken from the original to serve as templates for its reproduction as item number 910, "the finest and earliest American cupboard" (fig. 5.16).[41]

Although it is not clear how many reproductions of the monumental cupboard were completed, at least five survive (fig. 5.17).[42] Even the most casual examination of one of these cupboards reveals Nutting's workers to have been highly skilled cabinetmakers using modern construction techniques rather than joiners employing historical methods of the seventeenth century. The Ashland hands used dimensioned oak stock with low moisture content rather than riving components from "green" oak in historic manner. Nutting was quite explicit about these methods and, though he cloaked his enterprise in traditional imagery, readily admitted the use of modern technology—often on the same page. "You would get the picture if you were to look into the Wallace Nutting Studios and see the hand-carvers, the hand-turners, the hand assemblers, all skilled in their craftsmanship, and which is the only way in which much of the work necessary to the manufacturer of these true Colonials can be encompassed." Had the reader not glanced down the page, he or she might have missed the contradictory prose that followed this ode to traditional craftsmanship. "We do not mean to say that we don't use machinery, for we do. We feel inclined to believe that there is no finer equipment represented by any other country manufacturing a product in any ways comparable to ours, but the point is that machinery is used only where it can be used without sacrificing those things for which we strive."[43]

The Ten Commandments

Nutting's ambivalence toward machine production ran far deeper than confusing advertising copy. In a letter to William Sumner Appleton, Nutting made his feelings known about the effects of mechanized labor. "Up to say, 1815 furniture was made generally in good taste, partly because the seventeenth and eighteenth centuries were distinguished for better taste than ours, but principally for another reason: the nineteenth century furniture was made by machinery and it never can by any possibility come to have a value. . . . It lacks individuality, the touch of the hand and the feeling of the artificer. . . . It is inherently bad, owing to its coarseness, without any quaintness to redeem it."[44]

In spite of such frank words, Nutting's woodworking concern was fully equipped with the latest equipment by the mid-1920s. An inventory taken when the factory was broken up after Nutting's death included tools by Porter-Cable, Tannewitz, Gardner Machine Tools, and Grand Rapids Machinery.[45] Again, Nutting was quite open about this technology, writing that "the shop is also equipped with many motor driven machines, each the best of its kind."[46]

5.18
Factory interior showing
dimensioned stock, 46 Park
Street, Framingham,
Massachusetts, c. 1927.
Local History Collection,
Framingham Public Library

5.19
Factory interior showing
tooling and Windsor
components, 46 Park Street,
c. 1927. Local History
Collection, Framingham
Public Library

"Motor driven machines" made for confusing advertising copy, however, and Nutting's own feelings about modern production techniques compelled him to write out and place a copy of his own "Ten Commandments" at each work station in his new Framingham factory in 1925.[47] These injunctions, while biblical in format, were decidedly secular in content. Some commandments were more bon mot than gospel (number 8, for instance: "The hand

and the mouth do not work effectively together"). Others, however, reveal Nutting's position on machines in the factory. He felt compelled, for example, to enjoin his workers, "If the old method is best, use it."[48] Interior photographs and insurance maps of the Framingham factory reveal that this commandment was inverted as often as it was followed. Although the minister persisted in referring to the Park Street facility as his "studio," Wallace Nutting furniture was clearly made in a factory (figs. 5.18, 5.19).[49]

Even though industrial woodworking machines were widely used in the Park Street shop, Nutting clung to certain tenets of Arts and Crafts thinking. In his Ten Commandments, for example, Nutting reminded his workers to "use long and large mortises, and large square white oak pins." The bold, even overt, use of a traditional fastening technique clearly symbolized quality to Nutting and his buyers—a legacy of the Arts and Crafts ethos, wherein consumers learned that exposed construction details equaled honesty and value. Nutting summed up his Ten Commandments with another echo of John Ruskin and William Morris: "Let nothing leave your hands until you are proud of the work." Nutting's final and highly self-righteous rationale for issuing this craft doxology bears further witness to his debt to the nineteenth-century theorists of the Arts and Crafts movement. Appearing just after commandment 10 and over the minister's signature is the motto "To Insure Individuality and Make Men While Making Furniture."[50]

The Center of Old American Life

Nutting's concern for the moral fiber of his employees—a legacy of the socialist underpinnings of the Arts and Crafts movement—is ironic, for by 1925 Wallace Nutting, Incorporated, was a complex corporation serving numerous markets. Gone were the days of the Broadhearth compound in Saugus where Nutting cloaked his manufactory in historical guise. The physical plant inhabited by the company in the mid-1920s could not be mistaken for anything but a factory. Nutting purchased 46 Park Street, a straw-hat factory from the last quarter of the nineteenth century, in 1924 and consolidated his endeavors under one large roof.[51] Attracted to Framingham's location and its connection to an excellent network of roads and railways, Nutting sought to turn the city into the "center of Early American life."[52]

Period references to Nutting's hoped-for "center" paint the minister as somewhat of a dreamer. Arthur Train, a New York writer, traveled to Framingham in the late 1920s "in search of a grandfather" and failed to recognize the old New England town. "He [Train] had vaguely recalled the town as a cluster of low wooden and red-brick buildings—blacksmith shop, a tavern, a

The piece above, No. 918, has just been made to order and will be available for the public, together with 300 other exquisite reproductions of all early periods

{ *An exquisite catalogue with 355 pictures will be mailed for $1 — refundable with the first purchase* }

WALLACE NUTTING

46 PARK STREET   ::   ::   ::   FRAMINGHAM, MASSACHUSETTS

5.20
Wallace Nutting, Incorporated, Advertisement for a block-front chest of drawers. From *Antiques* (June 1928): 16

few high-stooped stores and a bank—at the turn of a narrow, dusty road beside an embowered 'common,' the tops of whose fanlike elms were pierced by several spires." Motoring up from the great metropolis, Train drove right by Framingham. "This peaceful New England village," he recalled, "had become standardized with a vengeance." "Nothing," he declared, "had so shaken his ostrich-like concept of modernity as this unexpected experience."[53]

The Park Street Studio

Forty-six Park Street in Framingham was Nutting's largest production facility. Joel Dodge, an employee who worked for Nutting in the early 1940s, recalled the factory's floor plan and organization. "Two cabinetmakers and one foreman and myself worked in the shop one was a man named Ernest Gerstan and a Latvian named Joe. I forget the shop foreman's name and the finishing dept. on their floor. Shop was on the 1st floor. Ernest John Donnelly was in office at that time and also his secretary the rest of the floor was picture dept. 3rd and part of 4th were furniture show rooms. All the pieces he had pictures in Final Edition of Catalogue were on exhibition at that time."[54]

The "pieces on exhibition" represented the final expansion of Wallace Nutting furniture. Nutting's catalogs had grown steadily from the days of Windsor chair-making in Saugus, through the Pilgrim Century era in Ashland, to the elaborate 160-page *Supreme Edition General Catalog* of 1930. By this point, Nutting offered reproductions of close to two centuries' worth of styles and types. The most important change, however, came when Nutting embraced mahogany and developed a line of eighteenth-century designs.

Nutting introduced mahogany furniture around 1926, according to Franklin Gottshall, a Park Street employee who went on to an important career as an author of woodworking books.[55] The first piece reproduced, according to Gottshall, was a monumental Townsend-style chest-on-chest. Nutting's public announcement of the new line came quietly in an *Antiques* magazine advertisement in September 1927, when he offered an upholstered chair, followed in April 1928 with a simple Chippendale chair and then in July 1928 with a block-front chest of drawers (fig. 5.20).[56] By the time the *Supreme Edition* catalog of 1930 shipped, Nutting's offerings included more than three hundred pieces of furniture, in addition to wrought iron and treenware.

The Museum and the Market

Nutting patterned these reproductions on furniture in his own collection as well as objects from the newly organized American collections at major museums.[57] As early as 1920 Nutting had access to the collections of the Wadsworth Atheneum and in that year received permission to photograph certain pieces for reproduction.[58] In 1930, he noted the "source of my copies" in the *Supreme Edition* catalog: "1. The Wallace Nutting Collection at Hartford, 2. The former collection, with much mahogany, 3. The collections of the Metropolitan Museum, of which I have the honor of being a member, 4. The collections of many friends who have been kind enough to give me access for measurements."[59]

Nutting secured photographs of these prototypes, made drawings, and created patterns to facilitate reproduction. Franklin Gottshall remembered that "Nutting's own drawings were often inadequate and poorly detailed, and his workmen . . . had trouble following them." Gottshall described one visit to inspect a chest. "Nutting did take six of us workmen to Providence to study the piece as well as others in the collection, but then Nutting and I returned alone to make the drawings. Despite my protestations that it was unnecessary, Nutting insisted that I make these working drawings full-size, so that workmen building the piece could take measurements directly from them."[60] Nutting may have been an inadequate draftsman, but he certainly knew his mind. Surviving patterns, parts, and cardboard templates show Nutting's intimate involvement in the process (figs. 5.21, 5.22). The minister's distinctive handwriting is scrawled across many, briskly specifying a certain angle, relief, or taper for the final component.

5.21
Wallace Nutting, Incorporated,
*Templates for Carving Chair
Crests*, c. 1925, pencil on
cardboard. Wadsworth
Atheneum Museum of Art,
American Decorative Arts
Purchase Fund, 1999.47

5.22
Wallace Nutting, Incorporated,
*Crests for #340, #380, and #394
Chairs*, c. 1925, mahogany,
maple, and walnut. Wadsworth
Atheneum Museum of Art,
American Decorative Arts
Purchase Fund, 1999.47

Old American Stock

Nutting's Framingham employees, the men who used these templates and translated the cryptic remarks into wood, were a crucial resource (fig. 5.23). Though he claimed that the "[work] force consists of fine American mechanics, men of character, whom it is a privilege to know," the Park Street workers were a decidedly international lot.[61] "One of my employees once wittily characterized the shop as the league of nations," he boasted, and the description was apt. "We have Catholics and Protestants and Jews," he continued. "We have natives, Italians, Scotch, Swedes, Canadians, Irish and have had French, German, Finns, Syrians and so on."[62] A snapshot of Nutting's employees from the 1930s bears a careful inscription and records workers with the surnames Nelson, Gerstan, Thomas, Turgeon, Carboneau, Ferrell, Kelley, Donnelly, Sterling, Libertini, Brackett, Bortolusi, Newcomb, Raustrom, Ball, Kimball, and Cacciola.[63] "I think it utterly wrong to pay American workers above immigrants," he wrote. Reflecting perhaps on the lot of John Nutting, his seventeenth-century ancestor, he piously declared that our "fathers were all immigrants and when they came they were poorer and less educated than those who come now."[64]

Of note among this "league of nations" were a handful of Scandinavian immigrants who worked for Nutting in Framingham. Part of a long-standing tradition in New England furniture factories, Scandinavian workers accounted for 0.7 percent of Boston's population in 1880 yet comprised 3.2 percent of furniture workers.[65] Nutting commented on the desirability of this population in a letter of 1933. "The modern American workman is so imbued with the commercial spirit," complained the minister, "fostered by the usual contractor, that it is difficult to get quality." The answer, for Nutting and others, came from northern Europe. A "man working part time for us now, a Swede, who teaches at the Wentworth Institute, Boston, is demanding the proper quality of his pupils."[66]

The Swede of whom the minister approved was one Peter Johnson, an important cog in the Park Street machine, for he produced many of the carvings needed on Wallace Nutting's early American designs (fig. 5.24). Johnson lived in Cambridge and acted as a subcontractor, working from photographs, templates, and shop drawings presumably produced by Ernest John Donnelly, Nutting's illustrator and all-around factotum.[67] Johnson's contribution not only reveals that highly skilled tasks were farmed out from the Park Street facility but provides a window into an economy of specialty woodworking in New England in the early twentieth century.

Johnson's work was supplemented by carved elements provided by E. J. Dunn of Hartford, Connecticut.[68] Dunn ran a well-established firm. His largest

5.24
Wallace Nutting, Incorporated,
*Carved Panels, Side Rail,
and Drawer Front for a #911
Cupboard, #910 Cupboard, and
#991 High Chest of Drawers,*
c. 1930, oak and maple.
Wadsworth Atheneum Museum
of Art, American Decorative
Arts Purchase Funds, 1999.47

customer was the Austin Organ Company, followed by Nathan Margolis and Company, a high-end manufacturer of colonial furniture. As early as 1928, Dunn shipped elaborate pieces for Nutting's expanded furniture line to 46 Park Street. For the next three years, Dunn's carvers fabricated sample desk moldings, created table legs with claw-and-ball feet, and rendered eagles for looking glasses. At times, it appears that Dunn's hands completed whole chairs and shipped them to Nutting, again revealing the minister's participation in a well-organized network of custom woodworkers rather than relying on a fully staffed facility in Framingham.

Shop Practice

Documentary, physical, and photographic evidence all indicate that limited runs of individual designs were the order of business in the Park Street factory, with the notable exception of Windsor production. Libraries and financial institutions in particular were frequent customers for large sets of seating furniture, and batch production perfectly suited this market. Interior photographs of the factory clearly show stacks of roughed-out Windsor seats, a jig for bending multiple bows, and substantial orders cued for final production and shipping (fig. 5.25).

5.25
Factory interior showing
Windsor chairs, 46 Park
Street, c. 1927. Local History
Collection, Framingham
Public Library

More elaborate pieces, such as the number 910 Parmenter Cupboard and the number 918 block-front chest of drawers advertised in *Antiques* in July 1928, appear to have been made to order. The very language of the advertisement implies that items were added to the Nutting line after a single commission.[69] The lack of sturdy metallic templates and production-line machinery, however, suggests that 46 Park Street operated as a large custom shop rather than a mass-market factory.[70] As a result, Nutting employed a number of multiskilled generalist woodworkers. In 1928, at the height of the furniture business before the stock market crash dramatically curtailed the demand for consumer durables, Nutting's woodworking concern employed twelve men. Six are identified as cabinetmakers and two as finishers. In the group there is also a carver, a Windsor chair assembler, a packer, and an "office manager and artist."[71]

The workers' rate of pay, and to a certain extant their ethnicity, indicates a hierarchy of labor in the Park Street facility. A surviving pay scale from 1945 (perhaps the final payroll) gives a sense of the organization of Wallace Nutting, Incorporated.[72] Ernest Gerstan, cabinetmaker, was paid $1.02 per hour. Wallace Nelson, also a cabinetmaker and Nutting's long-time shop foreman, made 98 cents an hour. The turner Gerard B. Thomas was paid at the same rate as Nelson.[73] George Turgeon, the valued Windsor chair maker, rated 90 cents an hour. The finishers Tom Carboneau and Charles Ferrell received 79 ¾ cents and 75 cents, respectively. An unnamed night watchman made 40 cents per hour.

Nelson and Turgeon had been with Nutting since the 1920s, and given the

5.26
Brand on a #910 cupboard.
Wadsworth Atheneum
Museum of Art, Purchased
through the gift of Charles A.
Goodwin, 2002.15

highly skilled nature of their vocation, it comes as no surprise to find them at the top of the payscale.[74] The employment of Thomas Carboneau, also a long-term employee, suggests an ethnic hierarchy within the factory, for Carboneau worked in the finishing department. Although Nutting was far more liberal in attitude toward immigrants than many of his class and background, it seems clear that workers of Scandinavian and Anglo-Saxon descent performed the most highly skilled tasks in the factory, such as carving, whereas Carboneau, presumably of French Canadian ancestry, worked in a more repetitive job in a less hospitable environment, the finishing shop.[75]

Original Finish

As with most aesthetic choices, Wallace Nutting held (and offered) strong opinions when it came to selecting an appropriate finish for his furniture. Although he was frequently asked to "antique" or add false patina to his wares, he steadfastly refused. Nutting furniture was sold complete with either a painted ebony topcoat or a carefully built-up shellac surface.[76] The minister was particularly proud to offer Old American forms gleaming as new.

For all his interest in honestly "redeeming" historic forms for the modern era, Nutting was equally fond of repeating the story of a certain Windsor chair. "A child's high chair made by us and sold for nineteen dollars, was artificially aged and resold for a cool thousand. Nobody but the maker could have discovered the imposition," he chortled.[77] Others were less amused. SPNEA's

William Sumner Appleton wrote to Nutting about this very point, no doubt playing on his ego. "Let me urge you very strongly to mark every piece that leaves your shop—whether iron work or furniture, or anything else—in such a way that it can never be confounded with the old."[78] In the early days of the business, Nutting had employed an "old time" paper label on the bottom of his furniture, often with a series of punches to indicate the item's model number. Perhaps as a result of Appleton's hectoring, Nutting began to brand his furniture in the early 1920s, first with a script logo and then with a bold, block brand (fig. 5.26).[79]

Surface finish referred to issues of honesty and quality in Nutting's thinking in the same way that construction details bespoke of Arts and Crafts morality. He wrote with disdain of the "cheap furniture [that] floods the American market.... Far more attention is given to the finish than to the form or the substance. For instance, I see before me as I write a table of oak, on which is stamped by machinery a design intended to make the buyer suppose that the table is quartered oak. The old scheme of imitating the grain of wood with paint was bad enough, and this is still worse. It is a falsity and is intended to deceive. It isn't an honest thing for children to see."[80]

Furniture for Modern Pilgrims

If the impact of grain-painted furniture on the youth of America concerned Nutting, then he certainly would not have wanted children to lay eyes on the forms he introduced to keep his company afloat during the Great Depression. Although the company outlived Nutting and survived until 1945, the stock market crash of 1929 dramatically affected the small company and left Nutting looking for new customers. Themselves reeling from the economic downturn, banks and other financial institutions proved to be important clients throughout the 1930s.[81] Esther Svenson, Nutting's last head colorist and secretary, noted of one request from the National Shawmut Bank of Boston, "our best profit has always been made on these orders."[82] Nutting recognized this and, despite his stance on hybrid colonial furniture ("It is Jack"), moved to capitalize on the market for institutional furniture.[83]

Not only did Nutting provide furnishings for such institutions as State Street Bank in Boston, First National Bank in Kansas City, and Aetna Property and Casualty Insurance Company in Hartford, but in a move that no doubt caused him considerable distress, he began to offer adaptations of his designs for the modern workplace (fig. 5.27).[84] As early as 1930, just one year after the stock market crash, Nutting included designs such as the number 495 "Tip and Turn" executive chair and the number 747 "Oak Chest Desk" in his catalog (fig.

5.27
#490 chairs installed in "The Pine Room" at Aetna, Incorporated, Hartford, Connecticut, c. 1935. Courtesy of Aetna Incorporated Archives

5.28
Office display showing Pilgrim Century desk, Nutting photographs, and "Great Peacock and Floral Rug by Mariet G. Nutting." From *Wallace Nutting Final Edition Furniture Catalog* (1937), 37

5.28). To add insult to injury, market demand led the minister to note that the desk was "adapted for typewriter."[85] Although he was willing to make furniture "the new way" by using modern tools, objects such as number 749, "Desk adapted from Connecticut Chest Pattern," could not have registered as anything but "humbug" with Nutting.

A man of considerable contradictions, Wallace Nutting hoped to provide honest furniture—"fit for children to see." Preaching an Arts and Crafts ideology that equated hand craftsmanship with quality, Nutting was also the proprietor of a fully equipped modern factory. A businessman who misjudged his market, the flinty Yankee minister was again the victim of geopolitical forces when the Great Depression stunted his furniture initiative just as World War I had ended his foray into house museums. In the course of building his furniture business, however, Nutting pursued collateral activities as a collector, lecturer, and writer that made him into a leading popular voice on early American life.

Chapter 6   *Beauty, Construction, and Style*

OLD AMERICA ON MADISON AVENUE

*F*or a man interested in the quiet beauties of the past, Wallace Nutting proved ever willing to adopt the latest, most modern, marketing techniques to encourage sales of his products. From the earliest days of simple magazine advertisements to elaborate crossover schemes whereby different product lines advertised each other in house museums, mail-order catalogs, and department stores, the road to Old America was paved with up-to-date methods of promotion (fig. 6.1). The minister's advertising practices, public lectures, and department store displays provide a vivid picture of how Nutting responded to and influenced middle-class taste while helping to organize a culture of consumption in early-twentieth-century America.[1]

Nutting's initial foray into the field of advertising challenges the notion of "amateur" photography. Like many avocational lensmen, Nutting began to submit his photographs to national journals while following another career path. In Nutting's case, he mailed off his prints in 1902 while still serving as a minister in Providence, Rhode Island. His work subsequently appeared as illustrations in a number of popular journals, including *Harper's Monthly Magazine*, *Pilgrim*, *Woman's Home Companion*, and *Country Life in America*. Typically accompanying a sentimental article about the beauties of rural life, such as "A Fallow Field" by Fannie Barnes in *Harper's*, Nutting's images helped to fix the myths of country living in print.[2] Pastoral views of farm animals, rustic houses, and venerable shade trees comprised the vocabulary of Nutting's early magazine work.

Dabbling in publishing was clearly part of the amateur photography scene. Others, including Mary and Frances Allen, also submitted their work to periodicals with like success. Nutting's photography, however, shows how amateur efforts could be quickly coopted to become "professional." The minister's photo, *The Start—Coaching in the Country*, proudly appeared as the center-

Opposite: Detail of fig. 6.9

The Birthplace of a
Distinctive American Art

At Nuttinghame, in historic New England, a new influence in American art had its beginning about fifteen years ago. Here Wallace Nutting produced the first pictures which won him art recognition. Appealed to by art lovers for examples of his work, this genuis of the lens and brush developed a typical and true American art.

Wallace Nutting has preserved for all time the interior and exterior art of America's Colonial Days and the beauties of this country's forests, streams and waters; he has caught the breath of Spring in her fragrant blossoms and the indescribable beauty of the winding country lane and shaded woodland path.

Wherever there is appreciation of the really beautiful and truly artistic—Wallace Nutting pictures in Nature's own colors are hung to be admired constantly. They are pictures that have brought new beauty into American homes.

Wallace Nutting pictures may be obtained in many sizes. Those measuring eleven by fourteen inches, and larger, show the subjects to the best advantage. As gifts, Wallace Nutting pictures meet every requirement and occasion most admirably; and they are not as expensive as their appearance indicates. Visit the store in your city which displays Wallace Nutting pictures.

Wallace Nutting

hand colored

PICTURES

Autumn Exhibit and Sale ~ September 20th to 30th

DEALERS: DISPLAY WALLACE NUTTING PICTURES PROMINENTLY BETWEEN THESE DATES

Wallace Nutting True Colonial Reproductions

All of the qualities which have made Colonial furniture serviceable for more than two hundred years are characteristic of Wallace Nutting True Colonial Reproductions. They are made for the discriminating few; necessarily somewhat higher priced than factory-made Colonial adaptations, Wallace Nutting Colonial Furniture represents infinitely greater value. The Wallace Nutting Colonial Furniture brochure sent upon receipt of ten cents, stamp or coin.

WALLACE NUTTING STUDIOS . . ASHLAND, MASS.

6.1
Wallace Nutting, Incorporated,
"The Birthplace of a Distinctive American
Art," *Good Housekeeping Magazine*
(October 1921)

STOCKING THE HAMPER

After a swinging drive, a tramp through the woods, a splashing canoe trip or any other outdoor diversion, nothing is so good to take the edge off the sharpest appetite as

Underwood's Deviled Ham

For many years it has been the mainstay in every country-bound hamper. It is appetizing and nourishing. For luncheon at home, a late supper or a chafing dish party, there is nothing better. On every can of Underwood's Deviled Ham a little red devil grins; you will see him in rows on your grocer's shelves.

A Little Booklet of Receipts sent on request.

WM. UNDERWOOD COMPANY, Boston, Mass.

COUNTRY LIFE IN AMERICA.

6.2
Wallace Nutting, "Underwood's Deviled Ham," *Country Life in America* 2 (July 1902). Courtesy of The Winterthur Library, Printed Book and Periodical Collection

fold in the June 1902 issue of *Country Life in America.* Depicting a formal group preparing to take to the open road in a carriage, *Coaching in the Country* portrayed the pastime of touring as genteel, dignified, and highly fashionable. So successfully did Nutting define the scene that the photograph appeared in *Country Life* again the following month (fig. 6.2)—but this time as an ad for Underwood's Deviled Ham![3] In one short month, Nutting's amateur effort had become an integral part of a professional advertising campaign.

6.3
Wallace Nutting, Incorporated, "Pictures on the Wall Make a House a Home," *Ladies' Home Journal* 39 (May 1922): 55

Advertising (A) Photography (Business)

Although Nutting supplied photographs for articles and advertising copy in major publications as early as 1902, he did not begin earnestly to advertise his own business interests until the early 1920s. Beginning in 1921, ads for the photography line began to appear sporadically in national magazines, including *Atlantic Monthly, Ladies' Home Journal*, and *Good Housekeeping* (fig. 6.3).[4] The platinotype business, it seems, needed little advertisement until this point. Indeed, Nutting's earlier boast of conducting a thousand dollars' worth of business a day suggests that his network of department stores, print shops, and "travelers" supplied customers faster than his rudimentary production methods could accommodate.

In 1921, however, Nutting stood at a crossroads. He had been forced to liquidate his Chain of Colonial Picture Houses some months before and was about to publish his first major volume, *Furniture of the Pilgrim Century*. He needed capital and as a result sought to increase the return from his photography line. He stepped up his advertising by sounding notes of tradition and longevity. "At Nuttinghame, in historic New England, a new influence in American art had its beginning about fifteen years ago." In typical purple prose, Nutting spun a tale of the early days of his business. After producing the "first pictures which won him art recognition" he was "appealed to by art lovers everywhere," and "it remained, then, for this genius of the lens and brush to develop a typical and true American art." Nutting continued to play on patriotic sentiment. He expounded upon "America's Colonial Days" and the "beauties of this country's forests, streams and waters," while promoting the "pictures that have brought new beauty into the American home."[5] To ignore his "Autumn Exhibit and Sale" was practically an un-American activity in 1921, a scant three years after the Armistice.

Advertising History

Nutting's penchant for cross marketing appears again in the 1921 ad campaign. At the bottom of his *Good Housekeeping* photography advertisement, the minister plugs his expanding furniture line. "A Wallace Nutting Colonial piece *is* Colonial in every detail," he reminded his customers. "They are made for the discriminating few." This admission is important, for it signals Nutting's awareness of the market. The platinum prints were for the masses, selling for as little as $1.25 in 1921. The furniture, by contrast, "necessarily somewhat higher priced than factory-made Colonial Adaptations," represented a considerable investment. As a result of this up-market placement, Nutting's furniture business demanded a concerted advertising campaign from the beginning.

Although Nutting advertised his furniture in a number of shelter magazines, *Antiques* was his principal forum. The initial publication of the journal roughly coincided with the expansion of Nutting's business and suggests a broadening of the Americana market as a result of postwar economic growth.[6] In 1921 the minister moved his furniture business from the Old Scott Mill to Ashland and expanded his catalog of offerings. The first issue of *Antiques* arrived the following year. From its inception, *Antiques* was the official organ of the Americana market, shaping taste and creating community for generations. It also provided the most cost-effective vehicle for reaching Nutting's constituents, "collectors and others who find interest in times past and in the articles of daily use and adornment devised by the forefathers."[7]

Nutting's advertisements in *Antiques* chronicle the development of the furniture business in high relief. "Once we have placed advertisements in the same category as many traditional historical documents," writes historian Roland Marchand, "it may be possible to argue that ads actually surpass most other recorded communications as a basis for *plausible inference* about popular attitudes and values.[8] Nutting's advertisements, according to this paradigm, provide much information about the attitudes and values held by the *Antiques* reader, filtered, of course, through the worldview of the minister from Rockbottom. The ads represent Nutting's perceptions of his customers' wants and needs and expose an important dialectic between producer and consumer. In this way, the advertisements provide a richer understanding of the "attitudes and values" of Nutting's Old American customers.

Nutting's initial pitch offered his reproductions as the "antiques of tomorrow." The accuracy of his designs, he claimed, guaranteed "distinction and dignity to the home."[9] In this way Nutting extended Clarence Cook's early argument for decorating with antiques, *The House Beautiful*, published in 1877. Cook, a writer for *Scribner's Monthly* and an important arbiter of taste in the late nineteenth century, applauded interest in venerable furniture as "returning good taste in a community that has long been the victim to the whims and impositions of foreign fashions." Noting that "everybody can't have a grandfather, nor things that came over in the 'Mayflower,'" Cook proposed that "those of us who have not drawn these prizes in life's lottery must do the best we can under the circumstances." His answer to those suffering from poor pedigree? "We must go down to Hawkens', or Sypher's, or Drake's," a who's who of early dealers and reproducers of antique furniture.[10] In recommending Sypher's to his readers, Cook anointed colonial furniture as appropriate for homes of good taste.[11] Yet Cook was not calling for wholesale decoration with ersatz ancestral antiques; he was advocating select objects, chairs, cupboards, and tables to serve as mnemonics of ancestral virtue in the modern Victorian home—be they from "grandfather's" house or Sypher's showroom.

Nutting took up the call a generation later, providing these symbolic domestic accessories for a population even less likely to enjoy furniture that belonged to grandfather or "came over in the 'Mayflower.'" Indeed, one of Nutting's trump cards by the 1920s was availability. "If you can find an old Court Cupboard like this," claimed one ad, "you can probably obtain $25,000.00 for it. If you want a new one, as this is, at a modest price, it is something you can get."[12] Another ad read, "If you cannot find the old, the reproduction should be obtained from the most perfect design, constructed in the most perfect manner."[13]

Beyond availability, Nutting promised value. His furniture, he assured the gentle reader, could be counted on as a commodity, just like a *real* antique. "In your own lifetime," read a series of advertisements in 1926, "this furniture, my name burned in, will be worth several times its cost."[14] Nutting thus sought to differentiate his product from the poorly aging "showy parlor suites" of shoddy furniture that saturated the market to Edith Wharton's horror in 1897 and survived into the 1920s to make up the back-room stock of the used furniture market.[15] Purchase a Nutting chair and the minister promised "Beauty, Construction, Style" (fig. 6.4).[16]

BEAUTY   CONSTRUCTION   STYLE

The above is a very perfect and important reproduction of the Connecticut Sunflower and Tulip two-drawer chest. The stools are examples of our minor pieces.

It is a beautiful drive to Framingham. You will find there 120 different patterns of reproductions. Also there is on the floor one of the finest old court cupboards of American origin.

Interested persons may, by sending a postal, be waited on with pictures at their homes.

Shown at my Studio, Framingham, 46 Park Street (close to Station)
21 *miles to Boston*

WALLACE NUTTING

6.4
Wallace Nutting, Incorporated, "Beauty, Construction, Style," *Antiques* (December 1926): 508

Christmas Greetings from Nuttingholme

Ad Men

If Wallace Nutting had not existed, Wallace Nutting's advertising agency would have invented him (fig. 6.5). The heyday of Old America coincided with the rise of nostalgic, personality-based advertising in popular middle-class periodicals. As "ancestral authority grew culturally or geographically remote," T. J. Jackon Lears has noted, "advertisements replaced it with a merger of corporate and therapeutic authority." Further, this authority often came in "pseudotraditional guise."[17] The Mennen Company, for example, launched an advertising effort in *Good Housekeeping* in 1920. Under the folksy byline of "Aunt Belle's Comfort Letters," Mennen offered new mothers advice about child rearing. To allay doubts, the company assured the public that "Aunt Belle is a real person and that is her real name." Her authenticity established, Mennen offered Aunt Belle's down-home credentials—"she really understands babies."[18] Other companies followed suit and created what Roland Marchand has termed "personal advisors." Aunt Belle was joined in print by "Helen Chase" for Camay, "Mary Hale Martin" for Libby's, and "Janet Gray" for Lewis and Conger.[19] Wallace Nutting, a Harvard-educated Congregational minister, was tailor-made to serve as an antimodern "personal advisor" for Aunt Belle, Janet Gray, and the rest of middle-class America.

The rise of Old America also coincided with a consolidation of cultural authority in the hands of the advertising executive, known ubiquitously as the "ad man." To be an advertising agent in the mid-nineteenth century was to peddle trade cards produced by chromolithography. The ad man "worked in small shops with a rudimentary division of labor, cranking our sentimental genre prints [of] interchangeable images that could be used as trade cards by various retailers." By 1900, major ad agencies such as J. Walter Thompson and N. W. Ayer conducted market research, advised their clients, and managed "every detail of the advertising process from layout and copy to final insertion."[20] Nutting's choice of advertising agency not only affected how he sold his wares but firmly locates him within the professional milieu of the ad man in the early twentieth century.

Nutting employed the George Batten Company to place his advertisements in the early 1920s.[21] A surviving scrapbook of Nutting's promotions testifies to the firm's professional methods. Tipped into each page is a tear sheet, or proof, for a print ad. Each ad is identified by an individual job number, the size, and intended publication. Number 2206, for example, called for "2 cols." in *Good Housekeeping*. Other proof sheets provide the contours of Batten's efforts on Nutting's behalf. Number 2303, for instance, "Quarter Page Ladies Home Journal–Nov" indeed appeared on page 229 of the venerable periodical that fall, while 2204 purchased space on the "3rd cover" of *Vogue* (fig. 6.6). Number 2201 announced a "Spring Exhibition and Sale" in the unidentified "s. c. News." The use of the now-standard marketing technique of a "special" or advertised "sale" again suggests the modern methods Batten employed for the Nutting account.

Located in Manhattan in the Fourth Avenue Building at Fourth Avenue and 27th Street and later at 383 Madison Avenue, the Batten Company eventually became part of Batten, Barton, Durstine and Osborn—one of the largest and most influential advertising agencies in America.[22] At first blush, the relationship between the fusty minister-turned-antiquarian and Batten, the progressive spearhead of modernity, could not appear more incongruous. Nutting, it would seem, could not have been farther from Madison Avenue with his Windsor chairs and "Colonial" platinum prints. Yet the distance between Nutting and the advertising world of the 1920s was far shorter than first appearances might suggest. Indeed, not only was Nutting the sort of personality, fictitious or not, that Madison Avenue preferred to promulgate in the 1920s, but he was the sort of individual with whom advertising executives would have felt perfectly at ease.

White, male, and Protestant, Wallace Nutting could have been an ad man. At the time of the merger between the George Batten Company and Barton, Durstine, and Osborn in 1928, the former company listed a staff of sixty-five, of whom seven were women. Of the seven, all were "assistants." In 1931, according to Marchand, of the five thousand men listed in *Who's Who in*

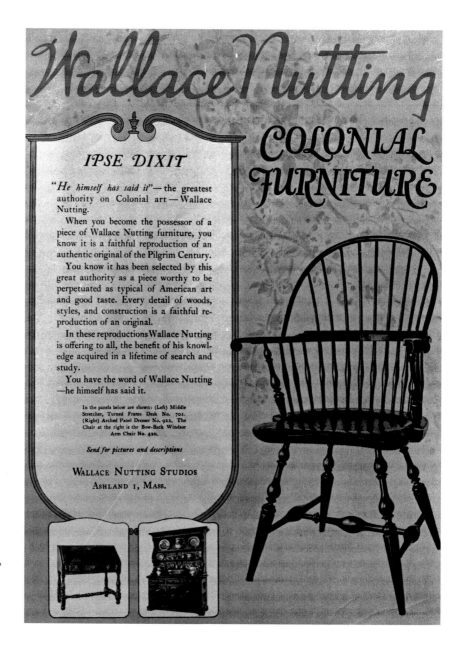

Advertising, only ninety-two were identifiably Jewish and there is "no evidence that blacks did anything other than janitorial work for the agencies during the 1920s and 1930s."[23] As a minister, Nutting fit neatly into the developing therapeutic notion of consumption. "By the 1920s," notes Lears, "religion and psychotherapy had merged to meet the needs of the educated middle and upper classes." Simply put, "therapies became more theological, theologies became more therapeutic."[24] The ad man, curiously enough, came along for the ride.

Bruce Barton, a prince among ad men and eventual partner to Nutting's own agent, George Batten, wrote a remarkable book in 1925 entitled *The Man Nobody Knows*. In his text, Barton offered a paradigm for the modern Christian in which Jesus emerged as the model businessman.[25] Barton's message was a popular one. *The Man Nobody Knows* topped the American nonfiction bestseller list in 1926.[26] Just as Nutting wanted to be a businessman, so Barton wished to preach. Not only did religious commonality make Barton and Nutting kith, but the two men shared another bond—an allegiance to Berea College in Berea, Kentucky. Nutting, a longtime supporter of the college, eventually left the bulk of his estate to Berea. Barton, following in his father's footsteps, was a trustee of the college from June 1931 until April 1965.[27] On the death of Nutting's widow, Mariet, in 1945, Barton interceded to ensure that the Nutting estate was properly wrapped up and that Berea received the maximum benefit from the minister's largesse.[28] Barton and Nutting, so easily assumed to inhabit opposite ends of the modern spectrum, appear to have been of similar hue and value. Given this affiliation, it comes as no surprise to find the minister lecturing about furniture in the 1920s just as the ad man preached about commerce. Nutting's lectures were yet another forum for him to broadcast his ideas and reinforced the professional advertising campaign laid out by the George Batten Company in popular magazines of the period.

The Man Nobody Knows

"When I preach," wrote Wallace Nutting in 1936, "I do not feel it to be ethical to receive payment, since I am earning my living in an other manner." "But lecturing," he quickly added, "is another matter." Indeed it was, for in public speaking Nutting again found a way to advertise his various business interests while getting paid for his time. To accomplish this feat he prepared some three thousand hand-tinted lantern slides, "at vast expense and long labor," and joined the lecture circuit.[29]

Nutting's illustrated lectures, first given in 1915, were arranged into a series of thematic courses.[30] At the height of his public speaking career he advertised a willingness to speak on twenty-four subjects, although three were "literary" in nature and did not require visual equipment.[31] With the exception of these latter topics, which included "Opportunity for the Young Generation" and "Beautiful Correlations in Nature, Science, Art and Religion," Nutting's talks focused on what he knew best—furniture and the moralizing landscape.

Lectures 1 through 4 delivered a course on American furniture. Each lecture consisted of about 180 images illustrating, for example, Dutch aspects of American furniture or "the Chippendale influence." Nutting recommended that an hour and a half be set aside for each presentation, which included a "homogeneous address . . . occupying thirty to forty minutes, followed by a forum" or period of question and answer.[32]

In a brochure devised to promote the lectures, Nutting advertised these presentations as appropriate for "Clubs, Architects, Schools or Decorators."[33] In his 1930 *Supreme Edition* furniture catalog, he offered the service and noted, "These lectures are popular for all sorts of organizations, and include courses for women's colleges."[34] Nutting targeted those professionals most likely to buy his furniture as well as women, traditional arbiters of middle-class taste. This latter audience was rapidly developing into the preferred consumers of the modern age and, as a group, was subject to constant market research and manipulation.[35]

The retired minister was quite clear about his thoughts on pro bono work. In his advertising brochure he stipulated that he required "one hundred dollars for a single lecture," though for "two lectures in the same town on successive days," he could be heard for the bargain rate of "one hundred fifty dollars."[36] To those who thought he should provide such education as a matter of course, Nutting had a ready retort. "Free doctoring is admirable where the patient has not wherewith to pay. If, however, he is not impecunious he is far more likely to take advice that he has paid for. I make it a rule except in hometown gatherings to require a fee. My appetite is still excellent and my clothing subject to ordinary wear. I think it entirely proper that I should live by my labor."[37]

Nutting was doing more than merely "living by his labor" in speaking to these groups, however. By his own admission he knew the value of promoting his products in the guise of education—he even boasted about his efforts. Del Gooding, his sometime chauffeur, recalled Nutting chuckling after a lecture in the Midwest. "What do you know about that," asked Nutting, "I got sixty dollars for advertising my own material!"[38] This method of advertising comes into sharp focus on several occasions, never more clearly than in Baltimore during the early spring of 1923.

Selling Tradition in the Department Store

By 1923 Nutting had been in the reproduction furniture business for some six years. He had issued two catalogs, *Correct Windsors* (1918) and *The Great American Idea* (1921), and was looking to expand his network of distributors. Following the patterns of his photography business, he began to look at department stores as one such outlet.[39] In March 1923, the *Baltimore Sun* began to run a series of advertisements for Mettee and Company, a local concern. Under the banner headline "Wallace Nutting Reproductions of Early American Colonial Furniture," the store proclaimed: "We are pleased to announce we have secured the exclusive selling agency for this very interesting collection of handmade furniture. All of us have admired and longed for one or more of the quaint old pieces shown in his beautiful pictures of Colonial Interiors and it was just this interest that prompted Mr. Nutting to reproduce his wonderful collection of antiques. The entire line will be shown on our floors."[40]

As a local firm, Mettee and Company seemed to need to reassure its customers as to the store's ability to pick a furniture line that represented the latest cosmopolitan taste. "With such names as John Wanamaker, Philadelphia & New York; Marshall Field & Co., Chicago; Jordan Marsh Co., Boston; and Sterling & Welch, Cleveland," continued the ad copy, "having secured the exclusive selling agency in their respective cities we feel very fortunate in having secured the line for Baltimore." Institutional pedigree aside, Mettee and Company enthused that "the prices are most moderate."[41]

Moderate price or not, Mettee and Nutting staged a remarkable public relations campaign around the opening of the line in Baltimore. Not only did the *Sun* run ads throughout the first two weeks in March, including one that appeared on the society page and another that announced "a 10% to 20% discount on our entire stock including Wallace Nutting colonial furniture, mahogany furniture and brasses," but on 11 and 13 March, respectively, two short articles promoted and reviewed his lecture at the YWCA. Nutting added authority to the hyperbole of his print advertising through the public address at the "Y," a national institution of known moral caliber. As an act of salesmanship, Nutting's Baltimore lecture, like his addresses to countless groups throughout the country, boosted his reputation while increasing sales.

A list of department stores that carried Nutting's furniture reads like a roster of early-twentieth-century retail giants.[42] Besides Mettee and Company in Baltimore, by the early 1920s the furniture (and often the platinotypes as well) could be purchased in Philadelphia at John Wanamaker's flagship and the Bellevue-Stratford department store. Wanamaker also offered Nutting furniture in his New York emporium, while Jordan Marsh served Boston, and Marshall Field's held the Chicago account. Nutting sunflower chests, Windsors, and elegant Federal card tables were also available in smaller cities. Well-to-do residents of Cleveland could buy a piece of Old America at Sterling and Welch, just as Denholm and MacKay served Worcester, Massachusetts—a retail outlet not far from Nutting's headquarters in Framingham.

By 1923 Nutting had even made inroads into North Carolina. Soon to be second only to Grand Rapids as the furniture-making center of the United States, the North Carolina corridor served as home to some of the premier manufacturers of colonial revival furniture, such as Danersk and Drexel.[43] Nutting entered this competitive market when he placed his line with the Harlee Furniture Company, a concern with stores in High Point and Greensboro.

As "the colonial" became an important national style, Nutting's furniture

JUNE 18-23

Wallace Nutting

hand-colored PICTURES

See how the Brandeis Department Store, Omaha, Nebraska features a Store Exhibition of Wallace Nutting Pictures. The decorations are neat and simple, but surround the customers with an out-of-doors atmosphere. Few women could resist the temptation to buy one or more Wallace Nutting Pictures in surroundings like this. Study the picture. Perhaps there is an idea or two that you can improve upon for either store or window display.

Wallace Nutting Window Displays
Work Wonders

Next to a store exhibit itself, window displays are most effective in increasing sales. People love to stop before a Wallace Nutting Picture and lose themselves in the wonderful day dreams they invoke. Don't forget this—no window is simpler to arrange and tastefully decorate than a Wallace Nutting window. So—let the public see you've got the pictures they need in their homes.

6.7
Unidentified magazine advertisement
illustrating the Brandeis Department
Store, Omaha, Nebraska, c. 1925.
Wallace Nutting Scrapbook, Local History
Collection, Framingham Public Library

6.8
Nighttime photograph of an
unidentified department store
display window, Harrisburg,
Pennsylvania. Local History
Collection, Framingham Public
Library

appeared in smaller stores in smaller cities throughout the country. His line
was represented at the Brandeis Department Store in Omaha, Nebraska, as well
as at Henderson and Mong in Chambersburg, Pennsylvania (fig. 6.7). A surviving photograph from an unidentified store in nearby Harrisburg, Pennsylvania, illustrates how Nutting fit his product lines into current modes of display (fig. 6.8). Tastefully arranged in this nighttime photograph, Nutting
platinum prints rest seductively on Nutting Windsor chairs. "Pictures are the
jewels of the home," reads the placard, and Nutting was clearly hoping that the
good people of Harrisburg would agree.

Nutting's store window reflected the sales practices of his day. *Good Furniture* magazine, the semiofficial organ of the Grand Rapids manufacturers,
stressed the importance of "a harmonious background and furnished setting
for furniture displays."[44] Inside the store, the editors of *Good Furniture* recommended "completely furnished rooms within four walls" and suggested that
these display rooms be "furnished to simulate the home interior." Major department stores, such as Jordan Marsh and Marshall Field's, displayed their domestic goods en suite in this fashion, effectively creating showrooms that instantly
related to the domestic environment.[45] Nutting included similar displays in his

6.9
Room scene in *Wallace Nutting
Final Edition Furniture Catalog*
(1937), 23

furniture catalogs, albeit in photographic form (fig. 6.9). In this way, the retailers and Nutting hoped to achieve what anthropologist Grant McCracken has termed the "Diderot effect," or the happy situation whereby the purchase of one object in a certain style leads to the desire to furnish a room (or better yet a house) to match.[46]

The Diderot effect and *Good Furniture's* recommendations were both predicated on active consumer behavior. They no doubt worked in 1928 but presumably fell flat after the stock market crashed the following year. With the economic slump of the Great Depression a litany of financial complaints began to emanate from Nutting's pen.[47] *Antiques* advertisements listed sale after sale as he tried to move merchandise. Even the modern methods of advertising and sales could not keep the furniture factory from becoming an albatross carried by Nutting's more solvent photography business.

Each aspect of Nutting's business advertised another. His lectures advertised his books; the books promoted the photography; the photography sold the furniture. With the addition of contemporary marketing techniques and up-to-date advertising methods, Nutting's business adopted the progressive methods of a modern corporation. Through his advertisements in specialty magazines, public lectures, and department store installations, Nutting not only fueled popular interest in traditional modes of interior decoration but, more important, aided in the construction of a conservative, Old American ideology for the modern home.

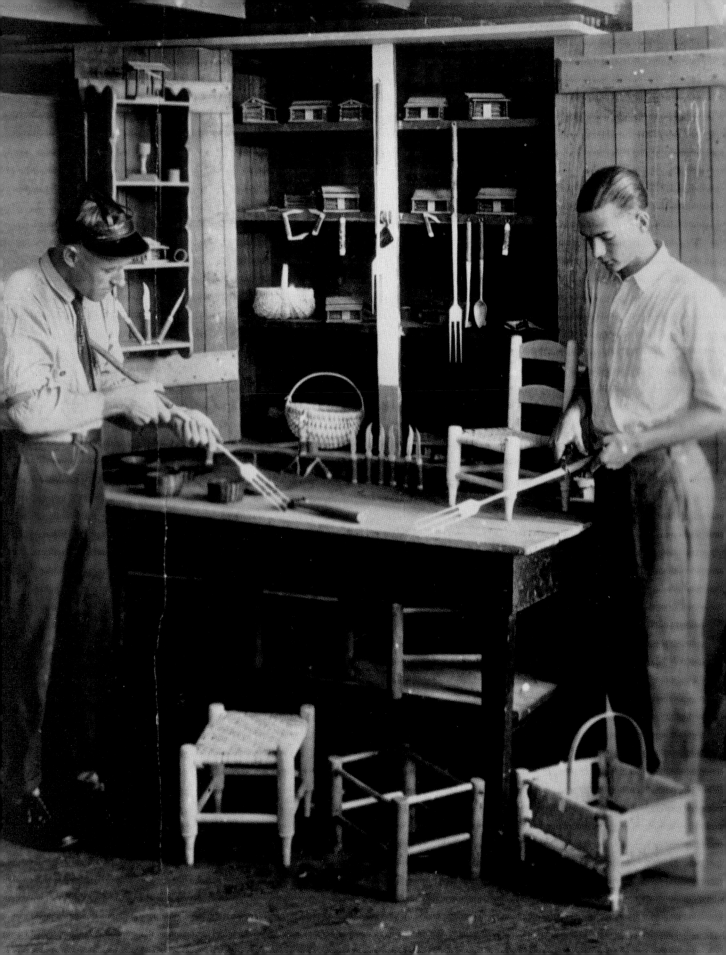

Chapter 7   *Contemporary Ancestors*

Berea College and the Past Progressive

"I t is a longer journey from northern Ohio to eastern Kentucky," wrote Berea College president William Goodell Frost in 1899, "than from America to Europe; for one day's ride brings us into the eighteenth century."[1] Intrigued by the notion of a place passed over by the modern age, Wallace and Mariet Nutting journeyed to Berea a year later to join the national search for a people Frost called "our contemporary ancestors."[2] The Nuttings were far from alone in their search for a preindustrial corner of the United States. As the nation evolved into a complex and heterogeneous body politic, boosters of the Southern Highlands promoted the region as a pure, timeless, Anglo-Saxon, culture, and Appalachia enjoyed a renaissance as a destination for those seeking authentic experiences to combat the vicissitudes of modern life (fig. 7.1).[3]

Berea College fueled the Appalachian renaissance by adopting a program of study that allowed students to work at a variety of traditional crafts as a means of subsidizing their education (fig. 7.2). This philosophy of "learning through doing" sat well with many people during the Progressive era, including Wallace Nutting, a vocal advocate of personal responsibility with a keen interest in craft. As a result, both Mariet and Wallace Nutting became moral and financial supporters of the college, serving as patrons, consultants, and ultimately major benefactors of the small school over forty years. Nutting took an active role in the development and refinement of Berea's woodworking program, supplying plans and criticism, offering the occasional student a position in Framingham, and finally leaving his business to the college in 1945.

Visiting Ministers

Nutting's first official visit to Berea came when, as pastor of the Union Congregational Church in Providence, Rhode Island, he delivered the college's

Opposite: Woodcraft View, Berea College (fig. 7.5)

7.1
Campus view of Berea College,
Berea, Kentucky, c. 1935.
Courtesy of the Berea College
Archives, Berea, Kentucky

7.2
One of Penelope's Daughters,
pamphlet from Berea College,
c. 1930. Private collection

commencement address on 6 June 1900.[4] He shared duty during the week-long exercises with the Reverend W. H. Hubbard of Auburn, New York, who gave the baccalaureate sermon.[5] The two clergymen lent an air of eastern establishment to the academic rituals, and the *Citizen*, a local newspaper, characterized Nutting's address as the "memorable feature" of a rainy commencement.[6]

Not only did Nutting's soggy address inaugurate a lifelong relationship with the college, but his visit came at a propitious moment in the little school's history. Berea, somewhat of an educational experiment from its founding in 1855, was rapidly evolving beyond its roots as a fledgling academy in need of church-sponsored financial assistance. Led by Frost, the college was moving to embrace a larger purpose and to forge a national reputation (with a commensurate development program). Nutting and Berea, then, were sailing a similar course in the earliest years of the twentieth century—away from idealized notions of liberal Protestant philanthropy and toward a more entrepreneurial stance for the modern era. It is no coincidence that both Berea and Nutting embraced the new age by looking backward.

An Oberlin in the Bluegrass

A liberal college in a conservative social landscape, Berea was born into troubled times and overcame a challenging institutional adolescence. Sponsored by the well-known politician Cassius Clay and chartered by J. A. R. Rogers and John Fee, Berea was to be, in Fee's words, "to Kentucky what Oberlin is to Ohio."[7] The new college would be "anti-slavery, anti-caste, anti-rum, anti-sin." Berea, he later elaborated, would provide "an education to all colors, classes, cheap and thorough."[8] A difficult mandate at any point in the nineteenth century, Fee's statements were fighting words in a restless and unsettled border state on the eve of the Civil War.

Fee's stand, however, secured national attention for Berea. As a result, the school enjoyed financial support from individuals as well as national organizations during the critical early years. In particular, aid came from Protestant philanthropic groups, notably the American Missionary Association, which underwrote the college president's salary. With this national backing, the college survived the sectional conflict and prospered in the second half of the nineteenth century. Unusual, and perhaps singular for its day, Berea dedicated itself to interracial coeducation.[9] Men and women, black and white—all attended Berea.

A Mountain School

Changing times, however, prompted Berea to focus its social and educational mission in the waning years of the nineteenth century.[10] Searching for a niche in the field of higher education, the college opted to provide an education to the poverty-stricken and underserved population of Appalachia. As early as 1895, Frost had publicly promoted this course of action and had begun to raise a new endowment to support the program. In 1911 Berea's trustees made the new mission official and formally amended the school's constitution to redirect Berea's aim "by contributing to the spiritual and material welfare of the mountain region of the South."[11]

The new mission placed unique demands on the institution. To provide an education to a population unable to pay tuition in a traditional manner, Berea had to develop ways for students to earn their keep. At the same time the administration was forced to increase fundraising efforts to cover the costs of faculty and infrastructure. Looking to the east coast, the college sought to build a network of institutional friends in moneyed (but moral) circles. To this end, Frost held a series of meetings in eastern cities, beginning with a dinner at the Thorndike Hotel in Boston in November 1894. In the years that followed, Frost systematically toured eastern cities where, aided by a number of well-known academics including members of the faculty at Harvard, Columbia University president Seth Low, and Princeton University professor Woodrow Wilson, he cultivated donors and raised Berea's profile.[12] On one of his many return trips back east, Frost came to know Wallace Nutting and converted him to the Berea cause.

Crafting Answers

The rise of regionalism gave Frost a pulpit from which to preach about Berea and pass the collection plate. Paralleling turn-of-the-century interest in old New England, the old South, Knickerbocker New York, and the rugged western frontier, Appalachia offered yet another organizing myth for the nation.[13] Urban dwellers unsettled by the conditions of modern life merely had to hop a train to book passage to the simple life, according to Frost. "At the close of the Revolutionary War," he wrote, "there were about two and one half million people in the American colonies. To-day there are in the Southern mountains approximately the same number of people—Americans for four or five generations—who are living to all intents and purposes in the conditions of the colonial times!"[14]

Frost, like many regionalists of his day, placed great faith in the mixture of myth and material culture that resulted in a full-scale revival of traditional

Appalachian folk culture in the early years of the twentieth century.[15] The southern highlands came to be regarded as a bulwark against degenerate foreign influences—a national reserve as important as any Fort Knox. "Another potent asset," stated an editorial in the *Carolina Churchman*, "that should appeal to the lover of America and American institutions, is that these southern Appalachian mountains are giving to the nation every year 100,000 new citizens of the purest American type." A drop in the bucket, conceded the journal, but "no inconsiderable item when we know that fifty per cent increase in many of our large cities is made up of a low type of immigrants from the slums of Europe."[16]

With nothing less than American character on the line, the phalanx of amateurs and specialists that queued up to catalog, interpret, and encourage native patterns of folklore and folklife stretched from the highlands back to every major northeastern city. By the turn of the century, the region was dotted with craft-producing social settlements, many of which possessed easily uncovered northern roots through they were located on southern soil. The Log Cabin Settlement in Asheville, North Carolina, was typical. In spite of being housed in and named after the most romantically traditional of Appalachian dwellings, the institution was founded by a Vassar College graduate.[17]

By 1908, so many craft-producing settlements were laced throughout the mountain landscape that the Russell Sage Foundation of New York embarked on a systematic survey to catalog the folk practices of the region.[18] A later foundation project, the grand-scale survey that culminated in sociologist Allen Eaton's monumental *Handicrafts of the Southern Highlands*, listed a formidable number of craft-producing social settlements in the upland South. Berea stood cheek and jowl with the Biltmore Industries, Penland, the Hindman Settlement School, the Berry Schools, Pine Mountain Settlement School, Rosemont Industries, Crossnore School, and a myriad of other similar institutions.[19] All shared a commitment to the notion that the revival of traditional handicrafts would provide answers to the problems raised by industrial capitalism.

Institutions such as Berea, Penland, and Pine Mountain hewed to a philosophy that blended Arts and Crafts ideology with the progressive pragmatism of the settlement house movement.[20] Twins born in mid-nineteenth-century England, these reform initiatives were familiar bedfellows by the time wealthy Americans imported them to the United States. Spearheaded in America by such organizations as Hull-House in Chicago and the Society of Arts and Crafts in Boston, local craft societies and village industries peppered the landscape from gritty urban neighborhoods to pastoral southern villages at the turn of the century. Discipline and handicraft, so it was thought, would renew the relationship between art and labor—a relationship torn asunder by the machine age.

Log House - Fireside Industries, Berea College   Berea, Kentucky

Log House Craft Gallery,
Fireside Industries, Berea
College, c. 1925, postcard view.
Private collection

The Fireside Industries

The lessons of the mountain settlements were not lost on William Frost and the trustees of Berea College. As early as 1893 Frost moved to found the Fireside Industries, a series of craft programs related to the college but staffed largely by the nearby population rather than students.[21] One story recounts that a local woman offered to sell a hand-loomed coverlet to the president's wife for three dollars so she could purchase medicine for her family.[22] The president saw an opportunity and requested that his wife organize local women into a weaving program, the products of which he could use as gifts for wealthy northeastern donors to the college. By 1896, the college was holding "Homespun Fairs" during commencement week and offering prizes for the best coverlets, blankets, and linsey-woolseys.[23] These textiles were promoted as "a most interesting survival of ancient Saxon handicraft."[24] The Fireside Industries not only wove Berea into the local community but became an important symbol of the college and, more important, an integral part of the college's development program throughout the early twentieth century.

By the 1920s the Fireside Industries and the college had become largely synonymous in the eyes of outsiders, although few if any students were directly involved in the program (fig. 7.3). Frost's successor, William J. Hutchins, determined that Berea could do more to integrate its various labor programs into the curriculum. As far back as the 1870s the college had offered students the chance to work on campus in the laundry, in janitorial service, or at office tasks. Students worked on the college farm, built roads, and supplied the labor for the college brickyard, literally creating the school from the earth itself. Frost, however, failed to marry the public image of the Fireside Industries to the college curriculum. In the early 1920s, the new president rectified this problem with the help of Wallace Nutting.[25]

Old America Moves South

In the years after World War I, William Hutchins moved to integrate craft into the curriculum at Berea College. In late November 1924 he wrote to Nutting, by then an old friend of the college. "I want to ask your advice," wrote the young educator to the aging antiquarian, while briefly outlining the labor situation at the college. "We have approximately twelve hundred men on the ground all the time; we have a broom factory which employs approximately one hundred and fifty of them; we employ, of course, a great many on the farm, in the garden, in the dining room, in our office, etc. etc." Despite this enviable record of student placement, he continued, "there is a large number of boys for whom we have not adequate employment."[26]

More worrisome to Hutchins was his concern that the college find the right sort of work for these surplus students. "We have an excellent corp[s] of men now in our Woodwork Department," he noted, "and they are trying various experiments to see about quantity production of certain woodwork articles which would have a ready sale." Not only did the product have to sell, but in Hutchins's mind it also had to relate geographically to the region and programmatically to the college. "I am very anxious indeed to have some article which would sell because of its relationship to the mountains or to our revolutionary ancestors," he continued.[27]

Looking for an appropriate student project that could also serve as a college product, Hutchins turned to local forms with some dismay. "As I go among the mountain homes, the distressing feature to me is that they have no articles which have any historic value," he lamented, although he made allowances for "the possible exception of the split bottom chairs." The actual possessions of the much-romanticized southern highlander failed to meet Hutchins's idealized notions of the simple life. "We have not discovered any really good design which our rather crude boys could manufacture." The one product that caught his fancy was the ubiquitous ladder-back chair (fig. 7.4). What the college needed, according to Hutchins, was a product line "which might have symbolic significance and which would find a ready sale, and which would not cost too much for transportation."[28]

Hutchins's letter to Nutting consummated the relationship between the Yankee minister and the bluegrass college. On 11 December 1924 Nutting sent Hutchins a copy of his book *Furniture of the Pilgrim Century*, noting, "I should

like to make references to pages in that book, as regards what might profitably be manufactured by the students."[29] Between 1924 and 1934, Nutting kept up a prodigious correspondence concerning the woodcraft program at the college, provided photographs and plans from his factory, and became a visiting lecturer and critic at the school.

Nutting's advisory role at Berea expanded considerably in the early 1930s. A raft of publications had secured the minister's reputation as an antiquarian in the 1920s, and the Nuttings had by this point become major contributors to the school. Nutting's opinion was one to be reckoned with at Berea. When Nutting expressed concern in 1933 over slipping quality in the woodcraft shop, Hutchins moved with alacrity. "Your present furniture is a serious discredit to the college when it is at all ambitious," wrote Nutting to Hutchins. "I think they [the students] could easily make simple *turned* chairs, like your own (some mine, and some 'copies') but they do not *hew to the line*." Most of all, wrote the testy benefactor, "they should not attempt tables, desks, and *least* of all chests of drawers without radical and [illegible] reform *or* training and hawk like inspection" (fig. 7.5). The crux of the problem, to Nutting's mind, was the head of the Berea woodshop, a gentleman named Ed Davis. "It is . . . painful for me to write this," he began, but "the parts of his mentality simply do not agree together."[30] Nutting's blistering critique was followed by the suggestion that Davis "come on" to New England and train at the Park Street factory in Framingham.

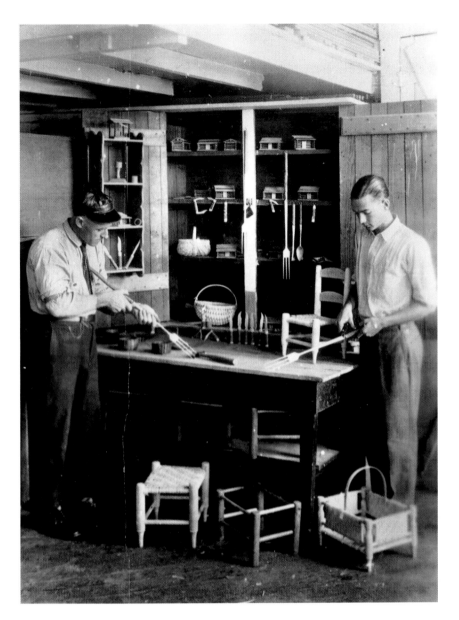

7.5
Woodcraft view, Berea College,
c. 1935. Courtesy of the
Berea College Archives, Berea,
Kentucky

Hutchins seized on Nutting's offer and immediately sent Davis to Framingham, "the center of Old American Life," according to Wallace Nutting, Incorporated, advertisements. Hutchins, ever frank in his exchanges with Nutting, noted, "I don't labor under any illusions. Doubtless Ed and we shall have to be 'gentled' up from time to time."[31] The minister was quite willing to "gentle up" his pet philanthropy, especially when it came to his favorite subject. Not only did Nutting take on Davis for a time, he immediately shipped prototypes from his furniture line to the college for use by the students in the woodcraft department. "Relating to the furniture I sent out . . . I think they should not sell untill [sic] they have copied all the parts and marked the models.

For identification purposes there is no objection to their using the same numbers to designate the pieces of furniture that we use here. From time to time if I go on here I shall be glad to furnish as far as possible sectional models of other things without charge and blueprints."[32]

Shortly after this exchange, Nutting began to receive feedback from Berea students, testifying to his impact on the woodcraft program. On 8 July 1934 student Victor McConkey wrote to Nutting that "making this chair was one of the most interesting pieces of work I have ever done." He assured Nutting that "while at work on the chair I had in mind that I must build every part just as you would do and that I really was trying to compete with your piece. Mr. Nutting I am very thankful to you for your trouble and kindness in getting the plans for me."[33]

By 1934 then, Berea College's woodcraft program featured a Nutting-trained director and worked from plans and prototypes out of the Framingham factory. A "family resemblance" between Berea Woodcraft furniture and Wallace Nutting's products comes as no surprise (figs. 7.5, 7.6). Although Berea furniture was intended to relate to local forms, the furniture was predominantly made from simplified Framingham designs, and by 1939 the college catalog looked much like a region of Old America (fig. 7.7).

Nutting as Customer

Not only did Nutting consult with Hutchins about woodcraft designs at Berea, his Framingham-based furniture company patronized craft departments at the college. "I have use for netted cotton canopies," the minister wrote the president on 10 May 1926. "If you have people in the college, or in the mountains there who would be benefited by making them . . . it might be quite a little source of revenue. As I understand it, you are interested to find work in your shops for men. This is something a woman can do, and help pay her way."[34] Nutting desired canopies for his ever-expanding furniture line. With the introduction of several new bed forms, a light canopy (for which Nutting charged extra) became a desirable accessory.[35]

Hutchins's prompt reply came via Western Union telegram. "Our Fireside Industries shall be happy to make netted cotton canopies."[36] After further discussion, a deal was struck, and Nutting was no longer a mere critic or benefactor but a minor business partner. The Berea canopies allowed Nutting to illustrate and offer a more complete suite of furniture in his catalogs. The integration of the Berea products into Nutting's catalog coincided with the expansion of the minister's line of goods. Hooked rugs designed by Mariet Nutting became an important component of the business by the time of the 1930 *Supreme Edition* catalog and, when illustrated with the Berea bed hangings, provided an attractive illustration of the Old American aesthetic (fig. 7.8).[37]

Mariet as Philanthropist

Both Wallace and Mariet Nutting considered Berea a pet charity. Laced throughout the Nuttings' correspondence with two Berea presidents are expressions of favor and indications that the small school was foremost in the couple's mind for almost half a century. Early in 1913, for instance, Nutting wrote to William Frost, saying, "I am interested in your work and so is my wife

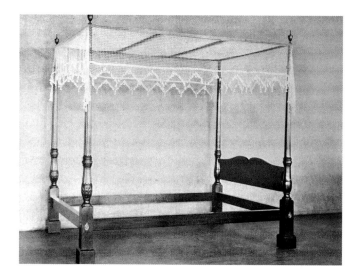

7.8
Wallace Nutting, Incorporated,
#832 Bed and Canopy. From
*Wallace Nutting Supreme Edition
General Catalog* (1930), 15

at whose suggestion I am enclosing check for $25.00 to help it along . . . I wish it were a thousand times as much."[38]

Nutting's words were prophetic. Thirteen years later the minister and his wife, riding a wave of success as collectors of seventeenth-century furniture, made their wish come true and presented Berea with a check for twenty-five thousand dollars.[39] A Berea official explained the circumstances of the gift to another friend of the college in 1926. "The donor of the $25,000.00 recently was Mr. Wallace Nutting of Framingham, the man of furniture fame. He had been interested for many years in Berea, and invited me several years ago to his home and then told me that as soon as his furniture was sold he would have a gift to give to Berea, but at the time did not indicate the amount of it."[40]

The college accepted the gift enthusiastically. "At any time in the history of Berea," wrote William Hutchins, "your gift would have been regarded as one of the most important benefactions coming to our College." The president continued his praise in an attempt to sway the Nuttings from the idea of endowing a museum and toward keeping the money for the general operation of the school. "I think you would wish to have me place this gift of yours in the Endowment," he wrote, "where so long as our present Industrial system lasts, it will be helping Berea to accomplish her task. I have indeed dreamed that we might place this money in the wing of a museum which contain the treasures of the ancient mountains, and the pictures which from time to time we might accumulate. Until, however, I can see my way somewhat more clearly, I think that the Endowment is the best place for your money, don't you?"[41]

The Nuttings could be excused for having museums on the mind in 1926, given the recent installation of their collection at the Wadsworth Atheneum, but Berea had no plans to enlarge their exhibition facilities at the time.

Hutchins, ever the good president, sought to celebrate the Nuttings' gift while maintaining maximum freedom to do as he pleased with the money.[42]

The End of Old America

Although Wallace Nutting died on 19 July 1941, the conclusion to the Nuttings' longstanding association with Berea came with the death of Mariet Nutting on 31 August 1944. After several small gifts to relatives, article 8 of her last will and testament transferred the majority of her worldly goods to Berea.[43] That the college was remembered in the will of a well-off congregational minister's wife was perhaps not unusual in the period. It is significant, however, that Berea inherited the Framingham furniture factory, including tools, equipment, plans, and templates, as well as the rights to the name "Wallace Nutting."

Upon execution of Mariet Nutting's will, Berea inherited the legacy of Wallace Nutting.[44] The college, after removing useful furniture and equipment from the 46 Park Street factory, moved to sell the business. Berea entertained offers from several suitors before selling Wallace Nutting, Incorporated, to the Drexel Furniture Company. Headquartered in High Point, North Carolina, with factories throughout the state in the company towns of Drexel, Marion, and Morgantown, Drexel cast a long shadow in the mass-market furniture business. The name "Wallace Nutting" thus passed from "the clergyman with a love of the beautiful" to the small Appalachian college he helped to mold and finally into the hands of a large corporation. For a time, Drexel used the minister's name on a high-end line of furniture, but in the words of a company executive, "changing living conditions produce different requirements for furniture." He continued, "People are building smaller homes . . . the public no longer wishes to buy such furniture as is listed in the Wallace Nutting catalog, issued in 1937."[45] Drexel folded the line as oak chests from the Pilgrim Century gave way to a taste for blond bedroom sets in the middle-class American home.

Chapter 8

Waiting for the Auto to Pass

Wallace Nutting and the Persistence of Sentiment

W*aiting for the Auto to Pass* wins no prizes as either the best or the most popular photograph by Wallace Nutting (fig. 8.1). Any number of pretenders vie for the crown of beauty, and the minister's self-described best-sellers, such as *The Swimming Pool*, far outstripped this rustic view in sales (fig. 8.2).[1] The image, however, is an archetype of the minister's initial foray into photography and foregrounds a number of issues raised by Nutting's subsequent endeavors. A romantic cliché, it ably serves as a coda and conclusion to any study of Nutting and his world.

Waiting for the Auto to Pass is an early Nutting effort from 1901.[2] It is a legacy of the nervous era that sent him fleeing urban life to seek salvation in the hills of northern New England. Closely allied to the efforts of well-known painters and amateur photographers, *Waiting for the Auto to Pass* is typical of the ruralizing imagery that found great favor as the United States fitfully came of age as an industrial nation between the Civil War and World War I (figs. 8.3, 8.4). As a nostalgic view, the photograph speaks volumes about the need for a seemingly simple past to combat the complexities of the modern era.

The photograph itself depicts a farmer and a pair of oxen yoked to a hay wagon. The man, a stereotypical old Yankee complete with whiskers, suspenders, and straw hat, leans on his hay rake, lips pursed, holding a switch. Posed as a stern patriarch, the human protagonist in *Waiting for the Auto to Pass* represents the tail end of the voyage of life, especially when bracketed by other, far more active, Nutting views.[3] Parked against the fence, the farmer has pulled his wagon off to one side to let the viewer past. The photograph is a thinly veiled allegory. The bounty of Old America is there for the taking, if only modern viewers would stop their cars and follow the farmer.

Waiting for the Auto to Pass had many lives. The image is typical of the work Nutting submitted to such magazines as *Country Life in America* and

Opposite: Detail of fig. 8.9

8.1
Wallace Nutting, *Waiting for the Auto to Pass*, 1901, hand-tinted platinum print.
Courtesy of the Society for the Preservation of New England Antiquities

8.2
Wallace Nutting, *The Swimming Pool*, c. 1910, hand-tinted platinum print. The Turney Collection

8.3
Winslow Homer, *The Nooning*, c. 1872, oil on canvas. Wadsworth Atheneum Museum of Art, The Ella Gallup Sumner and Mary Catlin Sumner Collection Fund

8.4
Wallace Nutting, *Fording the Upper Connecticut*, c. 1904. From *Vermont Beautiful* (1936), 129

Harper's Monthly Magazine at the height of the amateur photography craze. It later appeared as a cover illustration for *Farm and Fireside*, "an Illustrated Farm and Family Journal," on 15 March 1906 (fig. 8.5). That Nutting prized the image is clear, for he registered *Waiting for the Auto to Pass* as negative number 1349 in his office book and sought to protect the image by securing a copyright.[4] Nutting clearly felt he had a winner in 1901.

For reasons known only to himself, Nutting failed to include *Waiting for the Auto to Pass* in his 1912 and 1915 photography catalogs. Perhaps he thought it déclassé. The Barbizon-inspired image might have struck him as cloyingly out of date by 1912, and perhaps he felt there would be little call for number 1349. By 1922, however, Nutting dipped back into his trove of negatives and resurrected the image in his first travelogue, *Vermont Beautiful*.[5] Accompanied by a few spare lines of text, rife with double entendre, *Waiting for the Auto to Pass* is emblematic of the way Nutting wove his earlier photographs into the new publishing venture. The image became a visual manifesto for Old America.

"Perhaps the 'auto' will pass for good," begins his clever homily. Smarting yet from the voluntary gas rationing that spelled the end to his Chain of Colonial Picture Houses just three years earlier, Nutting observed that "the demand for fuel in all forms is beginning to sharpen until we may all take to the woods and chop our own and let the 'auto' go." Refining his wordplay, he sounded a prescient and clarion note of environmental concern. "The sources of coal and oil supply have only to become a little less, and civilization's wheel will take another turn; the rural life will be a necessity, and oxen will come back."[6]

Nutting, while waiting for the auto to pass, missed the boat when it came to reckoning with modernity. Savvy enough to engage the services of a Madison

FARM AND FIRESIDE.

AN ILLUSTRATED FARM AND FAMILY JOURNAL

EASTERN EDITION

Vol. XXIX. No. 12   SPRINGFIELD, OHIO, MARCH 15, 1906   TERMS { 25 CENTS A YEAR / 24 NUMBERS

Copyright, 1901, by Wallace Nutting

Guaranteed Circulation 400,000 Copies Each Issue

8.5
Wallace Nutting, "Waiting for
the Auto to Pass," *Farm and
Fireside*, 15 March 1906.
Courtesy of the National
Agricultural Library

Avenue advertising agency, he lacked the wisdom to engineer change into his product lines. His photographs and furniture, so popular in the 1920s, were embarrassments by the 1950s. Geriatric in appearance when compared to the new streamlined domestic interior, Wallace Nutting's Old America was consigned to the attic as modern forms found an enthusiastic middle-class audience in the postwar period.

"The old and the new generations have clashed very sharply in our age," observed Nutting in 1922.[7] The next generation brought a rout. Quaint villages turned into suburbs, genteel coastal cities into metropolitan centers. The upper Connecticut River, forever forded by hay wagons in Nutting's world, was impounded to generate electricity (figs. 8.4, 8.6). The auto passed. In short order it would speed by the "clergyman with a love of beauty." Americans (as of this writing) have not been forced to "take to the woods," nor have they had to trade in their cars for oxen. Indeed, given the centrality of the automobile to twentieth-century American culture, Nutting's paean to preindustrial modes of life and labor seems almost pathologically naive. And yet *Waiting for the Auto to Pass*, along with the rest of Nutting's tangible mnemonics of a glorious American past, never fully went away.

Although Nutting's business barely outlasted his own passing, his message has proven to be curiously persistent. The sentimental narrative of Old America, played out in countless platinum prints, Windsor chairs, and illustrated books, found a place in the cultural landscape as a dissenting opinion throughout the late twentieth century. "Modernism," writes Marshall Berman, is fundamentally "a struggle to make ourselves at home in a constantly changing world." As a continuum, "no mode of modernism can ever be definitive."[8] The split-level ranch may have replaced the cape as the symbol of the "American dream" in the 1960s, but by the 1980s many modern houses sported a fading Wallace Nutting platinotype in the front hallway as a new generation discovered the minister and his message.

Old America developed new relevance and gathered new followers with the founding of the Wallace Nutting Collectors Club. Organized in the fall of 1973 by Justine Monro and a small group of collectors to research the myriad photographs lingering in attics, closets, and antique shops, the club enjoyed a

8.7
Maxfield Parrish, *Dusk*, 1942,
oil on masonite. New Britain
Museum of American Art,
New Britain, Connecticut,
Charles F. Smith Fund.
Maxfield Parrish ® / Licensed
by AsaP and VAGA, New York,
NY

8.8
Wallace Nutting, *At Wallace
Nutting's Place*, c. 1914,
hand-tinted platinum print.
Courtesy of the Society for the
Preservation of New England
Antiquities

8.9
Wallace Nutting, *Home Charms*, c. 1910,
hand-tinted platinum print, tipped into
Old New England Pictures (1913). Auerbach
Library, Wadsworth Atheneum Museum
of Art

steadily growing membership throughout the 1980s. Nutting collectors began to congregate once a year, and a newsletter was inaugurated to seek out the minister's apostles. "I met a young girl when I went to buy matting board for our N.H. Nuttings," wrote Monro enthusiastically, "her grandparents knew a girl who posed for some of Dr. Nutting's interiors."[9]

The challenges of modern life crept their way into Monro's early newsletters and provide a hint as to the attraction of Nutting's sentimental worldview. "George," Monro wrote of her husband in 1973, "just said that our gas station is out of gas and won't have any for four days."[10] Beset by the OPEC energy crises and with yet another "old and new generation" clashing over the sexual revolution, the war in Vietnam, and questions about the body politic, a cadre of Americans found comfort in the imagery of a man who proposed waiting for the auto to pass.

The persistence of this sentimental vision throughout the twentieth century stands as one of modernism's dark secrets. Nutting—a failed tycoon— proved to be a successful prophet. Countless automobiles passed Nutting's old Yankee farmer with his hay wagon, but Americans' need for a historic collective memory has remained constant. A leading economic indicator, quoted quarterly in the financial pages, is the number of construction starts in the single-family housing market. One family in one (mortgaged) house on a small plot of land remains the goal for countless Americans. Wallace Nutting, in his own small way, enabled this dream by providing the necessary myths and symbols to embed the ideology of Old America into contemporary American culture. There is no question that countless others lent a hand in the process. A subsequent generation of artists, writers, bankers, and architects ensured the welfare of this vision from Nutting's day to the present (fig. 8.7). From Maxfield Parrish's dreamy views of northern New England to the "good things" purveyed today by Martha Stewart Omnimedia on television, in print, on-line, and at K-Mart to Thomas Kinkade's homogenizing images of small-town life—available at malls from coast to coast—sentimental culture remains the dominant middle-class idiom.

Old America gave Wallace Nutting a pulpit for the modern century. Taking full advantage of the developing culture of consumption, the minister provided his followers with motivation and opportunity to acquire talismans of a golden-age narrative of the American past. From Pilgrim furniture for the living room to photographic paths through the landscape of his ancestors, Nutting offered an interconnected series of goods and experiences that added up to a sum far greater than its component parts (figs. 8.8, 8.9). By inventing a sentimental past, imbuing it with moral significance, and selling it at every turn, Wallace Nutting made American history available, attractive, and useful for the modern era.

Notes

Chapter 1   *Consumed by the Past*

1. "Invented traditions," according to Eric Hobsbawm, are "a set of practices, normally governed by overtly or tacitly accepted rules and of a ritual or symbolic nature, which seek to inculcate certain values and norms of behavior." For more on this paradigm, see Eric Hobsbawm, "Inventing Traditions," in Hobsbawm and Ranger, eds., *Invention of Tradition*, 1, 9.

2. A telling exchange occurred in 1924 between Nutting and William Sumner Appleton of the Society for the Preservation of New England Antiquities. Appleton wished to use a Nutting photographic view and after several communications was reduced to asking his old friend, "Shall we print beneath the pictures 'courtesy of Wallace Nutting' or shall we use the 'Inc.' or 'Co.' or anything else after your name?" William Sumner Appleton to Wallace Nutting, 22 March 1924, William Sumner Appleton Correspondence, Library and Archives, Society for the Preservation of New England Antiquities, Boston. Hereafter cited as "Appleton Correspondence, SPNEA."

3. For a concise study of the rise of personality based corporations, see Jackson Lears, "Ad Man and Grand Inquisitor." For a perceptive investigation of Russel Wright, see Donald Albrecht, Robert Schonfeld, and Lindsey Stamm Shapiro, *Russel Wright: Creating American Lifestyle* (New York: Harry N. Abrams, 2001). For a critique of Martha Stewart, see Robin Pogrebin "Master of Her Own Domain," *New York Times* (8 February 1998): sec. 3, pp. 1, 14.

4. For a discussion of the role of the minister-historian in early America, see Kraus and Joyce, *Writing of American History*, esp. "The Era of Colonialism," 32–48.

5. Much ink has been spilled over the question of middle-class culture. I have in mind the white-collar professional and managerial middle-class of lawyers, doctors, and corporate executives. For an excellent group of essays on the subject, see Burton J. Bledstein and Robert D. Johnson, eds., *The Middling Sorts: Explorations in the History of the American Middle Class* (New York: Routledge, 2001).

6. Nutting served as a minister at Fryburg, Maine, in 1887; Passaic, New Jersey, in 1887–1888; Newark, New Jersey, 1888–1889; St. Paul, Minnesota, 1889–1891; Seattle, Washington, 1891–1894; and Providence, Rhode Island, 1894–1904. In his "retirement" he preached to dozens of congregations throughout the country. Nutting, *Wallace Nutting's Biography*, 283–287.

7. For more on the process by which citizens abdicated individual responsibility to ever-larger political and commercial structures, see Alan Trachtenberg, *The Incorporation of America: Culture and Society in the Gilded Age* (New York: Hill and Wang, 1982).

8. T. J. Jackson Lears spends much time defining the "weightlessness" of modern life in *No Place of Grace*, 32–47. For a magisterial critique of modernity, see Berman, *All That Is Solid Melts into Air*.

9. Richard Fox has written of the development of liberal Protestantism in the late nineteenth century as a negotiation with modernity and an accommodation of the new consumer culture. See Fox, "Culture of Liberal Protestant Progressivism."

10. Henry Mann, *Features of Society in Old and New England* (Providence, R.I.: Sidney S. Rider, 1885), 88.

11. The therapeutic nature of consumerism is explored in T. J. Jackson Lears, "From Salvation to Self-Realization: Advertising and the Therapeutic Roots of Consumer Culture, 1880–1930," in Fox and Lears, eds., *Culture of Consumption*, 3–38.

12. For more on this transformation, see the many excellent essays in Bronner, ed., *Consuming Visions*. For an excellent analysis of the importance of the department store in turn-of-the-century America, see Leach, *Land of Desire*.

13. For a perceptive study of the Victorian interior, see Katherine C. Grier, *Culture and Comfort: People, Parlors, and Upholstery, 1850–1930* (Rochester, N.Y.: Strong Museum, distributed by the University of Massachusetts Press, 1988). For more on American interest in Japanese decoration, see William N. Hosley, Jr., *The Japan Idea: Art and Life in Victorian America* (Hartford, Conn.: Wadsworth

Atheneum, 1990). For more on Anglos "playing Indian," see Elizabeth W. Hutchinson, "Progressive Primitivism: Race, Gender, and Turn-of-the-Century American Art" (Ph.D. diss., Stanford University, 1999).

14. Nutting's breakdown is itself a fascinating study in popular understanding of nervous disorders. At the time the minister's nerves would have been understood in the context of then current thinking on neurasthenia. When Nutting wrote his autobiography in 1936, he couched the unhappy episode in Freudian terms.

15. Douglass Shand-Tucci writes of this group, "Boston's ruling class as it approached the late nineteenth century did not doubt that . . . it was leading Puritan Governor John Winthrop's visionary city on a hill, America's first and brightest beacon, always testing, measuring, valuing, illuminating. There was no more judgmental place anywhere." Shand-Tucci, *The Art of Scandal: The Life and Times of Isabella Stewart Gardner* (New York: Harper-Collins, 1997), 10.

16. Berea College in Berea, Kentucky, was the principle beneficiary of Nutting's estate and received numerous papers relating to his businesses, including a ledger from which pages were carefully excised. John Barrow, presumably a Berea College librarian, typed out a careful note on 22 October 1941 and included it with a ledger noting that "Mr. Nutting himself had destroyed many of the ms pages. These are the only ones that had writing on them." RG 5-23, Archives of Berea College, Hutchins Library, Berea College, hereafter cited as "Berea College Archives."

17. Scholarship on Nutting is limited to a pair of doctoral dissertations and a handful of articles. For more on the minister and his world, see Thomas Andrew Denenberg, "Consumed by the Past: Wallace Nutting and the Invention of Old America" (Ph.D. diss., Boston University, 2002), and Marianne Berger Woods, "Visual Sermons: Wallace Nutting Photography" (Ph.D. diss., Union Institute, 2000). John Crosby Freeman, *Wallace Nutting Checklist of Early American Reproductions* (Watkins, N.Y.: American Life Foundation and Study Institute, 1969); Dulaney, "Nutting: Collector and Entrepreneur"; Barendson, "Nutting, American Tastemaker"; and Woods, "Viewing Colonial America." Nutting references also appear in broad cultural histories including Kammen, *Mystic Chords of Memory*, and Marling, *George Washington Slept Here*.

18. A useful theoretical text on self-invention and the complexities of human behavior in society is Goffman, *Presentation of Self*.

19. Nutting, *Wallace Nutting's Biography*, 9.

20. Stott, *Holland Mania*, 78, 79–89. Bok's stand no

doubt drew approval from the sitting president of the United States, himself a popular historian of Dutch extraction and fervent internationalist. For a discussion of Theodore Roosevelt as historian, see Kraus and Joyce, *Writing of American History*, 275–277.

21. Plymouth became known as the "Old Colony" in the mid-eighteenth century. In 1769 a civic organization called "The Old Colony Club" institutionalized the name. For more on the Old Colony Club, see John Seelye, *Memory's Nation: The Place of Plymouth Rock* (Chapel Hill: University of North Carolina Press, 1998), 25–27.

22. The term *Pilgrim* was first used in 1793 by the Congregational minister Chandler Robbins, according to Ann Uhry Abrams. By the 1830s the founders of Plymouth Colony were regarded as "patriarchs" of the new nation. Ann Uhry Abrams, *The Pilgrims and Pocohontas: Rival Myths of American Origin* (Boulder, Colo.: Westview, 1999), 5.

23. Nutting, *Wallace Nutting's Biography*, 9.

24. William H. Truettner and Roger B. Stein have demonstrated that arbiters of culture in Nutting's generation frequently shared this perspective. Stein goes into detail on this point in his essay "Gilded Age Pilgrims," in Truettner and Stein, eds., *Picturing Old New England*.

25. This patrimony was a typical circumstance for artists of the so-called Boston School among others. See the various biographies for Frank Benson, Childe Hassam, and Edmund Tarbell by Judith Maxwell, Thomas Denenberg, and Martha Norton in Truettner and Stein, eds., *Picturing Old New England*, 201, 212, 226.

26. Nutting, *Wallace Nutting's Biography*, 4.

27. That Nutting grew to maturity in a matriarchy is telling, for "women became the keepers of the nation's conscience," according to Mary Beth Norton, "the only citizens specifically charged with maintaining the traditional republican commitment to the good of the entire community." For more on the concept of "republican Motherhood," see Mary Beth Norton, "The Evolution of White Women's Experience in Early America," *American Historical Review* 89 (1984): esp. 615, and Lewis, "Motherhood and the Construction of the Male Citizen."

28. Jaffee, *People of the Wachusett*, esp. "Epilogue: The Myth of Town Settlement," 239–249, quotation on 247.

29. As late as 1936, Nutting referred to Rockbottom as his place of birth. In a manuscript for his Harvard College Fiftieth Anniversary Class Report, a classmate wrote, "Rockbottom is a village and Railroad station in an angle from the town of Stow, Mass. which projects into the town of Hudson. If he was born within a mile of this, his birth was in Stow. He was not, as has been stated, born in

Marlborough." Personal Folder HUD 287.505, Harvard University Archives.

30. Lawrence Buell, *New England Literary Culture: From Revolution to Renaissance* (Cambridge: Cambridge University Press, 1986), esp. chap. 13, "The Village as Icon."

31. For a study of the importance of success literature, see Hilkey, *Character Is Capital.* For more on the historical patterns and iconography of town settlement, see Joseph Wood, *The New England Village* (Baltimore: Johns Hopkins University Press, 1997), and William H. Truettner and Thomas Andrew Denenberg, "The Discreet Charm of the Colonial," in Truettner and Stein, eds., *Picturing Old New England*, 79–110.

32. Nutting, *Wallace Nutting's Biography*, 8, 283.

33. Nutting made explicit his familiarity with Bunyan and his aspirations for his own published efforts in *Vermont Beautiful* when he wrote, "Probably Bunyan's idea in picturing by allegory life as a pilgrimage had much to do with the popularity of his *Pilgrim's Progress.*" Nutting, *Vermont Beautiful*, 197.

34. Nutting, *Wallace Nutting's Biography*, 5, 6, 12.

35. Ibid., 283. Bigelow, Kennard and Company stood at 511 Washington Street, according to *The Boston Almanac and Business Directory, 1880*, vol. 45 (Boston: Sampson, Davenport, 1880), 319.

36. Nutting, *Wallace Nutting's Biography*, 283.

37. For more on the importance of the Philadelphia centennial, see Rodris Roth, "The New England or 'Olde Tyme' Kitchen Exhibit at Nineteenth Century Fairs," in Axelrod, ed., *Colonial Revival in America*, 159–184.

38. Nutting, *Wallace Nutting's Biography*, 283.

39. *Harvard College Class of 1887 Fiftieth Anniversary Report* (Cambridge, Mass.: Printed for the Class, 1937), 314. Harvard University Archives.

40. Wallace Nutting, Class of 1884, Academic Record, Phillips Exeter Academy Archives, Exeter, New Hampshire. All subsequent references to Nutting's high school record are from this document.

41. Williams, *Story of Phillips Exeter*, 63–67, 200.

42. Nutting's headaches had clearly subsided by the time he matriculated at Exeter. In his first term, he stood with four others at the top of his class of forty-eight students.

43. Nutting, *Wallace Nutting's Biography*, 12; Williams, *Story of Phillips Exeter*, 65, 200.

44. Williams, *Story of Phillips Exeter*, 64. Nutting later recalled the innate intelligence of this future secretary of the Interior. Nutting, *Wallace Nutting's Biography*, 13.

45. Edouard Desrochers, Phillips Exeter Academy archivist, to author, 30 April 1999.

46. Nutting, *Wallace Nutting's Biography*, 26.

47. Legend has it that the zeal of the Park Street Church led to its nickname as the "Brimstone Corner" of Boston Common. Church members preferred a story that assigned the name to a Revolutionary War episode involving the storage of gunpowder on the site. For more on Brimstone Corner, see Samuel Adams Drake, *Old Landmarks of Boston* (Boston, 1873), 300–301, and Michael Holleran, *Boston's "Changeful Times": Origins of Preservation and Planning in America* (Baltimore: Johns Hopkins University Press, 1998), 150–161.

48. Nutting is classified as belonging to the class of 1884 but left Exeter after three years. This was not unusual, as the school did not confer a formal degree until 1887. Nutting's Harvard record also lists him attending college for three years, from 1883 to 1886. Class of 1887 Class Files, HUD 287.505, Harvard University Archives.

49. *Harvard College Class of 1887 Fiftieth Anniversary Report*, 314.

50. For a critical assessment of this period, see Donald Fleming, "Harvard's Golden Age?" in Bailyn et al., eds., *Glimpses of the Harvard Past*, 77–97.

51. Eliot is quoted in Donald Fleming, "Eliot's New Broom," in Bailyn et al., *Glimpses of the Harvard Past*, 69.

52. Ibid., 74.

53. More cultural critic than academic, Norton painted with a broad brush about the moral nature of art and literature in his lectures. For more on Norton, see James Turner, *The Education of Charles Eliot Norton* (Baltimore: Johns Hopkins University Press, 1999).

54. For more on Norton's criticism, see Edward S. Cooke, Jr., "Talking or Working: The Conundrum of Moral Aesthetics in Boston's Arts and Crafts Movement," in Boyd, ed., *Inspiring Reform*, 20.

55. Fleming, "Eliot's New Broom," 72.

56. Nutting, *Wallace Nutting's Biography*, 13.

57. Ibid. Nutting referred to Mrs. Washburne as "the Governor's widow" but apparently conflated Elihu and his older brother Israel, who served as governor of Maine.

58. Kim Townsand describes Harvard as an academic community preoccupied with notions of masculinity during Nutting's tenure. Having declared an interest in the ministry, a feminized profession, it is easy to imagine Nutting's undergraduate discomfort. For more on this point, see Townsand, *Manhood at Harvard.*

59. Manuscript Biography for Fiftieth Class Report, Harvard University Archives, n.p. [p. 1].

60. Nutting, *Wallace Nutting's Biography*, 14. Nutting recalled meeting Abbott when looking after overnight guests at Pikes Peak. Abbott succeeded Henry Ward Beecher as the minister of the Plymouth Congregational Church

in Brooklyn, New York, in 1890 and served as the editor of the *Illustrated Christian Weekly*, the *Christian Union*, and the *Outlook*.

61. Manuscript Biography for Fiftieth Class Report, Harvard University Archives, n.p. [p. 1]. Nutting's wife was born Marrieta Griswold, but most records and accounts shorten her given name to Mariet.

62. Sidney E. Ahlstrom, *A Religious History of the American People* (New Haven and London: Yale University Press, 1972), 420.

63. Nutting, *Wallace Nutting's Biography*, 283.

64. Ahlstrom, *Religious History of American People*, 467.

65. Ibid., 458.

66. Record of Marriage, 5 June 1888, Vital Records, Town of Colrain, Massachusetts.

67. Nutting, *Wallace Nutting's Biography*, 20.

68. Mariet Griswold married her brother-in-law Albert Caswell in the fall of 1876 some three months after her sister's death. Albert Caswell, in turn, died on 6 February 1879, leaving her a widow. I thank Linda Palmer of Kent, Connecticut, for sharing her research on Mariet Nutting. See also Virginia Rose Wilde, "Octogenarian Widow Carries on the Business," *Springfield (Mass.) Sunday Union and Republican*, 19 October 1941, 5.

69. Nutting, *Wallace Nutting's Biography*, 22, 71, 76.

70. For examples, see Wallace Nutting, *Final Edition Furniture Catalog* (Framingham, Mass.: Wallace Nutting, 1937), 23, 26, 37, 99.

71. "Last Will and Testament of Mariet G. Nutting," RG 5-23, Berea College Archives.

72. The Nuttings were frequent visitors to resorts such as the Mohonk Mountain House, near New Paltz in upstate New York. There are no less than fourteen images of the Mohonk grounds in Nutting's studio log and he wrote a manuscript intended for publication entitled "Mohonk and the Smileys" in 1928. I thank Linda Palmer for giving me a copy of this manuscript. As for the minister's sartorial elegance, at least four portraits of Nutting survive in public collections and private hands. All depict him in pressed suit with starched collar. In one view Nutting holds a straw boater.

73. Nutting was not much of a driver. He owned an automobile as early as 1912–1913 but, as was typical of the time, required the services of a chauffeur to maintain and operate the vehicle. Keeping a chauffeur, however, proved difficult. There is an amusing exchange between Nutting and William Sumner Appleton of the Society for the Preservation of New England Antiquities (SPNEA) in the latter's papers. The two antiquarians vied for the services of the same driver, a Mr. Taylor, who seemed to oscillate between the two, causing sharp comments and bruised feelings. Wallace Nutting to William Sumner Appleton, 18 June 1917; Nutting to Appleton, postcard, 5 July 1917; Appleton to Nutting, 3 June 1918; all Appleton Correspondence, SPNEA.

74. *Wallace Nutting's Biography* reads like a catalog of the minister's many illnesses. See, for example, pp. 12, 19, 28, 32, 33, 284.

75. A vertically integrated corporation is one that expands into related businesses from point of supply to delivery. An automobile manufacturer that owns a steel mill, for example, is described as vertically integrated or organized.

76. Nutting first incorporated his business as the "Nuttinghame Company" in Maine on 26 October 1907. The corporation was excused on 24 December 1912. State of Maine, Department of the Secretary of State, Bureau of Corporations, Elections and Commissions, *Charter Volume 62*, 263.

77. Nutting's largest photography catalog, the so-called *Expansible* edition of 1915, contained inserts for his Chain of Colonial Picture Houses. The Cutler-Bartlet House in Newburyport, Massachusetts, for example, exhibited Nutting's platinotypes. Nutting's photographs included his wife's hooked rugs as well as forms of furniture reproduced by his Saugus, Ashland, and Framingham factories.

78. For a pointed critique of this process, see Andres Duany, Elizabeth Platner-Zyberk, and Jeff Speck, *Suburban Nation: The Rise of Sprawl and the Decline of the American Dream* (New York: North Point, 2000).

Chapter 2   *Spinsters, Widows, and a Minister*

1. Distracted perhaps by the development of fine art photography, the canonical works on the history of photography largely ignore the domestic art photograph. As a result, much ink has been spilled over Alfred Stieglitz and the Photo Secession, but little attention has been paid to what Americans displayed on their walls in the early twentieth century. Happy exceptions to this situation include Foy and Marling, eds., *Arts and the American Home*, and Marling, *George Washington Slept Here*.

2. Nutting, *Wallace Nutting's Biography*, 70. Nutting's claims, as mentioned in Chapter 1, are best taken with (un)healthy amounts of salt.

3. *Wallace Nutting Final Edition Catalog* (Framingham, Mass.: Wallace Nutting, 1937), 5.

4. Nutting, *Wallace Nutting's Biography*, 287.

5. The lack of business records has caused consternation for those few scholars who have reckoned with Nutting and is the subject of much speculation and folklore. Lee

Ford Swanson, curator of the Wayside Inn in Sudbury, Massachusetts, described seeing boxes of Nutting's records destroyed in the late 1960s or early 1970s. The records had been apparently stored in a farm building (personal communication, Swanson to author, 20 January 1999). Fragmentary records at the Framingham Public Library and Berea College suggest that Mariet Nutting destroyed a body of records after Wallace Nutting's death in 1941. Confirmation of this can be seen in the annotations to a dismembered ledger book in the Berea College Archives.

6. There are approximately seventeen hundred Wallace Nutting entries in the card files of the Copyright Office at the Library of Congress dated between 1901 and 1937. By way of comparison Alfred Stieglitz protected eight images in 1898, and Clarence White copyrighted a solitary view in 1920. Graphic Arts claimant files, Copyright Division, Library of Congress.

7. Nutting, *Wallace Nutting's Biography*, 74–75.

8. "Office Book," Wallace Nutting, Incorporated. Private Collection.

9. Nutting himself wrote, with typical hyperbole, "It is estimated, though count has been lost, that about a million of one subject has been called for." See *Wallace Nutting's Biography*, 75. Collectors and historians remain divided over the number of prints issued. Karal Ann Marling hedges her language but seems willing to accept Nutting's claim of ten million in *George Washington Slept Here*, 172. One of Nutting's least successful photographs, *The Guardian Mother*, is especially prized today for its rarity. Ironically, it is one of Nutting's most derivative images, resembling Abbott Handerson Thayer's *Caritas* of 1894–1895, now in the collection of the Museum of Fine Arts, Boston. Nutting could have seen such work in Sadakichi Hartmann's *History of American Art*, vol. 1 (Boston: L. C. Page, 1901), 273.

10. Nutting, *Photographic Art Secrets*, 113.

11. For an excellent study of Louis Prang and Company, see Michael Clapper, "Art, Industry, and Education in Prang's Chromolithograph Company," *Proceedings of the American Antiquarian Society* 105, no. 1 (1995): 145–161. Nutting went to great pains to establish the bonafides of his platinotypes. One surviving advertising placard reads "Wallace Nutting Pictures / Beware of Imitations / The Original Pictures are Known as Follows: 1. All are signed 2. Except where very small they are signed and titled 3. All signed and all handcolored 4. Wallace Nutting made all originals personally. He owns every negative existing of his pictures 5. No one has acquired any rights to copy, produce or reproduce any of my pictures / Wallace Nutting." Local History Collection, Framingham Public Library, Framingham, Mass.

12. Nutting, *Old New England Pictures*, copyright page.

13. David Davidson of Providence, Rhode Island, opened his own business in direct competition with Nutting. I thank Jeremy Adamson for sharing the illustrated Davidson advertisement with me. Along with Davidson, Fred Sawyer of New Hampshire, and Louis Prang and Company (better known as pioneers of chromolithography) sold a similar line of goods. Platinotypes should be distinguished from other processes, including less expensive halftones and proprietary processes like the Detroit Photographic Company's Photochrom process. For a history of early color photography, see Hughes, *Birth of a Century*. For a history of hand-tinted photography, see Henisch and Henisch, *Painted Photograph.*

14. Loren Baritz has cautioned, "Searching for the American middle class is a little like looking for air." See Baritz, *Good Life*, xi. For more on class formation in turn-of-the-century America, see Blumin, *Emergence of the Middle Class*, and Wiebe, *Search for Order*, esp. chap. 5, "A New Middle Class."

15. Suppliers of photographic equipment and supplies aided in the organization of Camera Clubs and underwrote the publication of a myriad of advice manuals for the amateur photographer. *The Modern Way in Picture Making: Published as an Aid to the Amateur Photographer* (Rochester, N.Y.: Eastman Kodak, 1905) is but one title in a seemingly limitless genre. Nutting's own contribution to this rubric came later on with the publication of *Photographic Art Secrets*. Although photographic how-to guides were ubiquitous in the marketplace by this point, Nutting's work was printed in a second edition in 1931.

16. For two excellent discussions of amateur photography, see Havinga, "Pictorialism and Naturalism," and Greenough, "Of Charming Glens." The first camera club in the United States, the Boston Society of Amateur Photographers (founded in 1881), provided a model for institutions throughout the region and nation. Havinga points out that Providence, Hartford, Manchester, Worcester, Cambridge, Lowell, Brockton, and Melrose all supported organized amateur activities by the end of the century.

17. As early as 1913, the *Amateur Photographer's Weekly* hosted weekly and biweekly competitions "open to any amateur photographer" and offering prizes ranging from one to three dollars. The periodical also advertised "The Wanamaker Annual Exhibition of Photography," promising to have works submitted "passed upon by competent critics." For more on these competitions see, *Amateur Photographer's Weekly* 1, no. 13 (4 October 1912): 254, and 2, no. 51 (27 June 1913): 257. For more on early photography exhibitions, see Havinga, "Pictorialism and Naturalism,"

136, in which the author notes that the Massachusetts Institute of Technology hosted the first exhibition of the Boston society in 1883, showing more than seven hundred prints. Amateur societies in New York and San Francisco staged inaugural exhibitions in 1885, Philadelphia followed suit in 1886 with more than eighteen hundred entries, and by the 1890s amateur exhibitions had become a fixture on the cultural stage throughout the country.

18. "Shall the Amateur Be Allowed to Sell His Pictures?" *Amateur Photographer's Weekly* 3, no. 59 (22 August 1913): 149. This was the age of professional associations, and it comes as no surprise to find photographers protecting their turf with the same intensity that medical doctors, architects, and engineers had exhibited before them.

19. George M. Beard used the term *Brain-Worker* to delineate the class of individuals most likely to suffer from neurasthenia. See Beard, *American Nervousness*. Ministers were often characterized as sickly in the late nineteenth century; see Ann Douglas, *The Feminization of American Culture* (New York: Avon, 1977), 104–123. Throughout "Adventures in Preaching," a chapter in *Wallace Nutting's Biography*, the author declaims on the constitutional prerequisites of the modern minister. Most of these attributes are defined against Beard's neurasthenic symptoms. In regard to dyspepsia, Nutting notes, "The pastor of a great church must have cast iron bowels and the heart of a pugilist." *Wallace Nutting's Biography*, 34.

20. George M. Beard, "Neurasthenia, or Nervous Exhaustion," *Boston Medical and Surgical Journal* 3 (1869).

21. Beard is quoted extensively in Gosling, *Before Freud*, e.g., 14.

22. Popular medical literature adopted Beard's diagnoses and disseminated information on the malady. For example, see "American Worry," in Marion Harland, *Eve's Daughters; or, Common Sense for Maid, Wife and Mother* (New York: John R. Anderson and Henry S. Allen, 1882), 226–246.

23. Lears, *No Place of Grace*, 50.

24. Charlotte Perkins Gilman, *The Charlotte Perkins Gilman Reader: The Yellow Wallpaper and Other Stories* (New York: Pantheon, 1980).

25. Nutting, *Wallace Nutting's Biography*, 70.

26. For a history of turn-of-the century athletic thought and practice, see Harvey Green, *Fit for America*.

27. This an interesting nexus, since neurasthenics, like consumptives earlier in the nineteenth century, seem more often than not to have been feminized. One historian has argued, "Neurasthenia itself was created out of strands of discourse on evolution and civilization [and] on gender." For more on this point, see Lutz, *American Nervousness*, 20.

28. "My Morning Spin," *Ladies' Home Journal* 9 (November 1892): 20. The question of bicycling as a gendered activity is discussed at length in Garvey, *Adman in the Parlor*; see esp. chap. 4, "Reframing the Bicycle: Magazines and Scorching Women."

29. Nutting, *Wallace Nutting's Biography*, 70.

30. The popularity of the combination is graphically illustrated in the 1897 *Providence City Directory*. The cover advertisement is a promotion for "Starkweather & Williams Co. / State Agents for the New Haven Bicycle / Chemicals, Dye-Stuffs, Paints, Oils / Materials for Artists and Photographers." *The Providence Directory and Rhode Island Business Directory* (Providence, R.I.: Sampson, Murdock, 1897). So wedded did the two pastimes become that in the late 1890s, the leading manufacturer of photography equipment began to market the "Bicycle-Kodak," a box camera designed to mount on the handlebars.

31. "Amateur Photography," *The Wheel: A Journal of Cycling and Recreation* 13, no. 9 (25 November 1887), 124.

32. The terms *modern* and *artistic* are highly loaded. By "modern" photography, I mean the movement for heightened aesthetic criterion within Pictorialism and the subsequent shift toward a "straight" medium. "Artistic" is a description claimed by portraitists since the mid-nineteenth century. Vernacular small-town commercial photographers, such as the Howes Brothers of Ashfield, Massachusetts, claimed to be "artistic" in the 1880s, but I refer here to the moderns, and protomoderns, of the Stieglitz circle. For a study of the Howes Brothers, see Alan B. Newman, ed., *New England Reflections: 1882–1907* (New York: Pantheon, 1981).

33. Alfred Stieglitz, "The Hand Camera: Its Present Importance," *American Annual of Photography* (1897), quoted in Goldberg, ed., *Photography in Print*, 214. The intertwined nature of the two hobbies can also be seen in Stieglitz's own Camera Club of New York, which "had given serious thought to becoming a bicycle club before Stieglitz became vice-president." See Margolis, *Alfred Stieglitz Camera Work*, ix.

34. The bibliography on Stieglitz is large and growing larger. Three helpful works are Whelan, *Stieglitz: A Biography*; Peterson, *Stieglitz's Camera Notes*; and Homer, *Stieglitz and American Avant-Garde*.

35. Wallace Nutting, "Photography as a Sport," *Frank Leslie's Popular Monthly* 50 (July 1900): 285–294.

36. Ibid., 285, 286, 294.

37. W. S. Harwood, "Amateur Photography of To-day," *Cosmopolitan: An Illustrated Monthly Magazine* 20, no. 3 (January 1896): 253. Cited in Havinga, "Pictorialism and Naturalism."

38. Emmons's career was made possible by chapter 248 of the Massachusetts General Statutes of 1870. This ruling mandated art education in the public schools of the commonwealth. For more on the history of art education in New England, see Korzenik, *Drawn to Art*, 153.

39. Peladeau, *Chansonetta*, 10.

40. For more on the Allen Sisters, see Suzanne Flynt, *The Allen Sisters: Pictorial Photographers, 1885–1920* (Deerfield, Mass.: Pocumtuck Valley Memorial Association, distributed by the University Press of New England, 2002).

41. Brown, *Inventing New England*, 9.

42. The Allen sisters shared a photo spread with Wallace Nutting and one Jane Dudley in the *Ladies' Home Journal* 23 (July 1906): 28–29.

43. "The Foremost Women Photographers of America," *Ladies' Home Journal* 18 (July 1901): 13. Flynt, McGowan, and Miller, *Gathered and Preserved*, 4–5, 10–11, 39, 50, 53. *Inspiring Reform*. Rosenblum, *History of Women Photographers*, 60–61, 291–92, 333.

44. Nutting, *Photographic Art Secrets*, 9.

45. *Women's Home Companion* 29, no. 11 (November 1902): 28–29.

46. *Country Life in America* 3, no. 2 (December 1902): centerfold and frontispiece.

47. Nutting, *Wallace Nutting's Biography*, 71.

48. Ibid., 57.

49. Nutting purchased the Southbury property from the estate of Truman B. Wheeler on 17 August 1906. Town of Southbury Deeds, Entry 473.

50. For a history of the movement, see William L. Bowers, *The Country Life Movement in America, 1900–1920* (Port Washington, N.Y.: Kennikat, National University Publications, 1974).

51. Henry Mann, *Features of Society in Old and New England* (Providence, R.I.: Sidney S. Rider, 1885), 54.

52. Kate Sanborn, *Adopting an Abandoned Farm* (New York: Appleton, 1892), 6.

53. Nutting, *Wallace Nutting's Biography*, 60.

54. For more on these utopian experiments, see Falino, "Monastic Ideal in Rural Massachusetts," and William S. Ayres, "A Poor Sort of Heaven; A Good Sort of Earth: The Rose Valley Arts and Crafts Experiment, 1901–1910" (M.A. thesis, Winterthur Program in Early American Culture, University of Delaware, 1982).

55. Ruth Flood Brown was interviewed in 1988 for *Wallace Nutting in Southbury, 1906–1912*, a video produced and narrated by Dorothy Manville and underwritten by the Southbury Historical Society. A copy of the video is available in the Framingham Public Library, Oral History Collection.

56. Ruth Brown expressed pride and satisfaction at having worked for Nutting and noted that being a colorist carried considerable status in the community.

57. Sarah Shortt was another early Nutting colorist who later dictated her memories of working in Southbury and Framingham to Rosemary Meyerott, a member of the Wallace Nutting Collector's Club from Los Altos Hills, California. The account survives in manuscript format in the Local History Collection, Framingham Public Library.

58. Sarah Shortt Dunn, Wallace Nutting Collector's Club manuscript newsletter, Local History Collection, Framingham Public Library.

59. Gertrude Brown, Wallace Nutting Collector's Club manuscript newsletter, Local History Collection, Framingham Public Library.

60. Nutting sold his Southbury property on 17 May 1912 to Francis H. Skelding of Pittsburgh, Pennsylvania. Deed, Town of Southbury Land Records, 318–321.

61. Nutting to Jennie M. DeMerit, 31 December 1917. American Decorative Arts Research Files, Wadsworth Atheneum.

62. For more on Nutting's coloring techniques, see Barendson, "Nutting, American Tastemaker," esp. 194–200.

63. Tinting photographs in the 1920s was little different than coloring maps in the 1880s, or earlier on, coloring prints—all traditional female jobs. I would like to thank Helena Wright for pointing out the significant role played by colorists earlier in the nineteenth century, especially in tinting prints and coding maps.

64. Videotaped interview, *Wallace Nutting in Southbury, 1906–1912*. Produced by Dorothy Manville, underwritten by the Southbury Historical Society, 1988.

65. Nutting, *Photographic Art Secrets*, 86, 108–109.

Chapter 3 *Middle-Class Art*

1. *The Wallace Nutting Idea*, advertising pamphlet (Ashland, Framingham, and Saugus, Mass.: Wallace Nutting Studios, 1921), n.p. Printed Book and Periodical Collection, Winterthur Library.

2. Nutting admitted familiarity with the "much ridiculed but often good Rogers groups" though he shared his generation's skepticism as "each was a molded copy produced a great number of times." *Wallace Nutting's Biography*, 221.

3. Michael Clapper, "The Chromo and the Art Museum: Popular and Elite Art Institutions in Late Nineteenth Century America," in *Not at Home: The Suppression of Domesticity in Modern Art and Architecture*, edited by

Christopher Reed (London: Thames and Hudson, 1996), 33–47.

4. Cited in ibid., 38.

5. For an excellent study of printmaking in turn-of-the-century New England, see David Acton, "The Flourish of Color Relief Printmaking in New England," in *Inspiring Reform*, ed. Meyer, 152–164.

6. *The Wallace Nutting Signed Platinotypes* (Southbury, Conn., 1906), n.p.

7. For a brief study of the transition from sentimental to modern art, see William S. Ayres, "Pictures in the American Home, 1880–1930," in *Arts and the American Home*, ed. Foy and Marling, 149–164.

8. Hand tinting was by no means a Nutting invention. A rosy blush painted on metallic cheeks banished the pallor from countless daguerreotypes and tintypes in the middle decades of the nineteenth century. For more on tinted photographs, see Henisch and Henisch, *Painted Photograph*. For more on modern longings for authenticity, see Orvell, *Real Thing*, esp. parts 2 and 3.

9. Nutting, *Wallace Nutting's Biography*, 77.

10. Orvell, *Real Thing*, 33–39.

11. For two succinct discussions of the rise of modernist "art" photography, see Peterson, "American Arts and Crafts," and Yochelson, "Clarence H. White."

12. *The Wallace Nutting Signed Platinotypes* (Southbury, Conn., 1906), n.p.

13. *Wallace Nutting Pictures* (Framingham, Mass.: Wallace Nutting, 1912), 3. Printed Book and Periodical Collection, Winterthur Library.

14. The catalog was issued in a small multi-ring binder to facilitate the addition of pages. Earlier Nutting catalogs had been hardbound quarto volumes.

15. An open letter dated 23 September 1910 from Wallace Nutting details the illness of one of his "travelers" or salesmen and provides instructions for one William Dolane to take over the route. Local History Collection, Framingham Historical Society.

16. Several advertising signs survive in public and private collections. These range from elaborate framed *églomisé* examples to simple silk-screen posters. Excellent photographs survive of Nutting window displays in department stores and local newspaper advertisements reflect the popularity of this sales technique. Local History Collection, Framingham Public Library. Two Nutting associates, Jane and Roberta Griswold, recalled the photographs being offered in jewelry stores in a 1989 interview. Jane and Roberta Griswold, interview by William N. Hosley, Jr., 19 February 1989, transcript, American Decorative Arts Department Files, Wadsworth Atheneum.

17. There is little variation among the four examples that I have studied. This leads me to believe that most of the catalogs were issued at one time with few subsequent additions.

18. Nutting was explicit about the relationship of his photographs to visual conventions of the day. "The question of originality is a ghost," he stated firmly. Nutting, *Photographic Art Secrets*, 1.

19. Sternberger, *Between Amateur and Aesthete*, esp. chaps. 1 and 2.

20. Frost wrote "Birches" in England in 1913–1914. It appeared in the *Atlantic Monthly* and was anthologized in Frost's third book, *Mountain Interval* (1916). For more on its symbolism, see Howard Nelson, "Birches," in *The Robert Frost Encyclopedia*, edited by Nancy Tuten and John Zubizarreta (Westport, Conn.: Greenwood, 2000), 31–32. I thank Dennis Marnon for reminding me of this poem.

21. Frank A. Waugh, "What the Birch Trees Do," *Country Life in America* 1, no. 2 (December 1901): 65. Waugh, a professor at the Massachusetts Agricultural College, is best known for his later writings, including *The Garden Beautiful* (New York: Orange Judd, 1912) and *The Natural Style in Landscape Gardening* (Boston: Richard G. Badger, 1917).

22. Nutting, *Wallace Nutting's Biography*, 284.

23. Nutting, *Vermont Beautiful*, 81.

24. Nutting, *Wallace Nutting's Biography*, 284.

25. Metcalf's work is often cited as commanding record prices in his lifetime. Although this is hard to prove, the painter did realize twenty-three thousand dollars for a single work in 1920. De Veer, *Sunlight and Shadow*. I thank Sandy Levinson for digging into the curatorial files at the Smithsonian American Art Museum on my behalf.

26. *Wallace Nutting Expansible Catalog* (Framingham, Mass.: Wallace Nutting, 1915; reprint, Doylestown, Pa.: Diamond Press, 1992), 5. Indeed the largest size, some 14 x 17 inches, cost only $6.50 in 1915.

27. For more on period response to three-deckers, see Richard M. Candee and Greer Hardwicke, "Early Twentieth Century Reform Housing by Kilham and Hopkins, Architects of Boston," *Winterthur Portfolio* 22, no. 1 (Spring 1987): 47–80.

28. As a category of historical analysis the New Woman is largely a question of historiographic interest today. Contemporary scholars of gender have pushed for a more nuanced understanding of the New Woman as a stereotype of well-off, educated, Anglo-Saxon behavior. My discussion,

however, is based specifically on the period stereotype of the New Woman. From satirical stereo cards to soap advertisements, the New Woman was ubiquitous in turn-of-the-century popular visual discourse. Charles Dana Gibson's Gibson Girl was the tip of the iceberg. Below the surface lurked the reality of the visual cliché that so preoccupied Nutting.

29. Carroll Smith-Rosenberg, "The New Woman as Androgyne: Social Disorder and Gender Crises, 1870–1936," in Smith-Rosenberg, *Disorderly Conduct*, 245.

30. Suffragettes particularly irked Nutting. Expounding on a wholly unrelated topic, he wrote, "The climb of Mt. Pisgah, not too severe for women who have the strength to vote, is an experience not to be missed." Nutting, *Vermont Beautiful*, 25. For a brief history of female suffrage, see Christine Stansell, *American Moderns: Bohemian New York and the Creation of a New Century* (New York: Metropolitan Books, 2000), esp. chap. 7, "Sexual Modernism."

31. Smith-Rosenberg, "New Woman as Androgyne," 245.

32. Henry Wadsworth Longfellow, "The Courtship of Miles Standish," in *The Complete Poetical Works of Henry Wadsworth Longfellow: Cambridge Edition* (Boston: Houghton, Mifflin, 1893), 164.

33. Ibid. See also Charles W. Elliott, *The New England History . . .* (New York: Charles Scribner's, 1857), and Alexander Young, *Chronicles of the Pilgrim Fathers of the Colony of Plymouth, from 1602 to 1625* (Boston: Charles C. Little and James Brown, 1841).

34. Longfellow, "Courtship of Miles Standish," 181. Longfellow drew on biblical imagery when sketching Priscilla, a point not lost on Nutting some years later. In *Vermont Beautiful*, Nutting notes, "One of the most beautiful and attractive chapters in the Bible deals with the ideal housewife and interweaves its thought with the twisted threads of her loom. She provides wool for her household." *Vermont Beautiful*, 185.

35. Whittier dedicated "Snowbound, a Winter Idyll" "To the Memory of the Household it Describes."

36. For a history of Priscilla at war, see Rodris Roth, "The New England or 'Olde Tyme,' Kitchen Exhibit at Nineteenth Century Fairs," in *Colonial Revival in America*, ed. Axelrod, 158–183.

37. Nutting, *Wallace Nutting's Biography*, 283.

38. William Dean Howells, "A Sennight of the Centennial," *Atlantic Monthly* 38 (July 1876): 100–101.

39. The definitive study of the iconography of spinning is Monkhouse, "Spinning Wheel as Artifact."

40. Metropolitan Opera House, program, "Dramatic and Scenic Reproduction of American History" (New York: National Society of New England Women, 1897). I thank Helena Wright for sharing this source with me.

41. For more on the myth of domestic textile production, see Laurel Thatcher Ulrich, *The Age of Homespun* (New York: Alfred Knopf, 2001), esp. chap. 1.

42. George Lunt, ed., *Old New England Traits* (New York: Hurd and Houghton, 1873), 35.

43. Nutting was certainly not alone in this line of thought. For more on the conservative nature of visual representation at the turn of the century, see Bernice Kramer Leader, "Antifeminism in the Paintings of the Boston School."

44. Nutting, *Wallace Nutting's Biography*, 77. Pajamas had become acceptable loungewear among fashion devotees in the 1920s. For more on this revolutionary moment, see Claudia Brush Kidwell and Valerie Steele, eds., *Men and Woman: Dressing the Part* (Washington, D.C.: Smithsonian Institution Press, 1989), 58.

45. Nutting, *Wallace Nutting's Biography*, 76.

46. "Thomas Dewing," wrote Sadakichi Hartmann, "is the only American painter who has succeeded in giving us pictures of women that might stand for the 'ideal American' type." Hartmann, *A History of American Art* (Boston: L. C. Page, 1901), 304.

47. Ironically, Nutting's composition pays tribute to a number of Dutch Old Master paintings of similar subject matter, images that have long been associated with sexual frisson because of their association with the lives of courtesans.

48. *Wallace Nutting Pictures* (Framingham, Mass.: Wallace Nutting, 1912), 6.

49. Dumenil, *Modern Temper*, 130.

50. Orvell, *Real Thing*, 73, 74.

51. The flexible format of the 1915 catalog makes exact counts impossible. The catalog's numbering scheme, outlined on page 3, provides a sense of the number of Dutch images. Numbers 5000 to 5499 are reserved for Holland.

52. Stott, *Holland Mania*.

53. David D. Hall, "Puritanism," in *A Companion to American Thought*, edited by Richard W. Fox and James T. Kloppenberg (Cambridge, Mass.: Blackwell, 1995), 559–560.

54. Wallace Nutting, *Photographic Art Secrets*, 105.

55. For a history of immigration restriction, see Solomon, *Ancestors and Immigrants*.

56. Nutting, *Vermont Beautiful*, 45.

57. Nutting, *Wallace Nutting's Biography*, 59.

58. *Expansible Catalog*, 701.

59. Nutting, *Vermont Beautiful*, 45.

60. Nutting, "Photographic Beauties of Objects in Motion," 307.

61. Gabriel, *Toilers of Land and Sea*, 297. I thank Bruce Robertson for calling my attention to this source.

Chapter 4 *Picture Houses, Period Rooms, and Print*

1. Fascinated by the storied entrepreneurs of the Gilded Age, Nutting often mentioned Carnegie, Vanderbilt, and others in his letters and sermons and later sought out Henry Ford, J. P. Morgan, Jr., and Henry Francis du Pont to further his position as an antiquarian. See, for example, Wallace Nutting, "The Obligations to Succeed in Business," Mss. Sermon, dated 1913 by a newspaper clipping integrated into the text, Local History Collection, Framingham Public Library.

2. For example, Nutting approached the antiquarian and curator George Francis Dow about the possibility of using the John Ward House and the Parson-Capen House, but he seems to have been all but summarily turned down. Nutting enlisted the aid of William Sumner Appleton of SPNEA to act as an intermediary to no avail. "Sure enough," recalled Appleton, "he said no before I could get the whole of the question out." William Sumner Appleton to Wallace Nutting, 23 December 1914, SPNEA Library and Archives. For more on Dow, see Stillinger, *Antiquers*, 149–154.

3. *The Wallace Nutting Chain of Colonial Picture Houses* (dated by hand 1915), Wallace Nutting Collection, Framingham Public Library. The pamphlet is designed to the graphic standards of the 1915 *Expansible Catalog* and was intended to be interleaved into the photography catalog, yet another example of the interconnected nature of Nutting's business efforts.

4. The other two links in the chain were the Hazen Garrison House at 8 Groveland Avenue in Haverhill, Massachusetts, and the Cutler-Bartlet House at the corner of Green and Washington Streets in Newburyport, Massachusetts.

5. For more on popular historical experience, see Mike Wallace, "Visiting the Past: History Museums in the United States," in Wallace, *Mickey Mouse History*, 3–32.

6. For an early history of the preservation movement, see Hosmer, *Presence of the Past*. More recent investigations include James M. Lindgren, *Preserving the Old Dominion: Historic Preservation and Virginia Traditionalism* (Charlottesville: University Press of Virginia, 1993); Lindgren, *Preserving Historic New England;* Diane Barthel, *Historic Preservation: Collective Memory and Historical Identity* (New Brunswick, N.J.: Rutgers University Press, 1996); and Holloran, *Boston's "Changeful Times."*

7. Associationism as a doctrine held sway in the late nineteenth century. In essential terms, proponents of the theory held that one's surroundings influenced one's character and behavior.

8. West, *Domesticating History*, 2.

9. Murtagh, *Keeping Time*, 34–35, 80–82.

10. For more on Chandler, see Lindgren, *Preserving Historic New England*, 71–79, 139–148, 170–185.

11. For more on this sea change, see James Lindgren, *Preserving Historic New England*, esp. chap. 7, "'Do Not Tear the House Down!': Establishing a Scientific Method in Preservation," 134–152.

12. For more on preservation and the Americanization of immigrants, see Wallace, *Mickey Mouse History*, 8–9, and William Rhoads, "The Colonial Revival and the Americanization of Immigrants," in *Colonial Revival in America*, ed. Axelrod, 341–362.

13. Nutting claimed that "the object of buying and fitting these houses was not commercial. It was a labor of love, to set forth the life of our fathers throughout our entire American history. It may be necessary later, when these picture houses are completely illustrated, to dispose of the latter two, in which large investments are tied up." *Wallace Nutting Chain of Colonial Picture Houses*, n.p.

14. Wallace Nutting to William Sumner Appleton, 7 April 1917, Appleton Correspondence, SPNEA.

15. See Lowenthal, *Past Is a Foreign Country*, esp. chap. 3, "Ancients vs. Moderns," 74–124.

16. For an excellent treatment of this phenomenon, see Myers, *Catskills*.

17. The Willey family of Crawford Notch, New Hampshire, was killed in 1826 in an avalanche that generated much publicity and subsequently turned their house into a tourist shrine. For more on the significance of the Willey disaster, see Eric Purchase, "The Willey Slide: The Problem of Landscape in Nineteenth-Century Narrative" (Ph.D. diss., University of Connecticut, 1994), esp. chap. 2, "The Tourism Frontier," 31–89.

18. Jakle, *Tourist*, 301.

19. Brown, *Inventing New England*, 201.

20. Dona Brown and Stephen Nissenbaum, "Changing New England, 1965–1945," in *Picturing Old New England*, ed. Truettner and Stein, 1–13.

21. MacCannell, *Tourist*, 40.

22. Brown, *Inventing New England*, 106.

23. *Wallace Nutting Chain of Colonial Picture Houses*, n.p.

24. Ibid.

25. Nutting was explicit about his debt to Appleton. Referring to SPNEA, he wrote, "I may say that without the

knowledge of the Society's work I should probably never have done any of this. The Haverhill house and the Saugus house I owe wholly to the Society, so far as calling my attention to them is concerned." Nutting to Appleton, 26 February 1915, Appleton Correspondence, SPNEA.

26. Appleton quoted in "Paul Revere Memorial," an undated and unidentified newspaper clipping. William Sumner Appleton's "Paul Revere House" Scrapbook, SPNEA. Cited in Lindgren, "'Constant Incentive to Patriotic Citizenship,'" 594.

27. Appleton to Nutting, 13 November 1914, Appleton Correspondence, SPNEA.

28. Ibid.

29. Ibid.

30. That Nutting was aware of the resources available to architects and preservationists is made clear in his correspondence with Appleton. See, for example, Nutting to Appleton, 30 December 1916, Appleton Correspondence, SPNEA.

31. Nutting to Appleton, 6 April 1915, Appleton Correspondence, SPNEA.

32. Nutting, *Wallace Nutting's Biography*, 151.

33. The State Street Trust Company in Boston was one customer. Allan Forbes, the States Street president, contacted Appleton in search of "a certain Norman Isham, architect of Rhode Island or Connecticut," for information about a doorway he had purchased from Nutting as "Wallace Nutting is abroad and I very much want to describe it for the opening of the new building." Forbes to Appleton, 23 July 1925, Appleton Correspondence, SPNEA.

34. The three architects often criticized one another to Appleton. Dean, for example, called Isham's work a "somber spectacle" and a "caricature." For an example of this behavior, see Lindgren, *Preserving Historic New England*, 147.

35. Appleton to Donald McDonald Millar, 20 March 1919, cited in Lindgren, *Preserving Historic New England*, 207. Millar was another clergyman turned antiquarian.

36. Both buildings were Joseph Everett Chandler restorations, the Paul Revere House in 1908 and the House of the Seven Gables in 1910.

37. Whitfield, *Homes of Our Forefathers*. Whitfield included the Iron Works house in the two subsequent editions of this text. Other important buildings include the Fairbanks House in Dedham, Massachusetts, and the Moffatt-Ladd House in Portsmouth, New Hampshire. Whitfield's sympathies are evident in his title page graphic—a depiction of the lamented Hancock House in Boston. The Hancock House was torn down in 1863 amid much publicity and is often cited as a harbinger of organized preservation campaigns. The standard work on Whitfield is Norton, *Edwin Whitfield*.

38. Nutting to Appleton, 26 February 1915, Appleton Correspondence, SPNEA.

39. As early as the fall of 1914 Nutting wrote, "I propose to buy for the Society the Coffin house, Newbury, if it can be purchased at a proper price, the Society in return for a deed to give me a 999 year lease . . . I to obligate myself . . . to undertake no repairs except with the consent of the Society." Nutting to Appleton, 16 October 1914, Appleton Correspondence, SPNEA.

40. Nutting to Appleton, 4 February 1915, Appleton Correspondence, SPNEA.

41. SPNEA's first three properties—the Swett-Ilsley House in Newbury, the Fowler House in Danversport, and the Cooper-Frost-Austin House in Cambridge—were all gifts to the society in 1911 and 1912. Lindgren, *Preserving Historic New England*, 185.

42. Deed, George Niven *et alia* to Wallace Nutting, Essex County Deed Book 2287, 365.

43. The Dean drawings are in the archives at SPNEA and are marked "Summer '08," but the date is lined out. The drawings presumably date to the period of Nutting's restoration but could have been an earlier speculative effort on the part of Dean and Appleton. Another incomplete set of postrestoration floor plans for four houses in the chain is at Winterthur in the registrar's files along with a number of templates from Nutting's furniture factory.

44. One of the photographs taken by Appleton is dated 20 September 1915, Ironworks File, SPNEA.

45. Clipping from the *Saugus Herald*, 4 October 1917, curatorial files, Saugus Ironworks National Historic Site. I thank Carl Salmons-Perez for his enthusiasm and assistance in researching the early history of the ironworks.

46. *Wallace Nutting Chain of Colonial Picture Houses*.

47. Nutting, *Early American Ironwork* (Saugus, Mass.: Wallace Nutting, 1919), 19.

48. Nutting, *Early American Ironwork*, 19, and "A Statement by Edward Guy, Maker of Hand Wrought Iron," 1 April 1922. The statement is a photomechanical reproduction of a letter interleaved in a copy of Nutting's *Furniture of the Pilgrim Century* (1921) in the library at Winterthur. Other copies of the Guy letter are in private hands.

49. Nutting, *Early American Ironwork*, 24.

50. Deed, Wallace Nutting, Inc., to Charles Cooney, 23 April 1920, Essex Country Deed Book 2382, 309. Cited in Joseph Albright, Orville W. Carroll, and Abbott Lowell Cummings, *Historic Structure Report—Saugus Ironworks* (Denver, Colo.: National Park Service, 1977).

51. The imbroglio set off a flurry of correspondence between antiquarians and curators. See, for example, the

many letters of Florence Paull Berger, the "general curator" of the Wadsworth Atheneum, to her colleagues at the Museum of Fine Arts, Boston, on the matter. Berger Correspondence, Archives of the Wadsworth Atheneum.

52. Appleton to Nutting, 15 April 1922, Appleton Correspondence, SPNEA.

53. Nutting to Appleton, 18 April 1922, Appleton Correspondence, SPNEA.

54. Deed, Wethersfield Land Records, vol. 60, 9 February 1916, 333.

55. Kendall, "Tea in Yorktown Parlor," 97.

56. Nutting to Appleton, 6 April 1915, Appleton Correspondence, SPNEA.

57. Appleton to Nutting, 1 December 1914, Appleton Correspondence, SPNEA.

58. Nutting to Appleton, 6 April 1915, Appleton Correspondence, SPNEA.

59. Appleton to Nutting, 8 April 1915, Appleton Correspondence, SPNEA.

60. "Account of Mr. Wallace Nutting," sporadic entries, April 1916 to July 1919.

61. Nutting to Appleton, 7 March 1916, Appleton Correspondence, SPNEA.

62. Ibid.

63. Kendall, "Tea in Yorktown Parlor," 100.

64. Nutting to Appleton, 6 October 1916, Appleton Correspondence, SPNEA.

65. Kendall, "Tea in Yorktown Parlor," 102.

66. "Account of Mr. Wallace Nutting," 24 June 1916, Webb-Deane-Stevens House.

67. Ibid., monthly entries, June 1916 to July 1917.

68. Kendall, "Tea in Yorktown Parlor," 108

69. *Wallace Nutting Chain of Colonial Picture Houses.*

70. For an excellent, albeit brief, exploration of the shock waves caused by labor unrest at the turn of the century, see David Demarest, Jr., *"The River Ran Red": Homestead, 1892* (Pittsburgh, Pa.: University of Pittsburgh Press, 1992), esp. chap. 9, "Legacy: The Next Hundred Years," 203–225.

71. Nutting to Appleton, 26 February 1915, Appleton Correspondence, SPNEA.

72. Nutting confided to Appleton that "the Haverhill house with all its improvements and land etc. cost me $9,000." Nutting to Appleton, 10 August 1918, Appleton Correspondence, SPNEA.

73. Nutting to Appleton, 26 February 1915, Appleton Correspondence, SPNEA.

74. Nutting to Appleton, 7 April 1917, Appleton Correspondence, SPNEA.

75. Several early architectural histories, including Joseph Everett Chandler's *Colonial House*, investigated Newburyport.

76. Wallace Nutting, "The Cutler-Bartlet House," unpaginated advertising pamphlet, Local History Collection, Framingham Public Library.

77. Nutting to Appleton, 10 August 1918, Appleton Correspondence, SPNEA.

78. "As built" floor plans for the first and second floors of the Gardner House are at Winterthur in the registrar's files. A letter from Appleton to Nutting comments on the "work now going on" at the house. Appleton to Nutting, 25 September 1915, Appleton Correspondence, SPNEA.

79. Nutting to Appleton, 6 May 1915, Appleton Correspondence, SPNEA.

80. Appleton to Wallace Nutting, 25 September 1915, Appleton Correspondence, SPNEA.

81. "Mrs. Wendell" was Mrs. Barrett Wendell, wife of the celebrated Harvard English professor and biographer of Cotton Mather. Appleton to Nutting, 25 September 1915, Appleton Correspondence, SPNEA.

82. Nutting to Appleton, 10 August 1918, Appleton Correspondence, SPNEA.

83. Ibid.

84. For a brief history of the fad for historic paneling in urban museums, see Hosmer, *Presence of the Past*, 228–232.

85. Nutting to Appleton, 10 August 1918, Appleton Correspondence, SPNEA.

86. Ibid.

87. For a succinct history of the founding of the American Wing, see Kaplan, "R. T. H. Halsey."

88. Lindgren, *Preserving Historic New England*, 108, 158–165.

89. Nutting to Appleton, 7 April 1917, Appleton Correspondence, SPNEA.

90. Citizens were urged to curtail petroleum consumption in the summer of 1917 with a call for "Gasless Sundays." Voluntary rationing caused considerable class tension. The *New York Times* devoted a number of column inches to the question of "joy riding" during the hostilities. On 24 July 1917, for instance, one J. Hemstreet took "exception . . . to Bedford's [A. C. Bedford of the Petroleum Committee of the Council of National Defense] appeal for the curtailment of motor touring . . . on the grounds that hotels in rural districts would suffer." *New York Times*, 24 July 1917, 20:1. I thank my father for ferreting out these citations.

91. Nutting wrote to Appleton, "In relation to my houses, it may please you to know that the Wethersfield

house has been sold to the Daughters of the Revolution to be their permanent acquisition." Nutting to Appleton, 30 June 1919, Appleton Correspondence, SPNEA.

92. For a history of the Wadsworth Atheneum, see Saunders and Raye, *Daniel Wadsworth.*

93. Seymour had earlier facilitated the Atheneum's 1920 acquisition of an important 1760s *beaufatt,* or corner cupboard, from the Captain Charles Churchill House in Newington, Connecticut. *Hartford Courant,* 11 November 1920. Newspaper clipping in annual scrapbook, Archives of the Wadsworth Atheneum. For more on Seymour, see Stillinger, *Antiquers,* 88–94.

94. "Rare Collection of Old New England Furniture," *Hartford Courant,* 16 October 1921. Newspaper clipping in annual scrapbook, Archives of the Wadsworth Atheneum.

95. Seymour's collection, as exhibited in the Morgan Memorial, represented the work of a second-generation collector. As a student at Hartford High School in the late 1870s, Seymour became known as a child prodigy in antiquarian circles. He sought out the acquaintance and advice of pioneer collectors, including Dr. Horace S. Fuller and Dr. Irving W. Lyon. Through Lyon, the author of *The Colonial Furniture of New England: A Study of The Domestic Furniture in Use in The Seventeenth and Eighteenth Centuries* (Boston: Houghton, Mifflin, 1891), Seymour was, in turn, introduced to a network of pickers and restorers, including Walter Hosmer and Edward Simons.

96. "Rare Collection of Old New England Furniture."

97. "Loan Exhibition of Pewter Shows Rare Examples," *Hartford Daily Times,* 21 February 1923. Newspaper clipping in annual scrapbook, Archives of the Wadsworth Atheneum.

98. "Colonial Houses to Be Discussed," *Hartford Daily Times,* 7 November 1923. Newspaper clipping in annual scrapbook, Archives of the Wadsworth Atheneum.

99. Morgan's half interest was noted in the *Hartford Daily Times,* 31 January 1924. Newspaper clipping in annual scrapbook, Archives of the Wadsworth Atheneum.

100. *Hartford Courant,* 12 December 1924. Newspaper clipping in annual scrapbook, Archives of the Wadsworth Atheneum.

101. *Hartford Courant,* 15 February 1925. Newspaper clipping in annual scrapbook, Archives of the Wadsworth Atheneum.

102. Eugene R. Gaddis, *Magician of the Modern: Chick Austin and the Transformation of the Arts in America* (New York: Alfred A. Knopf, 2000), esp. chap. 9 and pp. 235–238.

103. Advertisement, *Antiques* (July 1923): 38.

104. Nutting, *New Hampshire Beautiful,* 170.

105. A sample of this genre includes Clifton Johnson, *The New England Country* (Boston, 1893); Charles Goodrich Whiting, *Walks in New England* (New York: John Lane, 1903); and Helen Henderson, *A Loiterer in New England* (New York: George H. Doran, 1919).

106. For more on the role of Old America during the Depression, see William H. Truettner, "Small Town America," in *Picturing Old New England,* ed. Truettner and Stein, 111–142.

107. A democratic product, Nutting's books offered his invented world to those with imagination and four dollars.

108. Nutting, *Connecticut Beautiful,* 133.

Chapter 5   *Pilgrim Furniture of the Modern Century*

1. Wallace Nutting, *Correct Windsor Furniture* (Saugus, Mass.: Wallace Nutting, 1918), 44.

2. By "Americana market" I have in mind the demand for both period and reproduction domestic furnishings as well as the vast literature that identified, promoted, and interpreted such goods in the early twentieth century. Examples include N. Hudson Moore, *The Old Furniture Book* (New York: Frederick A. Stokes, 1903); Robert and Elizabeth Shackleton, *The Quest of the Colonial* (New York: Century, 1908); Carrick, *Next-to-Nothing House;* and Henry Hammond Taylor, *Knowing, Collecting, and Restoring Early American Furniture* (Philadelphia: J. B. Lippincott, 1930).

3. For a brief study of the significance of the Standard Oil Trust as a model of industrial capitalism, see Chandler and Tedlow, *Coming of Managerial Capitalism,* 343–372. For a more critical view, see Trachtenberg, *Incorporation of America,* esp. chap. 3.

4. Nutting also wrote numerous articles in this period, including two in *Antiques.* A representative sampling includes "Strength and Beauty in Our Earliest Furniture," *Art and Decoration* (December 1921): 96–98; "Colonial Bookcases," *Booknotes* (June–July 1924): 15; "Some Facts About Early American Furniture," *Woman's World* (April 1925); and "A Perfect Seventeenth Century Dwelling," *House Beautiful* (December 1926): 698–702.

5. As noted earlier, an exact accounting is made impossible by the destruction of Nutting's business records at the end of his life. Nutting himself frequently made reference to, and even made light of, the profitless nature of the business. Comparing the business records of Nutting contemporary Nathan Margolis of Hartford, Connecticut, in the Joseph Downs Collection at Winterthur and the remnants of a Nutting account book in the Berea College

Archives, it is clear that the Nutting's standards of accounting were far looser than Margolis's. Nutting, furthermore, seemed to be willing to hold onto stock and carry a larger payroll than Margolis, who maintained a core group of six to eight cabinetmakers and added two or three in times of need. More exact comparison is, of course, made academic by the lack of consistent records for Wallace Nutting, Incorporated.

6. Nutting's earlier photography company, a far more profitable enterprise, grew out of his efforts at combating neurasthenia, a disease of the feminized "brain worker." A decade later, stronger and wealthier, Nutting took up the more masculine role of company president and public authority on American furniture. For more on business success as masculine ideal, see Clark Davis, "The Corporate Reconstruction of Middle-Class Manhood," in *The Middling Sorts: Explorations in the History of the American Middle Class*, edited by Burton J. Beldstein and Robert D. Johnson (New York: Routledge, 2001), 201–216.

7. Nutting helped to define the ideology of the Small House Movement with his views of colonial interiors and hardy early Americans. For more on the Small House Movement, see Bridget A. May, "Progressivism and the Colonial Revival"; Gebhard, "American Colonial Revival"; and Rhoads, "Colonial Revival and American Nationalism."

8. For a time in the 1920s, Nutting offered furniture, wrought iron, braided rugs, hand-tinted photographs, and silhouettes, in addition to books on American decorative arts for the specialist and the states beautiful series for the generalist.

9. "Wallace Nutting, Incorporated" was owned almost wholly by Wallace Nutting. The Commonwealth of Massachusetts certified the corporation on 28 January 1914. Of the 1,250 shares of preferred stock issued, Nutting held 1,246. The remaining four shares were parceled out to three people, presumably to form a quorum. Records of the Corporations Division, Office of the Secretary of the Commonwealth of Massachusetts.

10. Nutting viewed inefficient production as a sign of commitment to craft. "A machine lathe leg 'nearly as good' could be made at one-twentieth of the expense we put on these turnings," he claimed in *Correct Windsor Furniture*, 2.

11. Nutting's ideas of craft and labor hardly precluded the use of industry standard power tools, however. His factory, as inventoried in 1945, was equipped with the latest machinery from major companies. Many of Nutting's suppliers provided tools for the large furniture companies of Grand Rapids, Gardner, and High Point, North Car-

olina (Wallace Nutting Collection, Berea College Archives). This seeming hypocrisy was also manifest in the Arts and Crafts movement, where, in the words of Edward S. Cooke, Jr., the "process" became a "product" when the style was divorced from the ideology and large companies began to produce lines of "mission" oak furniture. For a history of the commodification and commercialization of the Arts and Crafts aesthetic, see Cooke, Jr., "Arts and Crafts Furniture."

12. The average annual net income for a lawyer in 1929 was $5,534.00. A physician earned slightly less at $5,224.00. See Bureau of the Census, Series D 728-734, "Earning in Selected Professions, 1929–1954," *Statistical History of the United States*, prepared by the Bureau of the Census in cooperation with the Social Science Research Council (Washington, D.C., 1961), 97.

13. Top dealers, collectors, and students of Nutting, including Michael Ivankovich, William Hamann, and Roger Gonzales, estimate that perhaps as many as ten or twelve number 910 "Sudbury" court cupboards were reproduced by Nutting between 1922 and 1941. From surviving plans and templates at the Wadsworth Atheneum and Winterthur, it appears that the larger mahogany pieces were initiated as individual orders. This theory is buttressed perhaps by an advertisement on page 16 of the July 1928 issue of the magazine *Antiques* that illustrates a block-front chest of drawers, noting that "the piece above, No. 918, has just been made to order and will be available for the public, together with 300 other exquisite reproductions of all early periods."

14. That Nutting made money in this market is evident in the numerous surviving examples of the Windsor form. For a discussion of the expansion of the middle class, see Stuart Blumin, "The Hypothesis of Middle-Class Formation in Nineteenth-Century America: A Critique and Some Proposals," *American Historical Review* 90 (April 1985): 299–338.

15. *Final Edition Furniture Catalog*, 61, 62. Two initial templates survive from the Framingham factory. American Decorative Arts Research Files, Wadsworth Atheneum.

16. *Correct Windsor Furniture*, 1.

17. Nutting clearly viewed the Windsor as an "American" form though he acknowledged its English ancestry. In the narrative of *A Windsor Handbook*, he categorized the popular tale of King George discovering the chair as "mere legend." Of the English chairs themselves, Nutting notes, "The English Windsors lack grace." Nutting, *A Windsor Handbook* (Saugus, Mass.: Wallace Nutting, 1917), 5, 7.

18. Copyright Office, Library of Congress. In his autobiography, Nutting is quite explicit that he began his interior work in Greenwich, Connecticut, in 1904. See Nutting, *Wallace Nutting's Biography*, 284.

19. William H. Truettner and Thomas Denenberg, "The Discreet Charm of the Colonial," in *Picturing Old New England*, ed. Truettner and Stein, 91.

20. *The Wallace Nutting Collection of American Antiques* (New York: John Wanamaker, [1918]), 33. Catalog in Special Collections, Winterthur Museum Library.

21. Nutting to Appleton, 1 October 1918, Appleton Correspondence, SPNEA.

22. Nutting, *Windsor Handbook*, 127. What, exactly, Nutting thought were "early" forms remains to be discovered.

23. On 7 April 1917 Nutting wrote to William Sumner Appleton, "It is some advantage to have the houses shown as it is an advertisement of my pictures. I felt that our pictures did not look well in the houses and I have taken down every one except those in the upper stories at Newburyport." Appleton Correspondence, SPNEA.

24. Nutting, *Windsor Handbook*, 127.

25. Nutting devoted a page to "Education" in his 1915 photography catalog, because, he wrote, "taste in pictures develops slowly in most minds." *The Wallace Nutting Expansible Catalog* (Framingham, Mass: Wallace Nutting, 1915), 115.

26. For more on spinning-wheel chairs, see chapter 3. For more on "Centennial Furniture," see Roth, "Colonial Revival and Centennial Furniture." Roth's follow-up article, "The New England, or 'Olde Tyme,' Kitchen Exhibit at Nineteenth-Century Fairs," in *Colonial Revival in America*, ed. Axelrod, 159–183, continues her exploration of historicist furniture at the late-nineteenth-century fairs.

27. See, for example, Kenneth Ames, "Grand Rapids Furniture at the Time of the Centennial," *Winterthur Portfolio* 10 (1975): 23–50.

28. Nutting continued to damn the library chairs as "weak where they should be strong, and extremely clumsy and heavy in the arms." *Windsor Handbook*, 171.

29. Nutting, *Wallace Nutting's Biography*, 128, 127.

30. Nutting to Appleton, 30 September 1915, Appleton Correspondence, SPNEA.

31. Curiously, Nutting did not attempt to replicate the social vision of such Arts and Crafts theorists as Elbert Hubbard when it came to his furniture business. Nuttinghame, his early Southbury, Connecticut, photography concern, resembled the communal environment of such enterprises, but by the 1920s Nutting clearly placed his faith in industrial capitalism rather than seeking utopian alternatives. For two excellent studies of individual Arts and Crafts communities, see Falino, "Monastic Ideal in Rural Massachusetts," and George Thomas, "William Price's Arts and Crafts Colony at Rose Valley, Pennsylvania," in *Ideal Home*, ed. Kardon, 125–135.

32. For more on the history of high-volume furniture manufacturing, see Carron, *Grand Rapids Furniture*.

33. F. Scott and Son is identified as the mill owner in the *Historic Structure Report: Ironmaster's House* (Denver, Colo.: National Park Service Technical Information Center, 1977), 84–85, 419.

34. Appleton to Nutting, 24 November 1917, Appleton Correspondence, SPNEA.

35. Nutting, *Correct Windsor Furniture*, 2.

36. No records survive to document the tooling of Nutting's first factory, and the inventories for his later Framingham operation indicate that the majority of this equipment was purchased in the 1920s.

37. Unidentified Saugus newspaper clipping, Archives of the Saugus Iron Works, Saugus Ironworks National Historic Site.

38. Wanamaker purchased "largely the mahogany period" from Nutting in 1918. The department store magnate offered the collection to the public that same year in a special catalog entitled *The Wallace Nutting Collection of American Antiques*. Several copies are extant, including one in the Rare Book Collection at Winterthur Museum.

39. The Parmenter Cupboard is currently part of the Wallace Nutting Collection of Early American Furniture at the Wadsworth Atheneum.

40. Nutting relates the story of the cut-down cupboard as a caption to pl. 451 of *The Furniture Treasury*.

41. *Wallace Nutting Final Edition Furniture Catalog* (Framingham, Mass.: Wallace Nutting, 1937), 34.

42. Known examples are owned by Pine Manor College in Massachusetts, the Harvard Club in Boston, and three private collectors.

43. Nutting, *The Great American Idea* (Ashland, Mass.: Wallace Nutting, 1921), 2. Folio catalog in Special Collections, Winterthur Museum Library. *The Great American Idea* was issued in at least two formats. A staple-bound version seems to have been intended as a standard mail-order catalog, while the loose folio issue was possibly intended for department stores, salespersons, and others who required a more flexible format.

44. Nutting to Appleton, 7 July 1919, Appleton Correspondence, SPNEA.

45. There are several inventories and appraisals in the Wallace Nutting Files in Berea College Archives.

46. Wallace Nutting, *Seventh Edition Furniture Catalog*. Facsimile reprinted in John Crosby Freeman, *Wallace Nutting Checklist of Early American Reproductions* (Watkins Glen, N.Y.: American Life Foundation, 1969), n.p. [p. 2].

47. Nutting moved his operation from Ashland to

Framingham Center by 1926. Two copies of the "Ten Commandments" are in the Local History Collection, Framingham Public Library. Other framed copies are in private hands, lending credence to Nutting's claim that he posted the document throughout the Park Street factory. See Nutting, *Seventh Edition Period Furniture Catalog*, [p. 2].

48. Wallace Nutting, the "Ten Commandments," Local History Collection, Framingham Public Library.

49. Insurance maps record 46 Park Street as a modern industrial facility with up-to-date fire suppression equipment, steam heat, electric power, and lighting. Sanborn Fire Insurance Maps for Framingham, Massachusetts, Map Collection, Library of Congress.

50. Nutting, "Ten Commandments."

51. The structure was built between 1872 and 1875. Framingham Survey, Form Number 408, 25 June 1979, Massachusetts Historical Commission.

52. Nutting, *Seventh Edition Period Furniture Catalog*, title page legend.

53. Train, *Puritan's Progress*, 6, 8.

54. Dodge worked for Nutting from 1941 until 1942. Joel H. Dodge to Louis M. MacKeil, 31 December 1979, Local History Collection, Framingham Public Library.

55. Franklin H. Gotshall, "Nutting Revisited," *Fine Woodworking* 40 (May–June 1983): 24. Gottshall was employed by Nutting from 1926 until 1927 as "a furniture designer" in his own words. He also "did some woodcarving and cabinetmaking in [the] studio." See Franklin H. Gottshall to Abbott Lowell Cummings, 25 April 1973, Abbott Lowell Cummings Correspondence, SPNEA.

56. *Antiques* (September 1927): 249, (April 1928): 325, and (July 1928): 16. I thank National Museum of American History intern Brigham Bowen for ferreting out these advertisements.

57. For Nutting's involvement with the museum field, see chapter 4.

58. Florance Paull Berger to George Dudley Seymour, 16 August 1920, Berger Correspondence, Archives of the Wadsworth Atheneum. Berger served as "general curator" of the museum during this period.

59. *Wallace Nutting Supreme Edition General Catalog* (Framingham, Mass.: Wallace Nutting, 1930), 5.

60. Gotshall, "Nutting Revisited," 24, and Gottshall to Cummings, 25 April 1973, Cummings Correspondence, SPNEA.

61. *Wallace Nutting Period Furniture* (Framingham, Mass.: Wallace Nutting, 1930), 2. Nutting continued to wax patriotic about his employees, claiming at one point that "many live on their own little farms."

62. Nutting, *Wallace Nutting's Biography*, 246.

63. These employees are identified on the back of a photograph now at Winterthur. Registrar's files, acc. no. G 83.177.1, Winterthur Museum.

64. Nutting, *Wallace Nutting's Biography*, 246.

65. Sweeney, "Olof Althin," 13.

66. Nutting to William J. Hutchins, 18 November 1933, Hutchins Correspondence, Berea College Archives.

67. Johnson's Cambridge address is noted on correspondence in the Berea College Archives. Johnson appears in the Cambridge *City Directories* from 1910 to 1944. Though he lived at five addresses and worked in three shops in this period, he is always listed as a "wood-carver." Of interest is the fact that 4 Osborn Street, Johnson's work address from 1910 to 1916, was the factory of Allan and Endicott, a large furniture manufacturer bought by Kaplan and Company, maker of the popular Beacon Hill Collection of colonial revival designs for the B. Altman department store chain. I thank Susan Maycock of the Cambridge Historical Commission for her assistance in tracking Johnson.

68. All known information about E. J. Dunn is from an account book and small group of documents in the collection of John Baron, purchased from the estate of Hartford cabinetmaker Paul Koda.

69. The ad reads, "The piece above, No. 918, has just been made to order and will be available for the public, together with 300 other exquisite reproductions of all early periods." *Antiques* (July 1928): 16.

70. Most of the Wallace Nutting templates at the Wadsworth Atheneum and Winterthur are formed of cardboard. A high-volume factory would need wood or steel templates to prevent dimensional loss over time. Close examination of the Atheneum templates suggests that they were used several times, but not repeatedly. American Decorative Arts Study Collection, Wadsworth Atheneum.

71. These men are identified on the back of the group photograph of employees at Winterthur. Registrar's files, photo no. G83.177.1, Winterthur Museum. The cabinetmakers are A. Sterling, Everett Brackett, Wallace Nelson, John Raustrom, Bill Ball, and Joe Kimball. The finishers are Thomas Carboneau and Gus Bortolusi. The Windsor specialist is George Turgeon. Frank Newcomb is called a carver. One D. Libertini is the packer, and Ernest Donnelly the office manager and artist.

72. Unidentified Berea College official (probably George R. Kavanaugh, College Business Manager), notes on Framingham visit, 1945, RG 5-23, box 5, folder 6, Berea College Archives.

73. First name illegible, appears to be Gerard. The

handwritten nature of this manuscript makes the spelling of some names questionable.

74. These two employees are identified on the 1928 Winterthur photograph.

75. Looking back to the 1920s, the height of the furniture business, this ethnic hierarchy becomes even more evident, for Carboneau's associate in the finishing shop is listed as Gus Bortolusi. The only other Italian name in the shop is the packer, one D. Libertini.

76. Nutting would sell a piece "in the white," or unfinished, but refused to brand the piece or offer a guarantee because he feared the hydroscopic nature of the material. Wallace Nutting Incorporated, "Finish" hang tag, Local History Collection, Framingham Public Library.

77. This anecdote appears in both the 1930 and 1937 furniture catalogs. The chair itself was sold to Henry Francis du Pont and is now displayed at Winterthur after being remanded to storage as a fake for decades.

78. Appleton to Nutting, 24 November 1917, Appleton Correspondence, SPNEA.

79. Latter-day collectors of Wallace Nutting furniture are naturally interested in the subject of his marks. Generally speaking, Nutting used a paper label in Saugus and thereafter employed a series of brands. The shift may have been the result of unscrupulous dealers' soaking off the labels, distressing the surface, and representing the furniture as old. There is also a period in the early 1920s when Nutting furniture was produced with a branded script logo. Collectors identify this furniture with a temporary falling off in quality. On page 285 of *Wallace Nutting's Biography*, Nutting relates that he sold his company in 1922 and repurchased it a year later because he was "dissatisfied with conduct of business which bore my name." This may explain the mystery of the script brand, but incorporation documents filed with the Commonwealth of Massachusetts fail to record this change of ownership. After this interregnum, Nutting proceeded to mark his wares with a block-letter brand in different sizes. For more on Nutting's marks, see George J. Lovesky, "Signatures on Wallace Nutting Furniture" (Paper presented at the 1997 Annual Convention of the Wallace Nutting Collector's Club, Manchester, New Hampshire).

80. Wallace Nutting, "Early American Furniture," typescript, corrected in Nutting's hand, Local History Collection, Framingham Public Library, n.p. [p. 2].

81. "Business furniture" shows up in Nutting's 1927 catalog.

82. Esther Svenson to George Kavanaugh, business manager, 14 May 1945, RG 5-32, box 4, Berea College Archives.

83. Nutting, *Wallace Nutting's Biography*, 127.

84. Nutting provided furniture for the boardroom of the grand Colonial Revival Aetna headquarters in Hartford. An order from the First National Bank of Kansas City was received just as the Nutting factory was closing in 1945. The order refers to several pieces of furniture purchased previously. William Deuser to Ernest Donnelly, 21 March 1945, RG 5-23, box 5, folder 8, Berea College Archives.

85. *Wallace Nutting Supreme Edition General Catalog*, 143.

Chapter 6 *Beauty, Construction, and Style*

1. Consumption studies, long a subject of academic inquiry, reached maturity in the 1980s and continues to hold sway in the historical profession. Important works in this field include Jackson Lears, *No Place of Grace;* Fox and Jackson Lears, eds., *Culture of Consumption;* Bronner, ed., *Consuming Visions;* Cotkin, *Reluctant Modernism;* and Stanley Lebergott, *Pursuing Happiness: American Consumers in the Twentieth Century* (Princeton, N.J.: Princeton University Press, 1993).

2. Fannie Barnes, "A Fallow Field," *Harper's Monthly Magazine* 104 (January 1902): 295.

3. The two images appeared in *Country Life in America* in June and July 1902, 66–67 and lxix, respectively.

4. These promotions were infrequent when compared to the advertising program Nutting staged in the magazine *Antiques* for his furniture business. With rare exception, from 1922 to 1944 *Antiques* included a Nutting article or advertisement in every issue.

5. *Good Housekeeping* 73, no. 4 (October 1921): 80.

6. The postwar economic boom is chronicled in the number of permanent dwelling units started in the United States. Between 1918 and 1922, the number of starts increased by almost 600 percent. *Historical Statistics of the United States*, series N 106-115 (Washington, D.C.: U.S. Bureau of the Census, 1957), 393.

7. *Antiques* (January 1922): 7.

8. Marchand, *Advertising the American Dream*, xix.

9. *Antiques* (April 1928): 325.

10. Cook, *House Beautiful*, 163, 162. The chapters to *The House Beautiful* appeared as articles in *Scribner's Monthly* and were originally compiled in an 1877 edition.

11. Christopher Monkhouse has identified Sypher and Co. as a pioneer dealer in "bric-a-brac" in New York City. Dating to the 1840s, by the time Clarence Cook invoked the company's good name, Sypher employed approximately one hundred men. Writing in the *Curio* in 1887, Obadiah Sypher explained that his "strict principle is to sell goods for what they are, they are copies, originals when I am

lucky enough to find any. But, good faithful, honest, copies are of such worth in the market they do not need to be presented, and passed for what they are not." Sypher is quoted in Monkhouse and Mitchie, *American Furniture in Pendleton House*, 198–199.

12. The object illustrated is Nutting's well-known Parmenter Cupboard. In a 1932 price list, Nutting offered this piece for $645.00. *Wallace Nutting Supreme Edition General Catalog* (Framingham, Mass.: Wallace Nutting, 1930).

13. *Antiques* (June 1926): 448.

14. Ibid.

15. Edith Wharton and Ogden Codman, Jr., *The Decoration of Houses* (1902; reprint ed., New York: W. W. Norton, 1998).

16. The "Beauty, Construction, and Style" series of full-page ads ran throughout 1926 in *Antiques*.

17. T. J. Jackson Lears, "From Salvation to Self-Realization: Advertising and the Therapeutic Roots of the Consumer Culture, 1880–1930," in *Culture of Consumption*, ed. Fox and Lears, 24.

18. The "Aunt Belle" campaign is cited in Lears, "From Salvation to Self-Realization," 23–24.

19. Marchand, *Advertising the American Dream*, 355. Marchand notes that "Janet Gray" became so popular that the company found it "advisable to take legal steps to protect the use of her name."

20. Lears, "Ad Man and Grand Inquisitor," 112, 113.

21. The tear sheets for a handful of Nutting newspaper and magazine advertisements survive in a scrapbook made out of a binding designed to house the 1912 folio volume *Old New England Pictures*. Local History Collection, Framingham Public Library.

22. In 1927, according to Roland Marchand, the George Batten Company was the fourth largest advertising agency in America. Barton, Durstine and Osborne stood at seventh. The companies merged in 1928. Marchand, *Advertising the American Dream*, 32–33.

23. Ibid., 33, 35.

24. Lears, *Fables of Abundance*, 178.

25. Ibid. Lears discusses Barton and *The Man Nobody Knows* at length.

26. Marchand, *Advertising the American Dream*, 8.

27. Personal communication, Shannon Wilson, Berea College archivist, to author, 19 March 2001.

28. Three letters suggest the intimate involvement of Bruce Barton with the Nutting estate. In one dated 15 February 1945, George Kavanaugh, the Berea College business manager, thanks Frank W. Hatch, the manager of the Boston office of Batten, Barton, Durstine and Osborn, for his help in cleaning up Nutting's Framingham affairs. Remarkably, Kavanaugh quotes Whittier's *Snowbound* to Hatch in apparent reference to delayed travel plans. Another letter of the same date from Kavanaugh to Louise MacLeod, "Secretary to Mr. Bruce Barton," states that [Berea College] "President Hutchins and I wanted you and Mr. Barton to know of our appreciation of the favors shown." The final note, dated 30 July 1945 from Bruce Barton, congratulates Kavanaugh and notes that the ad man was "delighted with the outcome of the Wallace Nutting negotiations." RG 5-23, box 5, folders 8 and 9, Berea College Archives.

29. Nutting, *Wallace Nutting's Biography*, 225.

30. In a letter to William Sumner Appleton dated 30 September 1915, Nutting wrote that he was preparing an illustrated address on "Early American Homes and their Furnishings." He elaborated that for "$100.00, I seek, in my humble way to enlighten the public . . . the proceeds will be devoted to . . . the beautification of old homes [referring to the Chain of Colonial Picture Houses]." Appleton Correspondence, SPNEA.

31. "Wallace Nutting Lectures," RG 5-23, box 5, folder 8, Berea College Archives.

32. Ibid., 1, 3.

33. Ibid., 2.

34. *Wallace Nutting Supreme Edition General Catalog*, 139.

35. For two recent works on female patterns of consumption, see Laird, *Advertising Progress*, and Damon-Moore, *Magazines for the Millions*.

36. "Wallace Nutting Lectures," 4.

37. Nutting, *Wallace Nutting's Biography*, 225.

38. Gooding is quoted in Louis McKeil, *Wallace Nutting* (Saugus, Mass.: Saugus Historical Society, 1982), 36.

39. For more on department stores, see Leach, *Land of Desire*.

40. Wallace Nutting Advertising Scrapbook, Local History Collection, Framingham Public Library.

41. Ibid.

42. This list of department stores carrying Wallace Nutting furniture is compiled from advertisements, ad agency tear sheets and proofs, and manuscript notations in the ledger-scrapbook at the Framingham Public Library. Many of the entries in the ledger bear pencil annotation (dates and brief commentary) in Nutting's hand. Wallace Nutting Advertising Scrapbook.

43. Danersk, originally based in Connecticut, sold a broad line of colonial revival furniture manufactured in North Carolina. Drexel eventually purchased the rights

to use the name "Wallace Nutting" on a high-end line of furniture in 1945 but made little money on the deal and soon folded the enterprise.

44. "Display Features in the Wholesale Markets: Effective Methods Which the Retailer Can Use," *Good Furniture* 30, no. 3 (March 1928): 123.

45. Jordan Marsh was a frequent advertiser in *Old Time New England* in the 1920s and 1930s and promoted its "Little Colonial House," or furnished environment, in this journal. I thank former student Julie Cohen for pointing this out. Julie Cohen, "The Great Department Stores and the Popular Taste for Colonial Revival Furniture," typescript, Boston University, 2 May 1995.

46. "Diderot unities," according to McCracken, are "highly consistent complements of consumer goods." "The Diderot effect is a coercive force that maintains them." For more on this, see McCracken, *Culture and Consumption*, 118–129.

47. Nutting's financial agitation was soon laced throughout his correspondence. In a letter to the trustees of the Wadsworth Atheneum on 20 April 1933, he noted, "Money is exceedingly short. If you feel you can continue my subscription to the museum on account of this gift or on any other account I wish you would!" American Decorative Arts Files, Wadsworth Atheneum.

Chapter 7   *Contemporary Ancestors*

1. William G. Frost, "Our Contemporary Ancestors in the Southern Mountains," *Atlantic Monthly* 83 (March 1899): 311. This article is reprinted in W. K. McNeil, *Appalachian Images in Folk and Popular Culture* (Ann Arbor, Mich.: UMI Research Press, 1989), 92.

2. That Nutting read Frost's article is made clear in his own writings. Nutting mentions the "people president Frost referred to as our contemporary ancestors" in *Old New England Pictures*, 28.

3. For more on the importance of Appalachia in popular American thought, see Jane S. Becker, *Selling Tradition: Appalachia and the Construction of the American Folk* (Chapel Hill: University of North Carolina Press, 1998).

4. *Citizen* (Berea, Ky.), 23 May 1900, 1. This was Nutting's second commencement address. In 1895 he was the speaker at Wheaton College, a women's college in Norton, Massachusetts (Archives and Special Collections, Wallace Library, Wheaton College). Thirty years later Nutting officiated at Washington and Jefferson College in Pennsylvania, where he was honored with a Doctor of Humanities degree, his sec-

ond honorary doctorate. His first, in divinity, was presented in 1893 by Whitman College in Walla-Walla, Washington. See Nutting, *Wallace Nutting's Biography*, 284, 286.

5. *Citizen* (Berea, Ky.), 23 May 1900, 1.

6. Ibid., 13 June 1900, 4.

7. Fee was comparing his fledgling school to Oberlin College, a school founded in 1833. Coeducational from inception, Oberlin was then as now a bastion of liberal thought. For more on Oberlin's unique history, see Nat Brandt, *The Town That Started the Civil War* (Syracuse, N.Y.: Syracuse University Press, 1990). Fee's manifesto appeared in the magazine *American Missionary* on 9 November 1855 and is quoted in the standard history of the college: Elisabeth S. Peck, *Berea's First Century: 1855–1955* (Lexington: University of Kentucky Press, 1955), 8.

8. Peck, *Berea's First Century*, 8.

9. Although the sheer number of colleges and universities may have been on the rise in the postwar period, most were founded to serve discreet (and homogeneous) student populations. Examples include schools founded for African-American students such as Fisk University (1866), Howard University (1868), and Hampton Institute (1868), as well as the many colleges founded for women, such as Smith (1875), Wellesley (1875), Bryn Mawr (1885), Barnard (1889), and Radcliffe (1894). For a survey of African-American institutions, see Arnold Cooper, *Between Struggle and Hope: Four Black Educators in the South, 1894–1915* (Ames: Iowa State University Press, 1989), and Amy Thompson McCandless, *The Past in the Present: Women's Higher Education in the Twentieth-Century South* (Tuscaloosa: University of Alabama Press, 1999). For more on women's colleges, see Barbara Miller Solomon, *In the Company of Educated Women: A History of Women and Higher Education in America* (New Haven and London: Yale University Press, 1985), and Horowitz, *Alma Mater*.

10. This new direction was at least partially a response to government pressures. In 1899 the Supreme Court ruled on *Cumming v. Richmond County Board of Education* and sanctioned segregated public schools. More directly, a change in state law all but eliminated interracial education in Kentucky in 1904.

11. Peck, *Berea's First Century*, 70, 79.

12. Ibid., 71.

13. For an excellent history of myth and region, see Edward L. Ayers, Patricia Nelson Limerick, Stephen Nissenbaum, and Peter S. Onuf, *All Over the Map: Rethinking American Regions* (Baltimore: Johns Hopkins University Press, 1996).

14. Frost, "Our Contemporary Ancestors."

15. The principal text on the craft revival is Eaton, *Handicrafts of the Southern Highlands*. Eaton's retrospective, underwritten by the Russell Sage Foundation of New York, reinforced many myths as it sought to catalog traditional craft practice in the region. Subsequent scholarly attention has taken a more critical stance and includes Whisnant, *All That Is Native and Fine;* Jane S. Becker and Barbara Franco, eds., *Folk Roots, New Roots: Folklore in American Life* (Lexington, Mass.: Museum of Our National Heritage, 1988); and Becker's excellent *Selling Tradition*.

16. *Carolina Churchman* (March 1910), quoted in Whisnant, *All That Is Native and Fine*, 4.

17. Whisnant, *All That Is Native and Fine*, 7. For a history of the settlement movement, see Carson, *Settlement Folk*.

18. Whisnant, *All That Is Native and Fine*, 8.

19. Eaton, *Handicrafts of the Southern Highlands*, 69–91.

20. Helpful studies on the Arts and Crafts movement include Denker, ed., *Substance of Style;* Kaplan, ed., *Art That Is Life;* Kardon, ed., *Revivals!;* Boris, *Art and Labor;* Meyer, ed., *Inspiring Reform;* and Kardon, ed., *Ideal Home*.

21. Eaton, *Handicrafts of the Southern Highlands*, 60.

22. Peck, *Berea's First Century*, 116.

23. Eaton, *Handicrafts of the Southern Highlands*, 61.

24. Anna Ernberg, "Fireside Industries at Berea College," pamphlet, c. 1905, n.p., Special Collections, Winterthur Museum Library.

25. The Nuttings quickly bonded with the new president. The couple attended Hutchins's inauguration as president of the college, and Mariet Nutting later commented on the "lifting power" of the educator's first address. Mariet G. Nutting to William J. Hutchins, 11 January 1922, Hutchins Correspondence, Berea College Archives, hereafter cited as "Hutchins Correspondence."

26. Hutchins to Nutting, 26 November 1924, Hutchins Correspondence.

27. Ibid.

28. Ibid.

29. Nutting to Hutchins, 11 December 1924, Hutchins Correspondence.

30. Nutting to Hutchins, undated letter (summer 1933 by context), Wallace Nutting Biographical File, Berea College Archives.

31. Hutchins to Nutting, 14 November 1933, letter no. 23, Wallace Nutting Biographical File, Berea College Archives.

32. Nutting to Hutchins, 17 November 1933, Hutchins Correspondence.

33. Victor McConkey to Nutting, 8 July 1934, Wallace Nutting Biographical File, Berea College Archives.

34. Nutting to Hutchins, 10 May 1926, Hutchins Correspondence.

35. *Wallace Nutting Supreme Edition General Catalog* (Framingham, Mass: Wallace Nutting, 1930), 15.

36. Hutchins to Nutting, Western Union telegram, 10 May 1926, Hutchins Correspondence.

37. Curiously, Nutting fails to credit Berea in his catalogs.

38. Nutting to William G. Frost, 20 January 1913, Frost Correspondence, Berea College Archives.

39. The money came from the sale of the Wallace Nutting Collection of Early American Furniture to J. P. Morgan, Jr., who then donated the collection to the Wadsworth Atheneum. Conventional wisdom among students and collectors has been that Nutting used this money to purchase his furniture company back from the group of investors who had been running the business in the early 1920s and of whose methods the minister came to disapprove.

40. Charles Martin Hall to Cora McDowell, 3 March 1926, Hutchins Correspondence. Hall appears to have been a trustee or official of the college.

41. Hutchins to Nutting, 23 January 1926, Hutchins Correspondence.

42. Hutchins worked quite hard for the Nutting money, carefully cultivating the aging antiquarian and his wife. Several references in their correspondence note meetings in Boston or Hutchins's trips to Framingham. "We are very sorry, indeed, that we are going south before the date of your visit. We will probably return from the south about the first of March," wrote Nutting to Hutchins on 17 December 1923 in a typical exchange. Hutchins Correspondence.

43. Mariet G. Nutting, last will and testament, Berea College Archives.

44. Ernest John Donnelly and Esther Svenson, Nutting's right-hand man and last head colorist, respectively, were given the photography business in Mariet Nutting's will. For unknown reasons Donnelly decided to sell out to Svenson in the fall of 1945, leaving her to carry on in the photography business. Donnelly to George Kavanaugh, 7 November 1945, Berea College Archives.

45. Burton R. Tuxford to Kavanaugh, 24 February 1945, Berea College Archives.

Chapter 8 *Waiting for the Auto to Pass*

1. Nutting identified his "best sellers" in the 1915 *Expansible Catalog*.

2. The photograph was copyrighted 29 September 1901. Claimant files, Copyright Division, Library of Congress.

3. Nutting was well aware of such literary and visual

conventions. He frequently mentioned John Bunyan's *Pilgrim's Progress* in his lectures and sermons and commented on the work of Thomas Cole in *Vermont Beautiful.* "Thus the quaint old engraving, 'The Voyage of Life,' was very popular as depicting an advance." *Vermont Beautiful*, 172.

4. Nutting estimated that he exposed some fifty thousand negatives in his career, yet only approximately ten thousand appear in the office book, and of these about sixteen hundred were actually registered in Washington, D.C. Claimant files, Copyright Division and Prints and Photographs Files, Library of Congress.

5. The first edition of the states beautiful series, published by Nutting's own Old America Company, consisted of *Vermont Beautiful* (1922), *Massachusetts Beautiful* (1923), *Connecticut Beautiful* (1923), *New Hampshire Beautiful* (1923), *Maine Beautiful* (1924), *Pennsylvania Beautiful* (1924), *Ireland Beautiful* (1925), *England Beautiful* (1928), and *Virginia Beautiful* (1930). Curiously, *New York Beautiful* (1927) was issued by Dodd, Mead and Company of New York City. In the 1930s the series was published in an updated format by Garden City Publishing Company of Garden City, New York.

6. Nutting, *Vermont Beautiful*, 110.

7. Ibid.

8. Berman, *All That Is Solid Melts into Air*, 6.

9. Justine Monro, *Wallace Nutting Collector's Club Newsletter*, no. 3, 26 November 1973.

10. Ibid.

Selected Bibliography

Ames, Kenneth. *Death in the Dining Room and Other Tales of Victorian Culture.* Philadelphia: Temple University Press, 1992.

Arner, Robert. "Plymouth Rock Revisited: The Landing of the Pilgrim Fathers." *Journal of American Culture* 6, no. 4 (Winter 1983): 25–34.

Axelrod, Alan, ed. *The Colonial Revival in America.* New York: W. W. Norton for the Henry Francis du Pont Winterthur Museum, 1985.

Ayres, William. "Pictures in the American Home, 1880–1930." In *The Arts and the American Home, 1890–1930,* edited by Jessica Foy and Karal Ann Marling, 149–164. Knoxville: University of Tennessee Press, 1994.

Bailyn, Bernard, Donald Fleming, Oscar Handlin, and Stephen Thernstrom, eds. *Glimpses of the Harvard Past.* Cambridge: Harvard University Press, 1986.

Barendsen, Joyce. "Wallace Nutting, An American Tastemaker: The Pictures and Beyond." *Winterthur Portfolio* 18, no. 2–3 (Summer–Autumn 1983): 187–212.

Baritz, Loren. *The Good Life: The Meaning of Success for the American Middle Class.* New York: Alfred A. Knopf, 1989.

Beard, George M. *American Nervousness, Its Causes and Consequences, a Supplement to Nervous Exhaustion.* New York: G. P. Putnam's Sons, 1881.

Becker, Jane. *Selling Tradition: Appalachia and the Construction of the American Folk.* Chapel Hill: University of North Carolina Press, 1998.

Berman, Marshall. *All That Is Solid Melts into Air: The Experience of Modernity.* New York: Simon and Schuster, 1982.

Bermingham, Peter. *American Art in the Barbizon Mood.* Washington, D.C.: Smithsonian Institution Press, 1975.

Blumin, Stuart M. *The Emergence of the Middle Class: Social Experience in the American City, 1760–1900.* Cambridge: Cambridge University Press, 1989.

Bodnar, John. *Remaking America: Public Memory, Commemoration, and Patriotism in the Twentieth Century.* Princeton, N.J.: Princeton University Press, 1992.

Boris, Eileen. *Art and Labor: Ruskin, Morris, and the Craftsman Ideal in America.* Philadelphia: Temple University Press, 1986.

Brandimarte, Cynthia. "To Make the Whole World Homelike: Gender, Space and America's Tea Room Movement." *Winterthur Portfolio* 30, no. 1 (Spring 1995): 1–19.

Bronner, Simon, ed. *Consuming Visions: Accumulation and Display of Goods in America, 1880–1920.* New York: W. W. Norton for the Henry Francis du Pont Winterthur Museum, 1989.

Brown, Dona. *Inventing New England: Regional Tourism in the Nineteenth Century.* Washington, D.C.: Smithsonian Institution Press, 1995.

Burns, Sarah. *Inventing the Modern Artist: Art and Culture in Gilded Age America.* New Haven and London: Yale University Press, 1996.

———. *Pastoral Inventions: Rural Life in Nineteenth-Century American Art and Culture.* Philadelphia: Temple University Press, 1989.

Carrick, Alice Van Leer. *The Next-to-Nothing House.* Boston: Atlantic Monthly, 1922.

Carron, Christian G. *Grand Rapids Furniture: The Story of America's Furniture City.* Grand Rapids, Mich.: Public Museum of Grand Rapids, 1998.

Carson, Mina. *Settlement Folk: Social Thought and the American Settlement Movement, 1885–1930.* Chicago: University of Chicago Press, 1990.

Catalano, Kathleen. "The Longfellows and Their Trumpery Antiquities." *American Art Journal* (Spring 1983): 21–31.

Chandler, Alfred D., and Richard Tedlow. *The Coming of Managerial Capitalism.* Homewood, Ill.: Richard D. Irwin, 1985.

Chandler, Joseph Everett. *The Colonial House.* New York: Robert McBride, 1916.

Clapper, Michael. "Art, Industry, and Education in Prang's Chromolithograph Company." *Proceedings of the American Antiquarian Society* 105, no. 1 (1995): 145–161.

Colley, Marion. "I Never Learned to See Until I Was Fifty."

American Magazine 103 (January 1927): 38–42.

Comstock, Helen. "Wallace Nutting and the Furniture Treasury in Retrospect." *Antiques* 80, no. 5 (November 1961): 460–464.

Cook, Clarence. *The House Beautiful.* New York: Charles Scribner's Sons, 1881.

Cook, Marc. *The Wilderness Cure.* New York: William Wood, 1881.

Cooke, Edward S., Jr. "Arts and Crafts Furniture: Process or Product?" In *The Ideal Home: The History of Twentieth Century American Craft, 1900–1920,* edited by Janet Kardon, 64–76. New York: Harry N. Abrams in association with the American Craft Museum, 1993.

Cotkin, George. *Reluctant Modernism: American Thought and Culture, 1880–1900.* New York: Twayne, 1992.

Damon-Moore, Helen. *Magazines for the Millions: Gender and Commerce in the Ladies' Home Journal and the Saturday Evening Post, 1880–1910.* Albany: State University Press of New York, 1994.

Denker, Bert, ed. *The Substance of Style: Perspectives on the American Arts and Crafts Movement.* Winterthur, Del.: Henry Francis du Pont Winterthur Museum, 1996.

De Veer, Elizabeth. *Sunlight and Shadow: The Life and Art of Willard L. Metcalf.* New York: Abbeville, 1987.

Drake, Samuel Adams. *Old Landmarks and Historic Personages of Boston.* Boston: James Osgood, 1873.

Dulaney, William. "Wallace Nutting: Collector and Entrepreneur." *Winterthur Portfolio* 13 (1979): 47–60.

Dumenil, Lynn. *The Modern Temper: American Culture and Society in the 1920s.* New York: Hill and Wang, 1995.

Dyer, Walter. "The New Mission of an Old Farmhouse." *Country Life in America* 20, no. 2 (October 1, 1911): 35–38.

Eaton, Allen H. *Handicrafts of the Southern Highlands . . . .* New York: Russell Sage Foundation, 1937.

Erwin, Kathleen. "Photography of the Better Type: The Teaching of Clarence White." In *Pictorialism into Modernism,* edited by Marianne Fulton, 120–191. New York: Rizzoli, 1996.

Falino, Jeannine. "The Monastic Ideal in Rural Massachusetts: Edward Pearson Pressey and New Clairvoux." In *The Substance of Style: Perspectives on the American Arts and Crafts Movement,* edited by Bert Denker, 375–396. Winterthur, Del.: Henry Francis du Pont Winterthur Museum, 1996.

Finch, Grant E. *New England.* New York: Rand, McNally, 1933.

Flynt, Suzanne, Susan McGowan, and Amelia Miller. *Gathered and Preserved.* Deerfield, Mass.: Pocumtuck Valley Memorial Association, 1991.

Fox, Richard. "The Culture of Liberal Protestant Progressivism, 1875–1925." *Journal of Interdisciplinary History* 23 (Winter 1993): 639–660.

Fox, Richard Wightman, and T. J. Jackson Lears, eds. *The Culture of Consumption: Critical Essays in American History, 1880–1980.* New York: Pantheon, 1983.

Foy, Jessica, and Karal Ann Marling, eds. *The Arts and the American Home, 1890–1930.* Knoxville: University of Tennessee Press, 1994.

Gabriel, Ralph. *Toilers of Land and Sea.* New Haven: Yale University Press, 1926.

Garvey, Ellen Gruber. *The Adman in the Parlor: Magazines and the Gendering of Consumer Culture, 1880s to 1910s.* New York: Oxford University Press, 1996.

Gebhard, David. "The American Colonial Revival in the 1930's." *Winterthur Portfolio* 22, no. 2–3 (Summer–Fall 1987): 109–147.

Giffen, Sarah, and Kevin Murphy. *A Noble and Dignified Stream: The Piscataqua Region in the Colonial Revival.* York, Me.: Old York Historical Society, 1992.

Goffman, Erving. *The Presentation of Self in Everyday Life.* New York: Anchor, 1959.

Goldberg, Vicki, ed. *Photography in Print: Writings from 1816 to the Present.* New York: Simon and Schuster, 1981.

Goodyear, Frank H. "Constructing a National Landscape: Photography and Tourism in Nineteenth Century America." Ph.D. diss., University of Texas, Austin, 1998.

Gosling, F. G. *Before Freud: Neurasthenia and the American Medical Community, 1870–1910.* Chicago: University of Chicago Press, 1987.

Green, Harvey. *Fit for America: Health, Fitness, Sport, and American Society.* Baltimore: Johns Hopkins University Press, 1986.

———. "Looking Backward to the Future: The Colonial Revival and American Culture." In *Creating a Dignified Past: Museums and the Colonial Revival,* edited by Geoffrey Rossano, 1–16. Savage, Md.: Rowman and Littlefield, 1991.

———. "Popular Science and Political Thought Converge: Colonial Survival Becomes Colonial Revival, 1830–1910." *Journal of American Culture* 6, no. 4 (Winter 1983): 3–24.

Greenough, Sarah. "Of Charming Glens, Graceful Glades, and Frowning Cliffs: The Economic Incentives, Social Inducements, and Aesthetic Issues of American Pictorial Photography, 1880–1902." In *Photography in Nineteenth Century America,* 258–281. New York: Harry N. Abrams, 1991.

Halbwachs, Maurice. *On Collective Memory*. Edited and translated by Lewis Coser. Reprint ed., Chicago: University of Chicago Press, 1992.

Havinga, Anne. "Pictorialism and Naturalism in New England Photography." In *Inspiring Reform: Boston's Arts and Crafts Movement*, edited by Marilee Boyd Meyer, 135–150. Wellesley, Mass.: Davis Museum and Cultural Center, Wellesley College, 1997.

Heller, Adele, and Lois Rudnick, eds. *1915: The Cultural Moment*. New Brunswick, N.J.: Rutgers University Press, 1991.

Henisch, Heinz, and Bridget Henisch. *The Painted Photograph, 1839–1914*. University Park: Pennsylvania State University Press, 1996.

Hilkey, Judy. *Character Is Capital: Success Manuals and Manhood in Gilded Age America*. Chapel Hill: University of North Carolina Press, 1997.

Hirshler, Erica E. *A Studio of Her Own: Women Artists in Boston, 1870–1940*. Boston: Museum of Fine Arts, 2001.

Hobsbawm, Eric, and Terrence Ranger, eds. *The Invention of Tradition*. Cambridge: Cambridge University Press, 1983.

Holloran, Michael. *Boston's "Changeful Times": The Origins of Preservations and Planning in America*. Baltimore: Johns Hopkins University Press, 1998.

Homer, William Innes. *Alfred Stieglitz and the American Avant-Garde*. Boston: New York Graphics Society, 1977.

Horowitz, Helen L. A*lma Mater: Design and Experience in the Women's Colleges from Their Nineteenth Century Beginnings to the 1930s*. New York: Alfred A. Knopf, 1985.

Hosmer, Charles. *Presence of the Past: A History of The Preservation Movement in the United States Before Williamsburg*. New York: G. P. Putnam's Sons, 1965.

Hughes, James. *The Birth of a Century: Early Color Photographs of America*. London: Tauris Parke, 1994.

Ivankovich, Michael. *The Alphabetical and Numerical Index to Wallace Nutting Pictures*. Doylestown, Pa.: Diamond, 1988.

———. *The Guide to Wallace Nutting Furniture*. Doylestown, Pa.: Diamond, 1990.

Jaffee, David. *People of the Wachusett: Greater New England in History and Memory, 1630–1860*. Ithaca, N.Y.: Cornell University Press, 1999.

Jakle, John. *The Tourist: Travel in Twentieth-Century North America*. Lincoln: University of Nebraska Press, 1985.

Kammen, Michael. *Mystic Chords of Memory: The Transfor-mation of Tradition in American Culture*. New York: Alfred A. Knopf, 1991.

Kaplan, Wendy. "R. T. H. Halsey: An Ideology of Collecting American Decorative Arts." *Winterthur Portfolio* 17, no. 1 (Spring 1982): 43–54.

———. *Designing Modernity: The Arts of Reform and Persuasion, 1885–1945*. Miami, Fla.: Wolfsonian Foundation with Thames and Hudson, 1995.

———, ed. *The Art That Is Life: The Arts and Crafts Movement in America, 1875–1920*. Boston: Museum of Fine Arts, 1987.

Kardon, Janet, ed. *Revivals! Diverse Traditions, 1920–1945*. New York: Harry N. Abrams in association with the American Craft Museum, 1994.

Kendall, Douglas. "Tea in Yorktown Parlor: Wallace Nutting's Legacy at the Joseph Webb House." In *Creating a Dignified Past: Museums and the Colonial Revival*, edited by Geoffrey L. Rossano, 95–111. Savage, Md.: Rowman and Littlefield in association with History Cherry Hill, 1991.

Korzenik, Diane. *Drawn to Art: A Nineteenth-Century American Dream*. Hanover: University Press of New England, 1985.

Kraus, Michael, and Davis D. Joyce. *The Writing of American History*. Rev. ed. Norman: University of Oklahoma Press, 1985.

Laird, Pamela Walker. *Advertising Progress: American Business and the Rise of Consumer Marketing*. Baltimore: Johns Hopkins University Press, 1998.

Leach, William. *Land of Desire: Merchants, Power, and the Rise of a New American Culture*. New York: Pantheon 1993.

Leader, Bernice Kramer. "Antifeminism in the Paintings of the Boston School." *Arts Magazine* 56, no.5 (January 1982): 112–123.

Lears, T. J. Jackson. "The Ad Man and the Grand Inquisitor: Intimacy, Publicity, and the Managed Self in America, 1880–1940." In *Constructions of the Self*, edited by George Levine, 107–141. New Brunswick, N.J.: Rutgers University Press, 1992.

———. *Fables of Abundance*. New York: Basic, 1994.

———. *No Place of Grace: Antimodernism and the Transformation of American Culture, 1880–1920*. New York: Pantheon, 1981.

Levine, Lawrence. *Highbrow/Lowbrow: The Emergence of Cultural Hierarchy in America*. Cambridge, Mass.: Harvard University Press, 1988.

Lewis, Jan. "Motherhood and the Construction of the Male Citizen." In *Constructions of the Self*, edited by

George Levine, 143–159. New Brunswick, N.J.: Rutgers University Press, 1992.

Lindgren, James. "'A Constant Incentive to Patriotic Citizenship': Historic Preservation in Progressive-Era Massachusetts." *New England Quarterly* 64, no. 4 (March–December 1991): 594–608.

———. *Preserving Historic New England: Preservation, Progressivism, and the Remaking of Memory.* New York: Oxford University Press, 1995.

Lipsitz, George. *Time Passages: Collective Memory and American Popular Culture.* Minneapolis: University of Minnesota Press, 1990.

Lowenthal, David. *The Past Is a Foreign Country.* Cambridge: Cambridge University Press, 1985.

———. *Possessed by the Past.* Cambridge: Cambridge University Press, 1997.

Lutz, Tom. *American Nervousness, 1903: An Anecdotal History.* Ithaca, N.Y.: Cornell University Press, 1991.

MacCannell, Dean. *The Tourist: A New Theory of the Leisure Class.* New York: Schocken, 1976.

MacKeil, Louis. *Wallace Nutting.* Saugus, Mass.: Saugus Historical Society, 1982.

Marchand, Roland. *Advertising the American Dream: Making Way for Modernity, 1920–1940.* Berkeley: University of California Press, 1985.

Margolis, Marianne Fulton. *Alfred Stieglitz Camera Work: A Pictorial Guide.* New York: Dover and the International Museum of Photography at the George Eastman House, 1978.

Marling, Karal Ann. *George Washington Slept Here: Colonial Revivals and American Culture, 1876–1986.* Cambridge, Mass.: Harvard University Press, 1988.

May, Bridget. "Progressivism and the Colonial Revival: The Modern Colonial House, 1900–1920." *Winterthur Portfolio* 26, no. 2–3 (Summer–Autumn 1991): 107–122.

McCracken, Grant. *Culture and Consumption.* Bloomington: Indiana University Press, 1988.

McDougal, Elisabeth Blair, ed. *The Architectural Historian in America.* Washington, D.C.: National Gallery of Art, 1990.

McNeil, W. K. *Appalachian Images in Folk and Popular Culture.* Ann Arbor, Mich.: UMI Research, 1989.

Meyer, Marilee Boyd, ed. *Inspiring Reform: Boston's Arts and Crafts Movement.* Wellesley, Mass.: Davis Museum and Cultural Center, Wellesley College, 1997.

Miller, Marla, and Anne Digan Lanning. "'Common Parlors': Women and the Recreation of Community Identity in Deerfield, Massachusetts, 1870–1920." *Gender and History* 6 (November 1994): 435–455.

Monkhouse, Christopher. "The Spinning Wheel as Artifact, Symbol, and Source of Design." In *Victorian Furniture: Essays from a Victorian Society Autumn Symposium,* edited by Kenneth L. Ames, published as *Nineteenth Century* 8, no. 3–4 (1982): 154–172.

Monkhouse, Christopher, and Thomas Michie. *American Furniture at Pendleton House.* Providence, R.I.: Museum of Art, Rhode Island School of Design, 1986.

Murtaugh, William. *Keeping Time: The History and Theory of Preservation in America.* Pittstown, N.J.: Main Street Press, 1988.

Myers, Kenneth. *The Catskills: Painters, Writers, and Tourists in the Mountains, 1820–1895.* Yonkers, N.Y.: Hudson River Museum and University Press of New England, 1987.

Norton, Bettina. *Edwin Whitfield: Nineteenth-Century American Scenery.* Barre, Mass.: Barre Publishing, 1977.

Nutting, Wallace. *American Windsors.* Framingham, Mass.: Old America, 1917.

———. "Carved Spoon Racks." *Antiques* (June 1925): 312–315.

———. *The Clock Book.* Framingham, Mass.: Old America, 1924.

———. *The Clock Book.* 2d ed. Garden City, N.Y.: Garden City in cooperation with Old America, 1935.

———. *Connecticut Beautiful.* Framingham, Mass.: Old America, 1923.

———. *Connecticut Beautiful.* 2d ed. Garden City, N.Y.: Garden City in cooperation with Old America, 1935.

———. "Double-Purpose Furniture." *Antiques* (October 1940): 160–162.

———. "Early American House Hardware." *Antiques* (August 1923): 78–81.

———. *England Beautiful.* Framingham, Mass.: Old America, 1928.

———. *England Beautiful.* 2d ed. Garden City, N.Y.: Garden City in cooperation with Old America, 1936.

———. *Furniture of the Pilgrim Century.* Boston, Mass.: Marshall Jones, 1921.

———. *Furniture of the Pilgrim Century.* Rev. and enlarged ed. Framingham, Mass.: Old America, 1924.

———. *The Furniture Treasury.* 3 vols. Framingham, Mass.: Old America, 1928–1933.

———. *Ireland Beautiful.* Framingham, Mass.: Old America, 1925.

———. *Ireland Beautiful.* 2d ed. Garden City, New York: Garden City in cooperation with Old America, 1935.

———. *Maine Beautiful.* Framingham, Mass.: Old America Company, 1924.

———. *Maine Beautiful.* 2d ed. Garden City, N.Y.: Garden

City in cooperation with Old America, 1935.

_____. *Massachusetts Beautiful*. Framingham, Mass.: Old America, 1923.

_____. *Massachusetts Beautiful*. 2d ed. Garden City, N.Y.: Garden City in cooperation with Old America, 1935.

_____. *New Hampshire Beautiful*. Framingham, Mass.: Old America, 1923.

_____. *New Hampshire Beautiful*. 2d ed. Garden City, N.Y.: Garden City in cooperation with Old America, 1935.

_____. *New York Beautiful*. New York: Dodd, Mead, 1927.

_____. *New York Beautiful*. 2d ed. Garden City, N.Y.: Garden City in cooperation with Old America, 1936.

_____. "Notable Furniture of the Pilgrim Century." *Antiques* (August 1930): 138–140.

_____. *Old New England Pictures*. Privately printed, 1913.

_____. *Pennsylvania Beautiful*. Framingham, Mass.: Old America, 1924.

_____. *Pennsylvania Beautiful*. 2d ed. Garden City, New York: Garden City in cooperation with Old America, 1935.

_____. *Photographic Art Secrets*. New York: Dodd, Mead, 1927.

_____. *Photographic Art Secrets*. 2d ed. New York: Dodd, Mead, 1931.

_____. "The Prince-Howes Court Cupboard." *Antiques* (October 1922): 168–171.

_____. "A Sidelight on John Goddard. *Antiques* (September 1936): 120–121.

_____. "Turnings on Early American Furniture." *Antiques* (May 1923): 212–215.

_____. "Turnings on Early American Furniture, Part II." *Antiques* (June 1923): 275–278.

_____. *Vermont Beautiful*. Framingham, Mass.: Old America, 1922.

_____. *Vermont Beautiful*. 2d ed. Garden City, N.Y.: Garden City in cooperation with Old America, 1936.

_____. *Virginia Beautiful*. Framingham, Mass.: Old America, 1930.

_____. *Virginia Beautiful*. 2d ed. Garden City, N.Y.: Garden City in cooperation with Old America, 1935.

_____. *Wallace Nutting's Biography*. Framingham, Mass.: Old America, 1936.

_____. "The Windsor Chair." *Antiques* (February 1922): 74–76.

Orvell, Miles. *The Real Thing: Imitation and Authenticity in American Culture, 1880–1940*. Chapel Hill: University of North Carolina Press, 1989.

Peck, Elizabeth. *Berea College: A Brief History*. Berea, Ky.: Berea College, n.d.

_____. *Berea's First Century, 1855–1955*. Lexington: University of Kentucky Press, 1955.

Peladeau, Marius. *Chansonetta: The Life and Photographs of Chansonetta Stanley Emmons, 1858–1937*. Waldoboro, Me.: Maine Antiques Digest, 1977.

Peterson, Christian. *Alfred Stieglitz's Camera Notes*. New York: W. W. Norton, 1993.

_____. "American Arts and Crafts: The Photograph Beautiful, 1895–1915." *History of Photography* 16, no. 3 (Fall 1992): 189–232.

Reichlin, Ellie. "Emma Lewis Coleman, 1853–1942." Biographical manuscript, Society for the Preservation of New England Antiquities Library and Archives, 1981.

Rhoads, William. *The Colonial Revival*. New York: Garland, 1977.

_____. "The Colonial Revival and American Nationalism." *Journal of the Society of Architectural Historians* 35, no. 4 (December 1976): 239–254.

_____. "Roadside Colonial: Early American Design for the Automobile Age, 1900–1940." *Winterthur Portfolio* 21, no. 2–3 (Summer–Fall 1986): 133–152.

Rosenblum, Naomi. *A History of Women Photographers*. New York: Abbeville, 1994.

Roth, Rodris. "The Colonial Revival and Centennial Furniture." *Art Quarterly* 27, no. 1 (1964): 57–81.

Saunders, Richard. "American Decorative Arts Collecting in New England, 1840–1920." M.A. thesis, Winterthur Program in Early American Culture, University of Delaware, 1973.

Saunders, Richard, and Helen Raye. *Daniel Wadsworth: Patron of the Arts*. Hartford, Conn.: Wadsworth Atheneum, 1981.

Sears, John. *Sacred Places: American Tourist Attractions in the Nineteenth Century*. New York: Oxford University Press, 1989.

Smith-Rosenberg, Carroll. *Disorderly Conduct: Visions of Gender in Victorian America*. Oxford: Oxford University Press, 1985.

Solomon, Barbara Miller. *Ancestors and Immigrants: A Changing New England Tradition*. Cambridge: Harvard University Press, 1956.

Steinberg, Salme. *Reformer in the Marketplace: Edward W. Bok and the Ladies Home Journal*. Baton Rouge: Louisiana State University Press, 1979.

Sternberger, Paul Spencer. *Between Amateur and Aesthete: The Legitimization of Photography as Art in America, 1880–1900*. Albuquerque: University of New Mexico Press, 2001.

Stillinger, Elizabeth. *The Antiquers*. New York: Alfred A.

Knopf, 1980.

Stott, Annette. *Holland Mania: The Unknown Dutch Period in American Art and Culture.* Woodstock, N.Y.: Overlook Press, 1998.

Susman, Warren. *Culture as History: The Transformation of American Society in the Twentieth Century.* New York: Pantheon, 1984.

Sweeney, Erin. "Olof Althin (1859–1920): From Swedish Apprentice to Boston Businessman." M.A. thesis, Winterthur Program in Early American Culture, University of Delaware, 1998.

Townsand, Kim. *Manhood at Harvard: William James and Others.* New York: W. W. Norton, 1996.

Trachtenberg, Alan. *The Incorporation of America: Culture and Society in the Gilded Age.* New York: Hill and Wang, 1982.

Train, Arthur. *Puritan's Progress.* New York: Charles Scribner's Sons, 1931.

Truettner, William H., and Roger B. Stein, eds. *Picturing Old New England: Image and Memory.* New Haven and London: Yale University Press, 1999.

Wallace, Mike. *Mickey Mouse History and Other Essays on American Memory.* Philadelphia: Temple University Press, 1995.

West, Patricia. *Domesticating History: The Political Origins of America's House Museums.* Washington, D.C.: Smithsonian Institution Books, 1999.

Wharton, Edith, and Ogden Codman, Jr. *The Decoration of Houses.* 1897. New York: W. W. Norton for the Arthur Ross Foundation, 1997.

Whelan, Richard. *Alfred Stieglitz: A Biography.* Boston: Little, Brown, 1995.

Whisnant, David. *All That Is Native and Fine: The Politics of Culture in an American Region.* Chapel Hill: University of North Carolina Press, 1983.

Whitfield, Edwin. *The Homes of Our Forefathers: Being a Collection of the Oldest and Most Interesting Buildings in Massachusetts.* Boston: A. Williams, 1879.

Wiebe, Robert. *The Search for Order, 1877–1920.* New York: Hill and Wang, 1967.

Williams, Myron. *The Story of Phillips Exeter.* Exeter, N.H.: Phillips Exeter Academy, 1957.

Woods, Marianne Berger. "Viewing Colonial America Through the Lens of Wallace Nutting." *American Art* 8, no. 2 (Spring 1994): 67–86.

Yochelson, Bonnie. "Clarence H. White: Peaceful Warrior." In *Pictorialism into Modernism,* edited by Marianne Fulton, 10–120. New York: Rizzoli in association with the George Eastman House and the Detroit Institute of Arts, 1996.

Index